D1600812

PITTSBURGH IN STAGES

PITTSBURGH IN STAGES

Two Hundred Years of Theater

Lynne Conner

UNIVERSITY OF PITTSBURGH PRESS

Published by the University of Pittsburgh Press, Pittsburgh PA 15260

Copyright © 2007, University of Pittsburgh Press

All rights reserved

Manufactured in the United States of America

Printed on acid-free paper

10 9 8 7 6 5 4 3 2 1

Library of Congress Cataloging-in-Publication Data

Conner, Lynne.
  Pittsburgh in stages : two hundred years of theater / Lynne Conner.
     p. cm.
  Includes blbliographical references and index.
    ISBN-13: 978-0-8229-4330-3 (cloth : alk. paper)
    ISBN-10: 0-8229-4330-1 (cloth : alk. paper)
    1. Theater—Pennsylvania—Pittsburgh—History—19th century.
  2. Theater—Pennsylvania—Pittsburgh—History—20th century. I. Title.
    PN2277.P55C66 2007
  792.09748'86—dc22

                              2007005136

This book is dedicated to my parents, Nancy and Jesse Conner.
Home, it has been said, is wherever one prospers.
In your home I was given all the right ingredients:
love, respect, laughter, patience, imagination, and hope.

CONTENTS

ILLUSTRATIONS

PREFACE

Drama has long been a powerful metaphor for illuminating the human condition and a persuasive tool for influencing public opinion. Since the days of Plato's warning and Aristotle's praise, Westerners have been taught to both fear and honor a play's capacity to mirror current events, forecast the future, warn about the past, and, at least ideally, provide advice and counsel about the present day. But the practice of theater is much more than an attractive metaphor; it is a human industry that operates at the very heart of most communities. In many cultures the activity surrounding theatrical production—from acting to producing to writing to designing to watching and interpreting—has been an integral way for citizens to assemble, to talk, to argue, and ultimately to shape and re-shape their collective and individual identities.

This is certainly true of Pittsburgh, a city with over two centuries of indigenous theatrical activity to its credit. From the first garrison theatricals at Fort Pitt in the 1760s to the present array of professional, amateur, and community-based production, through economic booms and busts, through war, through periods of civic unrest and civic apathy, and through several urban "renaissances," Pittsburgh theater has remained a vital local industry with a rich evolving story. *Pittsburgh in Stages* tells that story in the form of a social history, weaving a chronology of Pittsburgh's theatrical past into the larger story of the city's evolving urban landscape. Here theater is seen as a vital component of the creation and growth of Pittsburgh—not just a product of the city's cultural life but an agent of social change. Indeed, the story of Pittsburgh's theater industry is really the story of the city itself—a tale of community activity, investment, and identity that closely reflects the evolution of a frontier village into one of the United States' major metropolitan areas.

I entered this territory by accident in 1996 when, as the resident playwright at the Senator John Heinz Pittsburgh Regional History Center, my job was to research and write plays using local history as subject and theme. In search of the details of my characters' lives, I spent a lot of time in the archives looking at institutional and family papers. Along the way I began encountering odd bits of Pittsburgh's theatrical past: an aluminum-plated souvenir program from 1903 honoring the opening of the Nixon Theatre, a downtown theater manager's account book from 1921 noting the "wretched business" of an appearance by Isadora Duncan, the hand-typed political theater manifesto of a local self-described "Afra-American" playwright from 1932, a short article by an anonymous "theater lover" describing the wooden theater built at Third and Wood in 1813, photographs of Yiddish theater skits performed at a Hill District settlement house from the mid-1920s, and literally hundreds of playbills and programs from Pittsburgh's plethora of nineteenth-century playhouses. At first I found these discoveries amusingly entertaining. But as the evidence of Pittsburgh's theatrical past piled up, I began to wonder if I had been missing something important. I was, after all, a trained theater historian, and yet I knew nothing about the regional history of my own city (except that it apparently did not warrant mention in the many national histories of the American stage). I had assumed, like everyone else, that nothing (theatrically speaking) had happened in Pittsburgh, or, more accurately, nothing that mattered. But here was a growing pile of evidence to the contrary—documentation of a vital regional industry.

My interest in telling this untold story has led me to several local archives, notably the Curtis Theatre Collection at the University of Pittsburgh, the Library and Archives of the Historical Society of Western Pennsylvania at the Senator John Heinz Pittsburgh Regional History Center, and the Pennsylvania Archives at Pittsburgh's Carnegie Library. These substantial (and largely unmined) collections include scrapbooks, playhouse and theater company business records, performers' memoirs, patrons' scrapbooks, extensive playbill and program collections, manuscripts, photographs, and newspaper clipping files. However, the lessons I've learned from feminist historiography (showing the inherent gender and class biases of the traditional archival process) have taught me to be cautious about relying solely on archived material. Therefore, *Pittsburgh in Stages* draws heavily from a variety of nontheatrical primary and secondary sources, including economic and regional histories (with publication dates beginning in 1807), diaries, memoirs, autobiographies, and biographies. I also rely on period newspapers, a plentiful repository of information about the city's theatrical industry and a rich source of data (ranging from advertisements and posted playbills to reviews, preview articles, columns, and letters to the editor). In addition, many secondary theater history sources provide data, context, and narrative models for this study.

In researching and writing this book I have been guided by standards for writing history that acknowledge the power of so-called grand narratives (histories purporting to explain the vagaries of historical development with universal explanations). I have tried to conduct my research, and to shape my narrative, with a willingness to accept incoming data even when it could upset, reverse, or otherwise mess up my story line. I have been equally guided by my belief in the possibility of plausible, rigorous historical storytelling and in the value of providing a coherent narrative arc. To that end I employ a fictional device at the opening of each chapter in the form of a snapshot designed to capture one specific moment in time. My use of this device is clearly set apart from the main narrative, however, so that there will be no confusion about the relationship between fact and fiction. I am indebted to the findings of scholars in theater history, both essayists and narrativists,[1] whose work provided structural and methodological guidance. However, because of my narrative goals, and because I write for a large readership, I engage in occasional dialogues with other theater historians only in the endnotes.

The definition of *theater* in this study covers a wide array of live stage entertainment; some examples may not fit traditional definitions of the form. My definition is inclusive because even though scholars may classify theatrical genres, audiences do not care if what they enjoy is "really" theater or not. Attempting to look only at what can be labeled "legitimate" theater would paint too narrow a picture of the city's theatrical history. In addition, the many hierarchical terms applied to theater (professional versus amateur, legitimate versus popular, serious versus merely entertaining) are to some extent dismantled here, since I do not see these divisions as absolute or always helpful in narrating the region's theatrical evolution. I avoid making my own aesthetic valuation and instead focus on how various contemporary stakeholders—critics, producers, investors, audience members—evaluated and absorbed the theatrical activity of their own time and culture.

Writing Regional History

Place-based comprehensive histories (as opposed to argument-based histories) of the American stage can be divided into two genres. The first is the hometown stage history, a generalized chronicle of a particular city's theatrical activity. Self-contained in perspective and approach, these works tend to be methodologically naive and resistant to intercultural and intracultural analysis. They often view a city's stage history as isolated from other cultural developments, both internally (they do not mention correspondences between a city's political profile, for instance, and the kind of theater it tends to produce) and externally (they often ignore altogether the hometown stage's history of exchange with other regional and national stages). The historians who created them have thus been guilty of treating the theater, to paraphrase Selma Jeanne Cohen, as a windowless room with mirrored walls. Partly because of these historiographical and methodological issues, the hometown stage history has, generally speaking, passed out of favor.

The second genre of place-based theater histories are studies that focus on the development of the national stage. While these studies are often more methodologically savvy than their regional counterparts, they tend to gloss over or ignore the contributions of regional theater in favor of launching a national discourse, and therefore they rarely investigate regional products thoroughly enough as evidence for the accumulating historical record. This is no doubt a circular problem: without a scholarly tradition, there have been few rigorously researched and narrated regional stage histories. And without credible texts to draw upon, historians working on large projects do not have the right kind of data and focus their attention elsewhere. Over time, glossing over regional theater has become the norm, gradually eroding the value of theater products from locations away from the center and effectively silencing many local events and practitioners within the national discourse.

Standard histories of American theater are filled with normative assumptions about the appropriate purview of serious theater history, including where the evidence is mined (the site of cultural products and production) and how much attention should be given to the physical site. This problem is especially pertinent to my study. Pittsburgh has long been ignored as a site of significant contributions to the "national" theater, and the city makes only rare appearances in histories attempting to document the evolution of American theater.[2] Because these histories cover a lot of ground and are not always thoroughly researched, they sometimes fall prey to the storytelling allure of regional myths. Pittsburgh has consistently played the role of the "working-class city with working-class tastes" in everything from biographies of Eleonora Duse to histories of the post-war regional theater movement.[3]

To transcend these limitations, *Pittsburgh in Stages* offers a detailed analysis that is both comprehensive and culturally informed. This reconstituted home-town stage history seeks to acknowledge the social determinants that affect the-atrical practice—economic, cultural, and demographic. Theatrical activity in Pittsburgh has been an integral part of the city's cultural life, and therefore I offer a narrative that is neither windowless nor mirrored but responsive to the connections between social behavior and theatrical output. I treat my local sub-ject matter with the deepest respect, which implies using a critical eye. As a re-sult, this book is not a piece of civic boosterism that romanticizes the city's contributions, as hometown stage histories often are, nor is it a personality-driven account of locals-made-good, as stage memoirs tend to be. (I do not, for example, discuss in any detail theater luminaries, such as George S. Kaufman, who were born in Pittsburgh but never practiced their art in the city.) Instead, I believe that a detailed history of Pittsburgh theater can offer some useful insights into the evolving story of our national theater.

ACKNOWLEDGMENTS

I offer thanks to many colleagues and friends who have, in a variety of ways, supported this project over the course of its nearly ten-year journey. Staff at the Heinz History Center and the Pittsburgh Public Theater encouraged the early stages of my research by sponsoring lectures on the topic. The University of Pittsburgh Department of Theatre Arts provided ongoing support in the form of a research leave and the help of graduate research assistants Michael Schwartz, Michael Cassidy, Jennifer Pierce, Devin Malcolm, Colleen Reilly, Insoo Lee, and Meredith Conti. Melanie Dreyer translated German-language material. Vernell Lillie and Maurice Levy shared their extensive knowledge about the arts community in Pittsburgh. Chris Rawson generously helped me to sort through the dizzying array of theaters and artists who came and went during the 1970s and 1980s. Miriam Meislik at the University of Pittsburgh's Archive Service Center, Art Lauderback at the Library and Archives of the Historical Society of Western Pennsylvania, and Jim Burke at the University of Pittsburgh's Center for Instructional Development and Distance Education helped with photo location and duplication. And a grant from the Edwards Endowed Publication Fund at the University of Pittsburgh supported duplication and copyright costs.

I am particularly indebted to Ellen Kelson, for the gift of her illuminating lens, and Bill Daw at the University of Pittsburgh's Curtis Theatre Collection, whose generous research support and good ideas have had a considerable influence on this book. The Curtis Collection, one of the most extensive of its kind, is an invaluable resource and a community treasure.

And finally, my gratitude to Miles and Roy de Klerk—for your patience and understanding on all those Saturday and Sunday mornings when I disappeared upstairs with a cup of coffee in one hand and my laptop in the other—and to Peter, still with me, day in, day out.

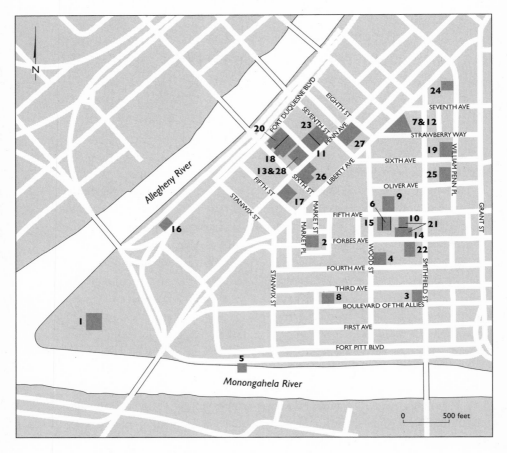

Fig. 1. Map of major downtown playhouses, 1812–2006. Source: Bill Nelson.

KEY:

1. Theatre in the Garrison, assembly room inside Fort Pitt. Opened ca. 1763.
2. Theater in the Courthouse, performance space on the second floor of the County Courthouse on Market Street between Fourth and Fifth streets. Opened ca. 1803.
3. Theatre on Third Street at 310 Third Street. Opened 1813. Razed ca. 1830.
4. Concert Hall on Wood at Fourth Street. Opened ca. 1830. Renamed Lafayette Hall in 1851. Burned May 1, 1866.
5. Floating Theatre, a flatboat theater docked on the Monongahela River. Opened 1831.
6. Pittsburgh Theatre (the "Old Drury") at 306–310 Fifth Street. Opened 1833. Razed 1870.
7. Melodeon at 810–812 Liberty Avenue at Strawberry Way. Opened ca. 1840. Later called the Atheneum and the Gaities. Burned 1865.
8. Philo Hall on Third Street at Market Street. Opened ca. 1850.
9. Masonic Hall at 335 Fifth Street. Opened 1851. Renamed Foster's Gaities in 1857. Burned 1887.
10. Odd Fellows' Hall on Fifth Avenue between Wood and Smithfield. Opened 1856–57. Renamed Foster's National, the Apollo, the National, Pittsburgh Opera House, Fifth Avenue Opera House, Fifth Avenue Lyceum, the Harris, and the Avenue. Burned June 2, 1905. New building erected on the spot in 1905 and incorporated into the Grand Opera House on Diamond Street.
11. Trimble's Varieties on Penn Avenue at Barker's Alley. Opened 1859. Renamed the Varieties by 1868, the American Variety by 1869, and Aim's Varieties by 1876. Razed 1878.
12. Academy of Music at 810–812 Liberty Avenue at Strawberry Way. Opened 1866. Renamed Harry Williams's Academy in 1877, later renamed the Follies and the Academy.
13. Library Hall at 611 Penn Avenue. Opened 1870. Called the Bijou in 1886, the Lyceum in 1910, the Academy by 1929, the Lyceum by 1936. Razed 1936.
14. Pittsburgh Opera House on Diamond Street (now Forbes Avenue) directly behind the Odd Fellows' Hall on Fifth Avenue. Opened 1871.
15. O'Brien Dime Museum on Fifth Avenue near Wood Street. Opened 1886. Renamed the Harry Davis Eden Musee in 1890.
16. Hippodrome in Exposition Hall on Duquesne Way near the Point. Opened ca. 1890.
17. Duquesne Theatre on Penn Avenue near Cecil Place. Opened 1890. Renamed the Belasco-Duquesne in 1905. Razed 1930.
18. Alvin Theatre at 115 Sixth Street. Opened 1891. Renamed the Shubert-Alvin in 1920, the New Harris-Alvin in 1934, the J. P. Harris ca. 1942, and the Gateway.
19. Nixon Theatre at 417–425 Sixth Avenue. Opened 1903. Razed 1950.
20. Gayety Theater on Sixth Street and Duquesne Boulevard. Opened 1904. Renamed the Fulton in 1930 and the Byham in 1991.
21. [10 & 14] Grand Opera House on Fifth Avenue and Diamond Street. Opened 1905. The new structure incorporated the Pittsburgh Opera House on Diamond Street (opened 1871) with a new entrance structure built in 1905 on the spot of Odd Fellows' Hall (then called the Avenue) on Fifth Avenue. The 1905 building burned to the ground in 1917. Rebuilt as the Million Dollar Grand in 1918. Renamed the Warner in 1930.
22. Harris Theatre on Diamond Street (Forbes Avenue) near Smithfield. Opened 1911.
23. Kenyon Opera House at 711 Penn Avenue. Opened 1912. Renamed the Pitt in 1913, the Miles in 1914, the Schubert-Pitt by 1918, and the Barry by 1940. Razed 1950.
24. Victoria Theater at 954–956 Liberty Avenue. Opened in 1912. Renamed the Sam S. Shubert in 1921, Loew's Aldine in 1923, the Senator by 1940, and the New Nixon in 1950. Razed 1976.
25. Davis Theatre on Oliver Avenue and William Penn Place. Opened 1915.
26. Loew's Penn on Sixth and Penn avenues. Opened 1927. Renamed the Penn by 1950 and Heinz Hall for the Performing Arts in 1971.
27. Stanley Theatre on Seventh and Penn avenues. Opened 1928. Renamed the Benedum Center for the Performing Arts in 1987.
28. O'Reilly Theater at 621 Penn Avenue. Opened 1999.

PITTSBURGH IN STAGES

THE THEATER AS COMMUNITY LIFE

1790 to 1830

Pittsburgh. December 11, 1818. By seven o'clock the Theatre on Third Street is filled with Pittsburgh's elite—local landowners, manufacturers, lawyers, and government officials—come to see the opening performance of the Dramatic Benevolent Society (actually a group of student thespians from the Pittsburgh Academy). The playbill posted on the front doors says that the show is to begin "promptly at quarter past seven." But no one seems inclined to quiet the house, not the building manager, who is busy counting receipts in the ticket office, nor the candle snuffer, wardrobe mistress, or property man, who are still trying to get the tiny backstage area ready, nor even the performers themselves, many of whom can be found, at this late hour, engaged in lively conversation with family and friends. Meanwhile, in the boxes on either side of the small proscenium stage (priced at one dollar per seat), an usher uses a filthy rag to wipe away the coal dust that has settled since the theater was last used nearly a month ago. In the orchestra pit members of the Apollonian Society warm up their instruments. And up in the gallery, where the decaying bench seats are selling tonight for seventy-five cents, a collection of keelboat drivers, wagon wheel makers, and glass blowers are crowding in, anxious to see if the town's so-called gentlemen can pull off a decent show. They jostle each other for position, spilling cups of ale and bags of pignuts as they squeeze to the front of the steeply raked seats, the better to yell out their jeers and boos when the opportunity presents itself, as it inevitably will.[1]

Leisure in the Western Country

As a European settlement, Pittsburgh dates to the 1730s when a thin stream of traders and land speculators began to arrive at a tiny western outpost between the Allegheny, Monongahela, and Ohio rivers. Originally these men (mostly English and French) came to trade with the indigenous tribes running the river routes between western New York and southwestern Pennsylvania. A decade later, English, German, Irish, and Scottish immigrants were using the site to rest after their difficult three-week journey across the Pennsylvania mountains and before heading into the vast Northwest Territory. By the time the Ohio Company was formed in 1847, the area had become a substantial trading and supply community. After the conclusion of the French and Indian War in 1763, the British reoccupied their abandoned Fort Pitt, and a small village of inns, taverns, supply stores, wagon shops, and horse traders developed along a carefully plotted diamond of land above the river banks. Over the next two decades, the Manor of Pittsburgh, as William Penn had named it, grew in population and productivity, becoming a thriving town and farming region under the military protection of the British garrison at Fort Pitt.[2]

The combination of labor-intensive daily living, especially for families working large farms, and security concerns—Indian attacks on the village were common —made life in the western country particularly challenging. But other factors of frontier existence were equally difficult. There was no cultural homogeneity among the odd mix of traders, retired soldiers, immigrants, free black migrants, and landed gentry who made up the population; they spoke a variety of lan-

Fig. 2. The Theatre on Third Street, 1813 (center building). Source: *Palmer's Pictorial Pittsburgh and Prominent Pittsburghers Past and Present 1758–1905*. Pittsburgh: R. M. Palmer, 1905.

guages and carried with them differing religious practices and political allegiances. Class anxieties, though somewhat different from those of the old countries, continued to arise. Retired British officers did not mix with former indentured servants. The gentry lived quite differently from the poor immigrants who farmed the rugged acres being parceled out in colonial land grants. And the region's migrant laborers—many of them first- and second-generation Americans—had little contact with the free black settlers attracted to Pennsylvania because of its Quaker tradition of tolerance.[3] If these first Pittsburghers had anything in common beyond their drive to succeed economically, it was a shared sense of isolation. In prerevolutionary Pittsburgh, a social life did not come easily. The concept of unoccupied time, defined as "freedom from business," was unknown to many settlers.[4] For others, opportunities for leisurely amusements were rooted in communal work activities—barn raisings and sewing circles—and in religious celebrations that steered well clear of the "vain amusements" decried by the Protestant clergy. For single male laborers, leisure time often meant drinking in taverns. In this environment, creative activities and performance events (recitations, singing, playing instruments, reading aloud) were rare outside the family

The Theater as Community Life

3

circle. Not surprisingly, ensemble art forms like theatrical performances were even more rare.

And yet, this odd collection of people who were the first Pittsburghers needed theater for the same reasons that all emerging communities do—as a means of sharing in the world of ideas, as a vehicle for expressing cultural identity, as a form of individual creativity, and, perhaps most important, as an acceptable excuse to convene in leisure hours. The editor of the *Pittsburgh Gazette*, the first newspaper west of the Allegheny Mountains, wrote in 1818:

> A complaint has frequently been made against the western country that we are so much occupied with the pursuit of gain as to have acquired a sordid and unsocial cast of character. . . . Whatever, therefore, has a tendency to mingle us harmoniously together, to soften the manners, to relax the brow of care; and to wear off those sharp points of character which seem to grow out of an exclusive devotion to business deserves attention. Nothing is better calculated for this purpose than a well regulated stage.[5]

Early Stage Entertainments

Before the Revolution, Pittsburgh's one clear social advantage was its proximity to the British military installation at Fort Pitt, situated at the confluence of the Monongahela and Allegheny rivers. A public assembly room was apparently in use at the fort at least from 1763, when Captain Simon Ecuyer was pleased to note, in a letter to another officer, the presence of "the most beautiful ladies of the garrison" at the Saturday evening balls. In 1765, a German doctor named Johann Schoepf recorded that "balls, plays, concerts and comedies" were being offered to the local community at the fort.[6] Another source reports that the British officers at Fort Pitt produced "some of Shakespeare's plays" in the early 1770s.[7] Garrison theatricals were common in British installations across the Americas. British officers, as members of the gentry, were responsible for setting standards of social protocol and helping to establish cultural activities in occupied territories. Participating in garrison theatricals was a crucial component of an officer's duty to his regiment and to the community; making theater both a way to model behavior for local inhabitants with social aspirations and a method for spreading British cultural traditions.[8]

In the early days of the Republic, leisure activities increased significantly, a change brought on by postwar prosperity and a new urge for civic assembly at both the national and regional levels. The call to "soften the brow" of the western country was made often, in and out of the pages of the *Gazette*, because the development of healthy forms of civic assembly (from military parades to agricultural fairs) was being linked to the "American spirit" rhetoric shared by both the Federalist and the Anti-Federalist parties. Not all of Pittsburgh's newly minted Americans were welcome, however; some were forced to create parallel public events such as the Saint Patrick's Day dinner, hosted by the overtly anti-British Sons of Hibernia, and the "Negro balls" sponsored by local African American congregations.[9]

In this new age of public assembly, commercial forms of amusement developed rapidly. Some of the most popular were also the most controversial. For some people, including the editor of the *Gazette*, horse racing topped the list of unacceptable amusements, because the "youth of both sexes run to harm, folly and debauchery at this fruitful seminary of all vice" (Oct. 16, 1801, 3). Still, the *Gazette* of the 1780s and 1790s was filled with advertisements for other types of leisure activity. Dozens of dancing masters offered to teach, for a fee, the "most fashionable Country Dances and City Cotillions" (June 20, 1798, 2). Public balls, usually following some kind of ticketed performance, were regular events in the great room at Fort Pitt. Outdoor fairs sponsored by the clerk of the Pittsburgh market began as early as 1796. These retail-oriented events (merchants paid a small fee to exhibit their wares) drew visitors by offering a variety of free entertainments, from "horse running" to "astonishing feats of Slack Rope, Wire Dancing, Balancing, Tumbling, &c. &c. &c." (May 14, 1796, 1). Small, family-operated traveling circuses made regular stops in the city and usually set up in the empty lots next to taverns and hotels. Menageries featuring exotic animals commanded a sizable entry fee, especially for a talented animal. The proprietors of the New England Hotel on Wood Street, for example, charged twenty-five cents for a brief look at the "first and only Male Elephant ever seen in this country. . . . He will take his Keeper with his foot or trunk, and place him on his back; but what is most curious among his maneuvers, he will dance to music, and very correctly" (June 18, 1819, 3).

Taverns and inns that had originally catered solely to travelers began serving a more crucial civic role. With their large public rooms, they quickly became de facto assembly halls for convocations of all sorts, legislative, religious, and cultural. Local residents in search of social intercourse and an evening's entertainment found them well suited for gathering and delivering news, celebrating important occasions, and sharing the performance traditions brought from home. Tavern owners in turn found their spaces well suited to a new source of income and began charging admission for a range of cultural events, from exhibitions of "curiosities and wonders" to musicales and dramatic readings. The Black Bear Tavern, for example, was well known in the 1790s for its lively evenings filled with a variety of entertainments—from chamber concerts to play readings to improvised farces. At William Irwin's popular inn, Punch and Judy shows played alongside circus acts. John Reed imported traveling curiosities and sold tickets to see "an elegant and extensive Collection of WAX WORK FIGURES AS LARGE AS LIFE." Mr. Carr's Tavern featured solo performances by local residents, including "Mr. Dwyer's Readings & Recitations" and a vocal concert by Thomas Sheldon, leader of the Apollonian Society, the city's first orchestra association. Mr. Morrow's Tavern also hosted dramatic readings and vocal concerts featuring "the most favorite pieces of music, among which are the *Yellow hair'd Laddie*, with variations."[10]

Dramatic Entertainment

In the early years of the Republic, dramatic stage entertainments were produced at a variety of spaces around the growing town. At Fort Pitt, for example, a room called the Theatre in the Garrison featured amateur work by the state militia occupying the increasingly dilapidated structure. The first to be announced in the *Gazette* was a production of Addison's *Cato* in April 1790. The story of the Roman leader, long a popular choice in the colonial theater, was first produced in the Americas at Charleston's Dock Street Theatre in 1735. During the Revolution George Washington quoted it often in his writings and speeches and even ordered a wartime production of the piece at Valley Forge in 1778. When *Cato* finally appeared on the western front in 1790, the four-year-old *Pittsburgh Gazette* proudly placed the news in a front-page box: "Ladies and Gentlemen are hereby informed, that a Theatrical Representation of the tragedy of Cato, with the farce of All the World's a Stage, will take place on Tuesday the 20th in the Theatre in the Garrison."[11]

The New Theatre over the Allegheny, which opened in 1795, seems to have been the first commercial space in Pittsburgh to call itself a theater. On February 27, 1796, the *Gazette* noted in a front-page editorial:

> The New Theatre over the Allegheny was opened last season under the direction of the Managers of the Population Company. The principal characters were ably supported by many of the leading and knowing ones of the State. . . . The Dresses, Scenery, and Decorations entirely new; Transparent Paintings, with shades after the Italian manner, were towards the close of the Season exhibited with astonishing effect, the colours so well applied as to be perfectly seen through.

The unsigned article reports that the Population Company Troupe, "having some time been moved to the Old Theater, Philadelphia," was currently being replaced by a strolling company from whom "the character of the actors much entertainment may be expected."[12] Among the new pieces the company was reportedly getting up were *Like Master Like Man, The Landlord Ousted, Who's the Dupe,* and *High Life Below Stairs.* In what was perhaps the first theatrical review published in Pittsburgh, the *Gazette* noted, "Although the taste of the whole audience may not be fully gratified, there is little doubt of the Gallery being much diverted." Since no other record of the Theatre over the Allegheny has been located, we do not know how long the venture lasted or who ran it. Nevertheless, the list of plays (short farces) indicates that its repertoire was populist in orientation.[13]

Another theater space that operated regularly during this period was the Great Room of the first county courthouse located in the Diamond (now Market Square), constructed in 1799. Before that time, all county business was conducted in various village taverns. During 1789, for example, the first Court of Common Pleas convened in Andrew Watson's tavern, while in the 1790s court proceedings were held on the third floor of William Irwin's inn.[14] Once legal proceedings had an official home in Pittsburgh, theater moved in as well: "The great room of the upper story of the courthouse, which from its size, and having several other contiguous apartments which serve for green room, dressing rooms, &c.,

is very well adapted to that purpose."[15] Over the next decade, newspapers advertised a wide array of performances at the courthouse, from amateur and traveling professional productions of popular English comedies, comic operas, and farces, to "Indian dances by the chiefs now in town."[16]

Thespian Societies

Like the officers and enlisted men stationed at Fort Pitt during the French and Indian War, native-born citizens of the new nation also enjoyed theatrical entertainment. After 1803 and into the 1820s, a number of thespian societies came and went, some dedicated to educational and charitable aims, others clearly re-flecting the creative urges of well-heeled lawyers, merchants, and other professionals with leisure time. In the early nineteenth century most American cities with growing economies and an established elite supported at least one community-based dramatic society, since the "thespian art" complemented other forms of aesthetic training and liberal education being established for members of the leisure class. By 1800, Pittsburgh supported many dancing academies, music schools, literary clubs, and lecture series. The Apollonian Society, for example, was founded in 1806 as the city's first semiprofessional musical organization. Led by S. W. Dearborn, a professional musician reportedly from Boston, the society consisted of twelve performers and a circle of subscribers willing to pay to hear the music of Bach and Mozart.[17] Other professional advancement clubs were the Mechanical Society, a "reputable tradesmen" group organized in 1788; the Columbian Society of Virtuosi, founded by a group of wealthy professionals in 1810 to collect specimens for a projected natural history museum; and four Freemason lodges in operation by 1815.[18] In addition, Pittsburghers attended lectures on a variety of subjects, most curiously a series on chemistry conducted by a Dr. Aigster "to be held at the Laboratory, corner of Smithfield and Second Streets, every Monday, Wednesday and Saturday" (*Gazette*, Dec. 27, 1811, 3).

Pittsburgh's first nonmilitary community theater troupe, made up of "Young Gentlemen of the Town," performed *The Poor Soldier* (a comic opera) and *The Apprentice* (a farce) at the courthouse in February 1803. According to an ad in the *Gazette*, the curtain would "rise precisely at half past six o'clock," with box seat tickets selling for "Three Quarters Dollar" and gallery seating at "Half a Dollar"

(Feb. 18, 1803, 1). Among the players that evening was the school-age son of Hugh Henry Brackenridge, the most prominent Pittsburgher of that era. Henry Marie Brackenridge recalled that he had "had the honour of delivering a letter to captain Glenroy [in *The Poor Soldier*] and appearing as a Scotchman in *Dick the Apprentice*." His account and several others suggest that the elder Brackenridge was so appalled at seeing his son on the stage (and in bit roles) that he immediately sent him off to a boarding school.[19]

Another thespian society was formed about this time among working-class Pittsburghers. According to Fortescue Cuming, a professional traveler, in 1803 a thespian group made up of "respectable mechanicks" began mounting joint productions with the courthouse club "in order to cast the pieces to be performed with more effect." By 1807 the two groups were being led by S. W. Dearborn, the Apollonian Society conductor, who in addition to his musical duties renovated the courthouse space and began offering monthly dramatic performances throughout the winter, with young men playing the women's parts. Though Cuming noted the "respectable manner" of these "rational entertainments," he had some criticisms: "The female characters being sustained by young men, are deficient of that grace and modest vivacity, which are natural to the fair sex, and which their grosser lords and masters vainly attempt to copy."[20]

Others must have shared Cuming's opinion, because in 1812 another thespian society was formed that included young women. This group, also called the Thespian Society, seems to have lasted in one form or another for nearly two decades, with several generations of Pittsburgh's young elite taking part. It appears to have evolved, in structure and purpose, into a semiprofessional theater company comprised of paid managers and unpaid performers with an operating budget, a governing board, a growing stock of costumes and properties, and a regular season of shows. According to an early historian, "The society numbered among its members the brightest and best bred young people of the city, most of whom took part in each performance."[21] The group performed in a small makeshift theater beneath the auditorium of the original Masonic Hall on Wood Street. A related group, sometimes referred to as the Academy Thespian Society, dates to about 1810, when students at the all-male Pittsburgh Academy (which later became the University of Pittsburgh) began producing plays.[22] The academy, which was essentially a secondary school for sons of the elite, operated out of a small wooden building on Third Street and Cherry Alley. An important part of the curriculum was classical literature, which meant memorizing passages from ancient dramas as well as performing recitations from the classical canon. The academy thespian group was an extracurricular organization with a mandate to produce full-length plays of literary merit, including those by Shakespeare and his contemporaries; Otway's *Venice Preserved* was a favorite choice.

By 1824, interest in amateur theatricals had evolved beyond their function as exercises for students and young men and women of the upper class. That year the Thespian Society was headed by Magnus M. Murray, chief magistrate of Pittsburgh (and in 1828, the city's fourth mayor) and included a list of members whose names are now attached to many Pittsburgh streets and localities: Richard Biddle, Matthew Magee, Morgan Neville, Alexander Breckenridge, William Wilkins, T. B. Dallas, and J. S. Craft. Murray not only managed the society's business affairs, he also acted and guided many of its productions with some skill. But he was apparently unable to solve the problem of the society's debts. After the 1824–25 season, in which only one production's receipts (*Tom and Jerry*) exceeded expenditures, the charitable institution was formally dissolved. The society's use of students from the Western University (the recently expanded Pittsburgh Academy) may have contributed to its demise, since the season's decidedly nonliterary repertoire—including *Who Wants a Guinea, Tom and Jerry, Who's the Dupe,* and *Day after the Wedding*—reportedly displeased the various clergymen who made up the faculty. According to the reminiscences of John Parke, "Many of the members of the company were students of the Western University, and the whole thing was suddenly brought to a full stop by the faculty taking the matter in hand."[23]

Early Professional Theater

By 1812, the population of the borough of Pittsburgh exceeded 5,000 people, not including an additional several thousand living in Birmingham (now called the South Side), Allegheny City (the North Side), and the Northern Liberties (roughly, the East End).[24] The act of incorporation chartering Pittsburgh as an official city was still four years away (March 18, 1816), but residents of the rapidly growing town were actively building an independent metropolis. The city was already well established as an industrial site producing glass, cannons, tinware, keelboats, wagon wheels, whiskey, cabinets, shoes, and Windsor chairs. Its geographic importance made it a leading trade center where waves of travelers stopped to rest from their long overland journeys and to exchange the wagons that had crossed the Alleghenies for keelboats in which to float down the Ohio. The impact of these travelers on the local inhabitants was both economic and cultural, since they brought with them not only money and goods for trading but also customs, habits, and opinions on everything from politics to art to social practice. This heady stream of outside influence brought information and ideas from Europe and the Atlantic seaboard, particularly Philadelphia. It must also have helped to establish standards of taste and to inform the cultural habits of the town's early inhabitants.

Among those who traveled through Pittsburgh were members of professional theater companies forging new performing circuits to the west and southwest. These routes complemented the well-established touring theater circuits along the eastern seaboard, from Boston to Charleston and beyond as far as Jamaica. The first established theatrical circuit west of the Allegheny Mountains dates to about 1811, when James Douglas brought his acting company from Canada to Lexington, Kentucky. But earlier troupes had been making their way to Pittsburgh at least since 1795 with the one-season residency of the Population Company at the Theatre over the Allegheny, already mentioned, and continuing with Bromly and Arnold, itinerant actors who performed at the courthouse in "the comedy of Trick Upon Trick" (*Gazette*, Jan. 20, 1803, 1).[25] Other traveling professionals performed in local inns and taverns, as shown in this ad: "The celebrated comedy of the Birth Day, Or Reconciliation will be presented by Mrs. Turner and Mr. Cipriani, ballet master from Sadler's Wells" (*Gazette*, Nov. 2, 1810, 3). Sophia Turner, an English actress, was the wife of William A. Turner, a theatrical manager whose traveling stock company frequently stopped in Pittsburgh en route to Cincinnati and Kentucky and who later became the director of the Theatre on Third Street (discussed below). The professional credentials of Mr. Cipriani, late of Sadler's Wells, are harder to verify. He seems to have been known primarily for his tumbling skills.[26]

Clear proof that substantial income-producing theater existed in Pittsburgh during this period are the borough and city ordinances "Concerning Plays, Shows and Theatrical Entertainments." Beginning as borough law in the late eighteenth century, these regulations were adopted by the newly formed city of

Pittsburgh in 1816 and published in the *Gazette*. The new ordinance (presumably based on earlier regulations) applied to "any show, spectacle, or natural or artificial curiosity, where money may be demanded for admission." The ordinance covered licensing and permissions ("to be obtained from the Mayor of the City"), content (plays were "to be of a decent and moral tendency"), performance conditions ("a Constable must attend . . . and prevent any outrage, or disturbance of the harmony of the citizens"), and the actors (those employing minors without consent "shall forfeit and pay the sum of Forty Dollars") (Sept. 6, 1816, 3).

The Theatre on Third Street

The most concrete indicator of Pittsburgh's growing interest in professional theater was the construction of the Theatre on Third Street, Pittsburgh's first freestanding playhouse, in 1813. The initiative was similar to other community-building efforts during this period. Municipal services, ranging from care for the indigent, child welfare programs, education, and circulating libraries, were supported entirely by privately funded groups sponsored by religious, ethnic, and professional organizations.[27] The construction of a theatrical playhouse was also seen as a private responsibility arising out of a common need. But it was, additionally, an entrepreneurial opportunity. Financed on a subscription basis by members of the wealthy elite, the effort was modeled on a shareholding system long used by theaters in Philadelphia, Boston, and New York. The goal was twofold: to promote the social advancement of the community while satisfying the cultural tastes of the subscribers; and to boost their economic interests, since a successful playhouse only increased a community's real estate value. To make the project happen, elite citizens (male, white, and property-owning) bought shares, became members of the board of directors, built the playhouse, and hired or leased the space to a professional actor-manager. The manager then formed a resident professional acting company, known as a stock company, which performed a rotating repertoire on a nightly basis.

The first record of the Theatre on Third Street is an advertisement in the *Gazette* from May 15, 1812, offering subscriptions at a cost of "one-third of the Season Ticket" (3). Another ad three months later noted that the building was "about to be erected" and requested subscribers to "attend a meeting to be held in the house of James Gibson" (Aug. 14, 1812, 3). Investors were guaranteed seating and a share of the profits. Since there is no record of production in the theater until a year later, in August 1813, subscription-style financing may have proved difficult. The shareholders eventually purchased a lot on Third Street near the corner of Smithfield and hired architect and builder Charles Weidner to erect a "substantial frame structure, sixty feet front, two stories in height."[28]

The Theatre on Third Street was completed in the summer of 1813, and Pittsburghers were proud of their new playhouse. A judge noted that the 400-seat interior was "tastefully fitted up with dress-circle, pit, gallery, and proscenium boxes," with a "fine" painting under the proscenium arch bearing the Latin motto "Veluti in speculum."[29] The space was immediately leased to the English-born actor-manager William A. Turner, who had started with James Douglas's troupe in Canada before founding his own traveling company in Cincinnati around 1811. By 1812 he was adding theaters to his western circuit stretching from Lexington, Kentucky, to Pittsburgh. Turner's company featured his wife and a Mr. Webster, billed as a "celebrated actor from Europe." Most of Turner's actors seem to have been little known, though a few had extensive London and New York credits.[30] Perhaps they joined the provincial company because Turner's circuit allowed for steady employment, as his troupe moved from city to city performing month-long seasons.[31] The Turner Company's Pittsburgh residency began in the fall of 1813 with *The Tale of Mystery*, Holcroft's popular adaptation of Pixérécourt's French melodrama. Other plays in the repertoire were comic operas or farcical short pieces such as *To Marry, or, Not to Marry* and *The Irishman in London*, featuring the singing talents of both Webster and Mrs. Turner.

Despite Turner's management experience, the Theatre on Third Street never achieved financial solvency. Almost immediately some of the original investors began attempting to sell off their shares. In November 1813 an ad appeared in the *Gazette* offering up a "half part" of the theater, "with the scenery, Decorations, Embellishments." Though described as "a very valuable property to a purchaser," it clearly was not, since attempts to resell shares continued to appear over the next decade. The theater had fallen into disrepair by the time the Samuel Drake Company took up a three-month residency in the fall of 1815. In the words of Noah Ludlow, an actor,

[It was] the poorest apology for [a theater] I had then ever seen. . . . It was situated on the eastern outskirts of the city. . . . It contained a pit and one tier of boxes, as they were called. The form was after the old style—two parallel elongations, with an elliptical curve at the entrance. The decorations, if such they might be termed, were of the plainest kind, and every portion bore the Pittsburgh stamp upon it—coal smut.[32]

It is not clear why the Theatre on Third Street failed to thrive. Some accounts suggest that with only 400 seats it was not large enough to make a profit, while others blame everything from the antitheatrical tendencies of the Presbyterian elite and the superstitious laboring class. Noah Ludlow clearly blames the latter in his memoir, *Dramatic Life as I Found It*. Recounting his difficulty in casting the supernumerary roles for his company's production of *Pizarro* in the fall of 1815, he noted with evident frustration, "Virgins (of course I mean stage virgins) were not to be had in Pittsburgh in those days. Seamstresses and shoe-binders would have as soon thought of walking deliberately into Pandemonium as to have appeared on the stage as 'supers' or 'corps de ballet.'"[33] Ludlow's memoir is not reliable, however, since there is ample evidence of a thriving amateur thespian community in 1815 made up of citizens willing to appear on stage. Perhaps the Drake Company failed to attract the attention of the city's established thespian societies, or perhaps local amateurs held their own prejudices about consorting with itinerant actors.

Despite its financial problems, however, the Theatre on Third Street continued to operate. In the winter of 1815 Turner and his actors (now the Pittsburgh Company of Comedians) produced *Richard III* and *King Lear*—no doubt the first professional productions of Shakespeare in the city (though not the first Shakespeare, as we have seen). An advertisement for *King Lear and His Three Daughters* "respectfully solicits the attendance of the patron of the Drama" to witness "Shakespeare's universally admired Tragedy."[34] There is no record of the Turner Company after this appearance.[35]

A few amateur productions were mounted at the Theatre on Third Street in 1816. Then, in the fall of 1817, another professional group took up residence. An itinerant company headed by John Entwisle, an actor and playwright, regularly traveled the western circuit offering "first rate talents, from the Theaters, New-York—Philadelphia—Boston and Charleston" in standard works from the popular repertoire. In August, Entwisle announced that considerable repairs to both the house and the stage of the Theatre on Third Street had been completed and that "neither pains nor expense has been spared to render the Theatre worthy the patronage of a liberal public" (*Gazette*, Aug. 5, 1817, 3). The Entwisle Company enjoyed a busy three-month season in Pittsburgh, then apparently never returned.

Over the next decade, a variety of traveling stock companies performed at the Theatre on Third Street, and a few more attempts were made to establish a resident stock company. In 1822, sixteen-year-old Edwin Forrest, later one of the most influential American actors of the century, came to Pittsburgh with a company organized by Joshua Collins, a former member of Turner's company, and William Jones, formerly with Drake's company. Forrest recorded his first impressions of the city in a letter to his mother in Philadelphia: "I arrived here yesterday at about eleven o'clock, and am much pleased with the place and its inhabitants. . . . Pittsburgh . . . is a sort of London in miniature, very black and smoky. The Alleghany River and Mountains surround it. The theater is very old." Forrest's biographer offers more detail:

> About the middle of October they began playing in Pittsburgh, in a building so ruinous and dilapidated that on rainy nights the audience in the pit held up their umbrellas to screen themselves from the leakings through the roof. The first performance was *Douglas,* Forrest sustaining the part of Young Norval with much applause. In the course of the season here he played many characters, in tragedy, comedy, farce, and ballet.[36]

Even the disgruntled Noah Ludlow repeatedly returned to the Theatre on Third Street after leaving the Drake Company. He appeared many times in Pittsburgh between 1818 and 1830 with his own barnstorming company and over the years developed close friendships with local residents. His final season at the theater began in June 1830, and, according to Ludlow, "worried along to fluctuating business."[37] He left Pittsburgh in November to join James Caldwell's company, leaving behind many of his actors. A Mr. Fuller briefly took over for Ludlow "with a very respectable stock-company, under whose management considerable changes and improvements were effected in scenery, decorations, etc."[38] Still, by the end of the 1820s the theater was often dark, its original purpose to "mirror the world" diminished to occasional productions by the various thespian societies and a series of one-night-only magic shows, circus acts, and "dramatic ventriloquists." The building itself was gradually being whittled away, as a traveler noted in 1824: "There was a day when a series of columns supported the projection of the upper story; but the rude and naughty boys, by occasionally whittling them with their pocket knives, have ruined the proportions of some, and left no traces of others" (*Gazette*, Nov. 17, 1824, 2). By 1830 the Theatre on Third Street had entered its final phase of useful existence, signified by a notice that ran repeatedly in the *Gazette* over the course of that year: "For Sale. The old Theater Lot . . . And a quantity of good seasoned boards" (Jan. 1, 1830, 2).

Early Theater Audiences

The poor financial history of Pittsburgh's first permanent playhouse and the failure to establish a lasting professional stock company at the Theatre on Third Street have frequently been interpreted as evidence of Pittsburgh's antitheatrical bias. This oft-cited "Presbyterian" characteristic is attributed to the city's Scots-Irish founding elite, their repugnance toward idleness, and a general disposition to "take their pleasures sadly."[39] These qualities predate the Scots-Irish, however, and are more characteristic of Pennsylvania's colonial Quaker culture. William Penn himself set the standard in 1682 when he declared playgoing to be "an offense against God [which incited] people to Rudeness, Cruelty, Looseness, and Irreligion."[40] Additional contributing factors were the realities of frontier living. As Zadok Cramer, Pittsburgh's first bookseller, noted around 1810: "The character of the people is that of enterprising and persevering industry; every man to his business is the prevailing maxim, there is therefore little time devoted to amusements or to the cultivation of refined social pleasures. . . . The amusements of these industrious people are not numerous."[41]

Yet a closer look at the late eighteenth century and early nineteenth reveals another Pittsburgh, many of whose citizens were not in the least opposed to idleness or an evening at the theater. As noted, the frontier town was settled by a varied mix of people who were anything but "Presbyterian" in their behavior, including former soldiers from Fort Pitt, Fort Lafayette, and Fort Duquesne, Indian traders and other economic adventurers, former indentured servants, religious exiles, and the ever-increasing number of immigrants from Western Europe. Population statistics show that the Scottish and Scots-Irish population

of the city was never greater than 29 percent and that the majority of early Pittsburghers were of English, German, and Irish stock.[42] Further, many seem to
have adopted a certain independence of behavior, regardless of their ethnicity or
religious beliefs. One diarist complained in 1773: "A great part of the people here
make the Sabbath a day of recreation, drinking & profanity. . . . The inhabitants
of this place are very dissipated. They seem to feel themselves beyond the arm
of government, & freed from the restraining influence of religion. . . . Drinking,
debauchery & all kinds of vice reign, in this frontier of depravity."[43] This criticism undoubtedly focused on traders and laborers but may also have included
craftsmen: nailers, shopkeepers, glass blowers, foundrymen, and brewers who
were able to afford the substantial prices being charged at taverns and other houses
of entertainment where drinking and other forms of vice, including theatergoing, were to be found. Though these varied settlers reflected a constantly shifting
mixture of cultural and ethnic identities, they soon began to take on a collective
"western" character, at least for journalists seeking to create a cultural profile for
the new nation's growing cities and towns. The rough, plainspoken, free-spirited
"western" label was the first of many tags to be applied to Pittsburghers—and by
extension, to Pittsburgh audiences.

Even among the Presbyterian founding elite there is no evidence of a consistent antitheatrical sentiment. The synod may have maintained an official
stance against "theatrical exhibitions and other vain amusements," but the mainstream presbytery did not prohibit theatergoing. Further, as the records of many
thespian societies make clear, members of the Presbyterian elite were among
the most prominent theater practitioners and consumers of the era, themselves
responsible for launching the city's first indigenous theater. The myth about an
antitheatrical bias among Pittsburghers is probably the legacy of the Covenanters,
a reformed branch of the Scots-Irish presbytery. In Pittsburgh, the Covenanters
were established in 1800 and led for nearly fifty years by Reverend John Black.
Though he was "identified with almost all the literary and charitable institutions
of his adopted city" and was a professor of ancient languages and classical literature
at Western University, Black shared the antitheatrical zeal of all Covenanters.[44]

Black led many attacks on the stage from his pulpit at the Covenanters'
downtown meeting house on Oak Alley and was the subject of many counter-
attacks led by commentators grown weary of his fire-and-brimstone rhetoric. In
1818 Morgan Neville, editor of the *Gazette*, took Black to task in a front-page ed-

itorial by touting both the "considerable spirit" of local amateur performers and the "intrinsic merit of their charitable enterprises." After echoing a passage from Ecclesiastes—"According to a very high authority there is a time for *all things*"— Neville ended with a satirical portrait of "Sombrius," a reference to Black: "He looks on a sudden fit of laughter as a breach of his baptismal vow. All the little ornaments of life are pomps and vanities. Mirth is wanton and wit profane. After all Sombrius is a religious man and would have behaved himself very properly had he lived when Christianity was under a general persecution" (Nov. 13, 1818, 1). Whereas Neville did not identify Black by name, others, including visitor Ann Royall, were not afraid to assign blame for a rhetorical posture they deemed both hypocritical and detrimental to Pittsburgh. In a travelogue written about 1828, Royall blames Reverend Black and his fellow "tract people" for the city's paucity of cultural amenities, exclaiming: "Every thing learned or liberal falls before the march of these priests."[45]

Although Black garnered attention in print, the majority of early Pittsburghers did not share his attitude or follow his advice. As this chapter recounts, from the colonial period Pittsburghers from all social classes and ethnic and religious heritages were eager for theatrical entertainment at markets, fairgrounds, taverns, the courthouse, and the Theatre on Third Street, enjoying everything from farces and dramatic ventriloquists to Shakespeare and Sheridan. When the Samuel Drake Company arrived in 1815 to produce *Pizzaro*, the itinerant actors may have had difficulty in finding extras to appear as stage virgins, but they had no trouble finding an audience. During the company's three-month residency, the theater's 400 seats were priced at the astonishingly high cost of one dollar. Yet, notes Ludlow, "the house was filled to its utmost extent" each night, the pit crowded with "foundrymen, keel-boat men, and sundry and divers dark-featured and iron-fisted burghers," the boxes filled "with dark-skinned yet beautiful ladies."[46]

2

THEATER AS COMMUNITY INVESTMENT

1830 to 1870

Pittsburgh. September 13, 1833. It is a special night for the 1,200 or so Pittsburghers now jamming Fifth Street on their way into the brand-new Pittsburgh Theatre, a playhouse the local newspaper claims "will safely vie with any other in the Union." And while most local theatergoers haven't the travel experience to make such a comparison, their eyes do not deceive. With its five arched entranceways, the outside of the brick structure is certainly impressive, especially in contrast to the mostly wood-frame buildings that surround it. The real splendor, though, is inside. The large proscenium arch bears the Pennsylvania arms. The two tiers of stage boxes are painted rose and ornamented with gold. The seats are covered with crimson, edged with velvet, and studded with brass nails. And the auditorium—the most lavish assembly hall in the city's brief history—is lighted with eighteen enormous chandeliers. The excitement over the new playhouse is further enhanced by the gala appearance of Edwin Forrest. And even though this newly crowned prince of American acting has seen fancier theaters and played for bigger crowds in bigger cities, tonight's performance is just as special to him, since it marks his triumphant return to a city where he once apprenticed as a boy actor. Since then Forrest has become the champion of a new, utterly American style of acting—muscular, energetic, and independent. And Pittsburghers, who fancy themselves equally muscular, energetic, and independent, are ready to yell out their approval the minute he walks on the stage in his signature role as the doomed Indian chief Metamora.[1]

"An Elegant Home to the Drama"

By 1830 the population of Pittsburgh had climbed to 12,568, with an additional 10,000 living in nearby towns and boroughs. This steady residential growth reflected a change in the city's status from an outpost for soldiers and traders to a destination for immigrants, land settlers, and entrepreneurs. Improvements in road building had helped to make the Pittsburgh-Philadelphia trip quicker and safer, and residents were anticipating the completion of the Pennsylvania Main Line Canal, a complex waterway and overland system (using canal boats, inclines, and short rail tracks) that stretched from the eastern seaboard and reduced the journey from nearly three weeks to about three and a half days. In addition, the industrial potential of the city was rapidly being exploited; instead of simply shipping and trading goods made in the east, manufacturers were beginning to use local resources to build essential items such as flint glass, boats, steam engines, and a variety of iron ore products. And as the permanent workforce increased to meet the city's new industrial mandate, so did its physical plant. By 1830, Pittsburgh's downtown area included hundreds of residential dwellings, two dozen churches, about 500 shops, mills, factories, and other industrial structures, a waterworks, a nascent university, government buildings, dozens of private academies, the offices of eight weekly and daily newspapers, several bookstores and print shops, a museum, a lending library, five assembly halls, scores of taverns, hotels, and public meeting rooms, and on Third Street, one small, decaying wood-frame theatrical playhouse.

Fig. 3. The Pittsburgh Theatre on Fifth Street, erected in 1833. Source: *Allegheny County: A Sesqui-Centennial Review*, 1938.

A few years earlier, James S. Stevenson, a local manufacturer and U.S. congressman from 1825 to 1829, had begun raising funds to build a new playhouse to replace the Theatre on Third Street, by then so thoroughly dilapidated that many considered it unsafe to enter. By 1826 Pittsburgh had several large assembly halls and even the country's first floating theater. Still, none was outfitted with stage machinery or a picture-frame proscenium. The original Masonic Hall on Wood Street, built in 1811 as a lecture hall, had a shallow stage floor that could not accommodate most commercial theater. Another public space, Mr. Bond's Concert Hall at Wood and Fourth streets, was also too small for most stage productions, although it did occasionally host recitals or small touring acts, such as the three-night appearance of Julia Lane, a "Celebrated Juvenile Actress, from the principal Theater in the Union" (*Pittsburgh Daily Gazette*, Apr. 13, 1830, 3).[2] And William Chapman's Floating Theatre, a craft fitted out with a stage, a pit, and a gallery, was in Pittsburgh for only a few months each season. The English-born Chapman had come to Pittsburgh in 1829 after working a stint at the Bowery Theater in New York City. He produced two seasons of plays in the dining room of the Monongahela Hotel before buying a large keelboat and erecting a stage at one end and a small auditorium at the other. Over the next eight years he and his family mounted productions of Shakespeare (*Othello, The Merchant of Venice, Hamlet*), opening each season in Pittsburgh before traveling down the Ohio and Mississippi, performing in small river towns along the way.[3]

Given the makeshift quality of these spaces, none was competitive with the state-of-the-art theatrical playhouses being built in other fast-growing cities. Pittsburgh's lack of a viable playhouse must have concerned the city's elite, as it did many traveling theater companies. Congressman Stevenson and the other subscribers envisioned a new "elegant home to the drama" as a way to enhance the city's cultural life and to bolster their own social positions. Stevenson, the single largest contributor, gave $500 and was selected to buy a lot for the new structure. In 1827 he purchased a plot of land at 306–310 Fifth Street in his own name, but there the project stalled. After Stevenson lost his bid for reelection to Congress, he was evidently short of cash. When the other subscribers demanded the deed to the Fifth Street property, Stevenson refused to "convey it or the interest in it to his partners."[4] After his death in 1831, a court order forced Stevenson's heirs to sign over the property to a newly elected board of directors, headed by George A. Cooke, which was to raise additional funds to cover building costs and to supervise construction of a theater.

The new board chose John Haviland, a Philadelphia architect, to design a new playhouse and hired a local contractor to build the two-story brick structure, which took more than a year to complete. In a key strategic decision, they leased the space to Francis Courtney Wemyss, a London-born actor who had begun his American career at Philadelphia's Chestnut Theatre in 1822 and eventually managed theaters and stock companies in Washington, D.C., Wheeling, Wilmington, Delaware, Baltimore, and Philadelphia.[5] Wemyss's management strategy was to establish a strong, professional resident company, to program regular "star" turns (while maintaining tight financial control over them), to keep gallery prices low, and to invest in elegant surroundings and stage machinery capable of special effects.

As Wemyss began his tenure at the Pittsburgh Theatre, he jobbed out the interior stage mechanics to a Philadelphia firm, Stafor and Hoffman, and the scenery to J. R. Smith, "a young Artist of great talent." He also began cultivating an economically diverse audience. First he promoted season ticket sales to the city's elite: "A few tickets of Admission, for the Season, may be obtained, if applied for immediately—the number being limited, to prevent disappointment, an early application is indispensably requisite" (*Gazette*, July 26, 1833, 3). A month later he began appealing to single ticket buyers—mostly factory workers willing to pay for a reasonably priced twenty-five-cent seat in the gallery. (The old Theater on Third Street had charged a dollar for similar seating.)

Wemyss's largest task, however, was to bring a sense of excitement to the city. A skilled publicist, he conducted a three-month advertising campaign touting his "advantageously known Regular Company" and the impending appearances of the "most distinguished Performers of the American Stage, who will appear in rapid succession" (*Pittsburgh Daily Gazette*, July 26, 1833, 3). Wemyss lived up to his promise. Edwin Forrest's sold-out run in September 1833 featured the muscular actor as Othello, King Lear, Macbeth, and Metamora, the doomed Indian chief.[6] He was followed by other notable stars, from Charles Parlsoe, a clown and pantomime famous for his portrayal of monkeys, to the Englishman Junius Brutus Booth, progenitor of a long line of American actors. Booth was very well received in the city (his Shylock and Richard III were favorites), though he was also remembered for being "beastly drunk" night after night during his Pittsburgh run.[7] Other notable performers and events from the Wemyss era include repeat appearances by the Irish comedian Tyrone Power (another progenitor of a famous line of actors) and Thomas Dartmouth Rice, later famous for his "Jump Jim Crow" song and dance routine. In 1838 Wemyss also produced the first full-length opera presented in Pittsburgh, *The Barber of Seville*.[8]

Wemyss's management style affected the city's cultural life in both positive and negative ways. Because of his Philadelphia connections, a regular flow of sophisticated performers, designers, and stage mechanics came to the city, mounting and remounting a rotating repertoire of popular plays, farces, operas, and short musical events. Wemyss quickly succeeded in establishing his playhouse as *the* cultural destination for both Pittsburgh residents and visitors.[9] Ironically, a series of cultural faux pas seems also to have been related to Wemyss's outsider status. Despite his considerable experience as an actor-manager, he was frequently unaware of or at odds with the cultural complexities of his audience. One such issue was segregation of the audience by race. A few weeks after the Pittsburgh Theatre opened, Wemyss began running the following notice in his daily bill:

> To the Gallery—Anxious to add to the comfort of the frequenters of this part of the Theatre, they are respectfully informed that two Boxes, from each side, have been thrown into the Gallery. The two on the left hand side of the house will be reserved exclusively for People of Color—the price of which will be the same as admission to the Pit. The subscriber hopes this arrangement will prove satisfactory (*Pittsburgh Daily Gazette*, Sept. 12, 1833, 2).

This information was prominently featured in the theater's weekly ads for the remainder of the fall season, indicating perhaps that Wemyss was adjusting his ticket policy in response to the increasingly tense racial atmosphere, especially among the white, working-class, male clientele in the gallery.[10]

Why a segregated gallery was not seen as a "necessity" before the theater opened is unclear. Wemyss may not have been prepared for the relative autonomy of free blacks in Pittsburgh—a vibrant, middle-class community living in an area known as Little Haiti or Arthursville (today's Lower Hill District). This free population dated to the prerevolutionary period, when African Americans were welcome conscripts in the Continental army. By the early 1830s, a number of black-owned businesses were operating in white and black neighborhoods in and around the downtown. And though blacks comprised a small percentage of the city's population, they would have been as eager as anyone else to attend performances at the Pittsburgh Theatre. Wemyss's sudden adjustment of the seating policy must have been in response to the demands of white patrons. This redistribution of the auditorium launched a segregated seating policy at the Pittsburgh Theatre that was maintained until its demolition in 1870.[11]

Ironically, even though Wemyss felt he needed to please his white audience, he also complained about them publicly, particularly frequenters of the upper

gallery. Like most nineteenth-century playhouses, the Pittsburgh Theatre was divided into three areas that tended to reflect class differences. Upper-class patrons
usually purchased seats in the boxes (sometimes called the dress circle) furnished
with upholstered wingback chairs priced at seventy-five cents. (One memoirist
recalled that "a very stout person, after squeezing into one, could easily walk
off with it attached").[12] Craftsmen and skilled laborers and their families usually
purchased fifty-cent seats in the pit, where rows of benches were placed directly
in front (and considerably below) the stage. Everyone else sat in the gallery, where
the cheapest seats were twenty-five cents. This section was almost exclusively the
domain of single men, African Americans, and prostitutes, who often circulated
during the performance.[13] This division by class was further achieved by two
front entrances (one for the boxes and pit and another for the gallery) and a tacit
agreement to observe protocols keeping the two groups apart. This attempt was
not always successful, however, as indicated by the spirit of class warfare implicit
in this 1838 editorial: "The Babel confusion and uproar, the yelling and cursing—
swearing and tearing—the friendly interchange of commodities—apples, pignuts,
etc., between the tenants of the upper boxes and pit, have become intolerable."[14]

As in most playhouses of the period, an ethos of self-rule governed the
white sections of the upper gallery; this crowd had a strong sense of ownership
over events in their part of the auditorium and on the stage. Wemyss was clearly
frustrated by the gallery patrons' habit of hissing actors off the stage. According
to one anecdote, the gallery audience once drove an actor from the stage because
he had been spotted wearing white gloves on the street earlier in the day, a habit
deemed overly "European." Another story recounts how Wemyss attempted to
stop the incessant hissing by putting a police guard in the upper gallery, only to
be hissed at himself when he next appeared in a role.[15] In his memoirs written
in the 1850s, Wemyss blamed his problems on this rowdy gallery crowd, complaining that the "Pittsburgh audience invariably selected the worst actors as
their favorites."[16] This characterization was overly general—he seems to have
conflated the gallery with other parts of the house. Moreover, Wemyss may
have ignored his own responsibility for the audience's discontent. A series of newspaper articles criticized the manager for casting untrained actors in Pittsburgh before moving them on to his theater in Philadelphia, a practice that amounted to
using the Pittsburgh Theatre as a site for actor training. According to the *Pittsburgh Times*:

General complaint is made that the manager of this affair treats his audiences with a great degree of contempt; that he takes their fips and levies without giving them bellowing to the amount agreed upon in return. It appears that the manager makes the Pittsburg Theatre the drill ground for the awkward squad, and as soon as the stage-struck boy is "put to trap" and has learned when to speak low, when loud, when to roll up the eyes, and when to clasp the hands expressive of love, anguish, etc., he is packed up and directed to Chestnut Street theatre, and a Johnny Raw is pressed to do duty in his stead. It would appear that this game has been going on for some time, and that our theatrical critics have only lately made this discovery.[17]

By the late 1830s, attendance began to decline in the wake of increasing attacks on the quality of Wemyss's productions. In 1841 he resigned his post and departed, leaving the Pittsburgh Theatre suddenly dark. Several local newspapers cited his practice of shoddy casting as the main reason for "the drama . . . sinking in the public estimation" (*Mercury and Democrat,* Oct. 27, 1841).[18] Only the *Gazette* saw the silver lining of Wemyss's departure. Editor Neville Craig, a well-known critic of the performing arts, refused to accept advertising notices from the Pittsburgh Theatre because he considered it a "school of vice." He is also said to have fired a young reporter for the crime of attending the theater during his free time.[19] When the Pittsburgh Theatre went dark, Craig did not blame Wemyss for the situation but instead concluded, "There is not enough of a drama loving population in this city to support a respectable theater, and we are glad of it. We think it speaks well for the good taste and morality of our inhabitants."[20]

The Playhouse Boom

Despite the artistic and financial ups and downs at the Pittsburgh Theatre, by the time Wemyss left the city in 1841 Pittsburgh was actually on the verge of a new, extremely productive era. From that time until the end of the Civil War, theater evolved from a small cottage industry sponsored by the elite and designed mostly for private entertainment into a large, profitable industry offering both variety-type and legitimate theatrical fare.[21] This rapid growth was spurred on by two forces: the appearance of a new entertainment capitalism based on the mass-market appeal of melodrama and variety formats, and the growing economic power of the city's laboring and professional classes.

By the early 1840s, Pittsburgh's transformation from trading site to production center was well under way. To be sure, many frontier towns along the country's interior travel corridors grew substantially in the early nineteenth century. But Pittsburgh's quick recovery from the economic panic of 1837–38 was part of a deliberate metamorphosis led by local businessmen, who "were avid to enter more daringly and extensively into competition with manufacturers of the world than they had ever undertaken, indeed, even dared to dream of. The rivers and the Pennsylvania canal had measurably emancipated them from the domination of the competitive advantages possessed by their eastern rivals, and the promised coming of railroads from Philadelphia and Baltimore . . . raised their hopes."[22] Though the great age of steel manufacturing was still in the future (Andrew Carnegie was then just a telegraph delivery boy who often sat in the upper galleries of the Pittsburgh Theatre), by 1850 the region had twenty-eight pig iron furnaces (turning out products ranging from nails to cannons), several glassworks, and scores of coal mines. The city's advantageous geographical position helped to spur growth and to foster a new industrial economy.

An important sign of change in the city's theatrical economy was the removal of much of its cultural activity away from the Diamond area (now Market Square) of the original eighteenth- century settlement. The farms along the two thoroughfares leading into the city—today Penn Avenue and Liberty Avenue— gradually assumed a residential and commercial character, with houses located mainly on Penn Avenue and storefronts and wholesale distributors on Liberty. As factories and foundries went up along the banks of the Allegheny, skilled iron-ore workers (or puddlers) settled in this section.[23] Beginning in the 1830s, amusement halls and concert saloons began filling the Penn-Liberty corridor. Most of them operated like the old tavern assembly rooms, selling alcohol and hosting musical performances and paid female companionship to a chiefly male clientele.

Soon, the new economic power of Pittsburgh's rapidly expanding working class, coupled with the growing mass appeal of variety-format theater, prompted a real estate boom in the theater industry. In 1842 the Melodeon (810–812 Liberty Avenue at Strawberry Way) was erected as the city's second legitimate playhouse, a home for full-length dramas to rival "Old Drury" (the Pittsburgh Theater's new nickname). Over the next two decades, many other new theaters opened in this section, including Foster's Gaieties (on the top floor of the Masonic Hall on Wood Street), Trimble's Variety (at Penn and Barker's Alley), Lafayette Hall (the old Concert Hall on Wood Street), Wilkins Hall, the new Masonic Hall (on Fifth Street), the Apollo–National Theater–Pittsburgh Opera House (in the Odd Fellows' Building near the Pittsburgh Theatre on Fifth Avenue), the Eagle Ice Cream Saloon (on Wood Street), Vierheller's Concert Garden (on Diamond Street between Wood and Smithfield), Sefton's Opera House (across from the Pittsburgh Theatre), and the Academy of Music (replacing the Melodeon after it burned in 1865).

Some of these venues, like the Melodeon and the Opera House, were lavish spaces with lounges, elegant interiors, and other accoutrements rivaling the country's leading playhouses. Others, like Trimble's Variety and Vierheller's Concert Garden, were closer to the concert saloon where a patron could buy a dozen oysters and a pint and not worry about spilling anything on the floor. Still others, like the new Masonic Hall, for instance, were multipurpose assembly halls with enormous auditoriums (1,500–2,000 seats) that were occasionally refitted to accommodate stage shows and special events. At the new Masonic Hall, Jenny Lind played her abbreviated Pittsburgh "season" of one night in April 1851. Though reports conflict, most agree that the Swedish Nightingale left the city after only one performance (literally under the cover of darkness) to avoid an angry mob of Pittsburghers unable to secure one of the 3,000 or so tickets Phineas T. Barnum had auctioned off at an average price of seven dollars per head.

Variety Theater

The wave of new construction and rehabilitation along the Penn-Liberty corridor between 1840 and 1865 produced a 500 percent increase in the city's theatrical capacity—from one dedicated playhouse, a handful of small concert saloons, and four assembly halls to roughly twenty-five dedicated and adaptive-use stages. This building frenzy reflected the growing popularity of variety entertainments, particularly the minstrel show, a national phenomenon by the 1840s. Minstrelsy in the United States had begun decades earlier as acts featuring white solo performers in blackface. Called "Negro songs" or "Ethiopian acts," they were usu-

Fig. 4. Odd Fellows' Hall (center), site of the Original Opera House
(1865), and the Avenue Theater (1897–1905). Source: *Pittsburgh Bulletin*,
1917.

ally performed as interludes between acts of plays. In Pittsburgh, references to
"Ethiopian entertainments" date at least to the 1820s, when local and strolling
performers appeared at Philo Hall, Nichols Amphitheater (Liberty near Ninth
Street), Masonic Hall (the original hall on Wood Street), and Concert Hall (on
Penn Avenue).

The first solo blackface performer to exploit the form in a nationally known
act was Thomas Dartmouth Rice, a skillful singer and dancer working with various troupes traveling the western circuit, including Pittsburgh, between 1828

and 1833.[24] Rice's claim to the national stage began in either Louisville, Cincinnati, Pittsburgh, Baltimore, or the Bowery (depending on the source), when he decided to offer a satirical song and dance portrait of a disabled black man, which he labeled Jump Jim Crow. Though there is a dispute about where Rice's character originated,[25] the first sheet music version of the "Jump Jim Crow" song was published in Pittsburgh by William Cummings Peters, a band leader and music dealer with a shop on Market Street.[26]

By the mid-1840s minstrelsy had expanded from a solo form to a full-length group production involving white actors, comedians, instrumentalists, dancers, and singers in blackface. Pittsburgh's first professional minstrel troupe was the Nightingale Ethiopian Opera Company, the resident company at Masonic Hall on Wood Street "composed wholly of home talent."[27] Companies that played regularly in Pittsburgh and nearby cities in the 1840s and 1850s were the Sable Harmonists, the Ethiopian Melodists, the Empire Minstrels, and the Ethiopian Warblers. In addition, the first well-known national touring troupes—including the Christy Minstrels and the Campbell Minstrels—made regular appearances in Pittsburgh.

The city's best-known connection to the minstrel phenomenon is of course Stephen Foster, who was born in Lawrenceville (now part of Pittsburgh) and raised in Allegheny City. Many of Foster's first "Ethiopian melodies" were introduced at the Eagle Ice Cream Saloon, a concert hall where minstrel acts were regularly staged by a resident company.[28] In 1847 Foster's songs won a song competition at the Eagle, and soon after they were being sung on minstrel stages all over the city and sold as sheet music at several downtown stores.[29] By the early 1850s, Foster's minstrel songs were famous throughout the United States.[30]

But while the minstrel show was extremely popular in Pittsburgh, no large theaters were dedicated solely to its production. In fact, none of the city's theaters could be labeled by genre—there was no grand opera or symphony hall, and the so-called legitimate playhouses were not particularly selective in their repertoires. Theaters constantly changed their bills of fare by offering one- or two-week seasons featuring both the resident acting companies and various traveling companies and their star players. This arrangement was not new; the Theatre on Third Street and the Pittsburgh Theatre had always rotated between seasons produced by the resident company (professional or amateur) and traveling shows. What was new was the city's capacity to offer local theatergoers a choice. Beginning with the real estate boom in the 1840s, Pittsburghers could select from a range of resident companies and traveling shows on any given night and throughout most of the year. They also had a growing choice of entertainment genres and styles. Even the term *variety* signaled a free-wheeling bill of fare that could include songs, orchestral numbers, dances, short plays, magic acts, circus performers, trained animals, freak show displays, and other "curiosities."

Theater notices from midcentury demonstrate this eclecticism:[31]

1845: At Masonic Hall: the Nightingale Ethiopian Opera Company; at the Pittsburgh Theatre: the Fakir of Ava's "Grand Soirees of Hindoo Miracles and Mysteries"; the Pittsburgh Theater Company in *The Soldier's Daughter*, *The Englishman in India*, and *The Married Rake*.

1849: At the Pittsburgh Theatre: Junius Brutus Booth and Edwin Booth in *Hamlet* and *Richard III*; the regular company in *Much Ado about Nothing* and *Romeo and Juliet* and three "local" burlettas: *A Squint at Pittsburgh*, *A Glance at Philadelphia*, and *1949, Or Pittsburgh 100 Years Hence*; at Philo Hall: "Jones, the well known colored tragedian, assisted by another young man designs giving his imitations of celebrated players at Philo Hall this evening. The Duquesne Band will add to the attraction by their music."

1859: At Masonic Hall: a festival of Schiller's plays, read and acted by local citizens; Miss Davenport "reads" *As You Like It* and *The Merchant of Venice*; Campbell Minstrels; at the Apollo-National: the Italian Opera Company, featuring Mlle. Piccolomini as Violetta in *La Traviata*; Miss Louise Wells's Equestrian and Dramatic Company; Buckley Serenaders and the Ethiopian Burlesque Opera Troupe; the Apollo-National resident company in *The Boy Martyrs of 1814*, "to conclude with *The Good for Nothing*"; at the Pittsburgh Theatre: Adah Menken in *The Soldier's Daughter*, *The Fate of a Coquette*, and *Lola Montez*; Mr. and Mrs. Yankee Locke in *The Spirit of '76* and *Our Vermont Cousin*; the Pittsburgh Theater Company in *The Poor of New York* and *Charcoal Burner*, "with the usual musical and terpsichorean interludes."

1868: At the Opera House: Edwin Forrest in a rotating repertoire of *Richard III*, *Macbeth*, *Othello*, *Virginius*, *Metamora*, *The Gladiator*, and *Damon and Pythias*; the resident company in *Our American Cousin*; at the Pittsburgh Theatre: Miss Leo Hudson and her "great trained steed, Black Bess, in the great Spectacular Play of *Mazeppa*"; Fred Aimes's Variety Combination Company in a "well selected programme rendered in the most excellent fashion . . . featuring a splendid Corps De Ballet and complete Dramatic Company"; at the Academy of Music: Rossini's *Stabat Mater* by C. Tetedoux and a chorus of fifty singers; at Trimble's Variety: "The dashing dancers, the Dumont Sisters"; "Miss Kate Raymond's most admirable rendering of 'Mazeppa'"; the "newest local sensation, the Cross Roads of Life, localized with remarkable skill and effect"; at Lafayette Hall: "Lecture by Fred. Douglass. This eloquent Orator, and most intelligent Colored Man in the world, will deliver a new and highly interesting Lecture. . . . Tickets only 10 cents to all parts of the Hall. No reserved seats."

The playhouses changed their programming on a weekly basis, moving freely from one genre to another and from the highbrow to the decidedly lowbrow while offering everything from Shakespeare to the latest melodramas to minstrel troupes to equestrian dramas to Italian opera. The performers were equally diverse, from local professionals to established touring stars. At midcentury, Pittsburgh helped to establish the careers of a number of famous American actors. Matilda Herron apprenticed in Pittsburgh and developed her famous rendition of Camille at the Pittsburgh Theatre in 1848. Other notable Pittsburgh apprentices were James Hackett, Lawrence Barrett, and the young Edwin Booth, who appeared with his father on several occasions. The Shakespearean actor Edwin Adams spent so much time in Pittsburgh during his salad days that he inspired the creation in 1865 of the Adams's Dramatic Association. It was formed "with the full consent of the distinguished young tragedian, Edwin Adams, to use his name, with his best wishes, for its success. . . . Some of the brightest stars in the theatrical firmament have learned the first rudiments of their professions in associations similar in character to the Adams' Dramatic Association" (*Pittsburgh Gazette,* Jan. 29, 1866, 4).

Pittsburgh's most intriguing coming-of-age story belongs to Adah Menken, the famous "naked lady" of the equestrian drama craze of the 1860s and an actress of international fame by the time of her death in 1868. In 1858, Menken was a small-time touring actress working the western circuit. While performing in Dayton, Ohio, she agreed to dine with members of the city's volunteer militia. Once details about the evening's events were reported to the press, Menken instantly developed a certain reputation. Recognizing an opportunity, William Henderson, the entrepreneurial lessee of the Pittsburgh Theatre, brought her to Pittsburgh and quickly capitalized on her notoriety with this ad: "Adah Menken, a daughter of Israel, and a charming actress, will be amongst us next week. She is quite eccentric and very beautiful."[32] Menken played several roles from the standard repertoire during her initial run and was acclaimed as a "charming young actress and danseuse." After that, Menken returned to Pittsburgh frequently and in 1861 became a regular member of Henderson's company, appearing in *Ivanhoe, Fast Women of Modern Times,* and *Mazeppa,* in which she gave Pittsburgh "a taste of her ability as an equestrian." By 1864 she had become world-famous as the first "naked" star of the equestrian drama craze.

The First Resident Professional Theaters

While visiting celebrity actors certainly contributed to the theatrical boom of midcentury Pittsburgh, the day-to-day survival of the city's downtown playhouses rested squarely on the shoulders of the professional actors who staffed the resident stock companies. They had two purposes: to mount a rotating repertoire of independent productions for the "stock weeks" and to support traveling stars who booked the theater and needed a cast of professionals in each city to flesh out their productions. Because of a constantly changing repertory, actors were identified with certain roles: leading dramatic, ingénue, light comic, old man, old woman, heavy, etc. Most nineteenth-century actors apprenticed in a particular line of business and remained in it throughout their careers. By midcentury the stock company had become well established in the American theater, with the average troupe employing from eight to ten actors, at least one stage manager and prompter, a scenic artist, a stage carpenter, a properties master, and sometimes an orchestra leader.

Between 1840 and 1870, during the heyday of the stock company, at least six of Pittsburgh's downtown playhouses supported large in-house troupes, while many more of the variety-format houses featured local performers in specialty acts. The longest-running stock company of the era was attached to the Pittsburgh Theatre between 1833, when it was built, and 1870. This was not one company, but a series of troupes organized and administered by several generations of manager-lessees. However, many actors stayed on through management changes and became a part of the Pittsburgh community. These working actors supported a long list of international acting stars that included William Macready,

Edwin Forrest, Junius and Edwin Booth, Charles Kean, Charlotte Cushman, James Hackett, and Edwin Adams.

The first resident company at the Pittsburgh Theatre was Francis Wemyss's regular company, debuting on September 6, 1833, when it supported Edwin Forrest in *Damon and Pythias*. Many of Wemyss's regular actors were eastern professionals who did not stay long in Pittsburgh (including Thomas Rice, later famous as Jump Jim Crow). Other company members became permanent residents of the city and launched several generations of professional actors. Among those were Mr. and Mrs. Eberle and their daughter, Annie, who went from playing ingénue and breeches parts in the 1830s to being a leading actor with the company in the early 1860s, to finally becoming the manager of the original Opera House. She was married to another Pittsburgh actor, English-born Joe Sefton, whose brothers John and William were also members of Wemyss's original company. John and his wife later managed Niblo's Garden in New York City during the 1850s, though apparently they returned briefly to Pittsburgh in the 1860s to open a short-lived "opposition" house directly across the street from Old Drury called the Sefton Opera House.[33]

The life of the average stock company actor during this era was neither easy nor particularly lucrative. Working conditions were strenuous, since an actor was required to keep many roles ready for performance and also to be ready to learn new roles very quickly. Actors attended rehearsals in the morning and often performed two shows a day, six or seven days a week. They were paid on a per-show basis, making it difficult to survive during the off weeks and much of the summer, when theaters were closed. In a letter written in 1865, Arthur Palmer, the resident scene painter for Old Drury, notes that in that year salaries were between $18 and $25 a week—similar to the salaries Francis Wemyss was paying thirty years earlier.[34] Many members of the company, according to Palmer, lived in rented rooms in a "nasty, dreary house, dark and uncomfortable" on Fourth Street. Palmer's letter also describes a repertory system in which actors were required to learn a dozen or more roles at one time: "William 'Old Chip' Chippendale . . . was an actor of some repute in old men and indeed was in some things very fine. But he was very queer and taking a dislike to a part would merely speak his lines and not then unless he got his exact cue [from the prompter]." And since actors were at the mercy of the audience (especially the gallery), stock actors had a vested interest in developing a popular acting technique. In Palmer's words, "J. O. Sefton . . . was our low comedian. As a comedian

Sefton was not considered first class but was a great favorite among the theater going public. He was a most peculiar man and as he depended a great deal upon funny faces—or as professionals call it mugging—he was almost constantly before the glass in the green room practicing this accomplishment."[35]

Stock actors also suffered the indignity of submitting to the outsized egos of traveling stars. Robert Dignam, a Pittsburgh native who apprenticed at Old Drury in the 1860s, noted during an interview:

> Charles Kean and Ellen Tree . . . stopped over in Pittsburg to play two weeks with us. . . . During their engagement they produced *Henry the Eighth, Merchant of Venice, Hamlet* and *Macbeth.* . . . I played Solonto in the *Merchant of Venice.* I remember it distinctly, for they had bought a new pair of slippers for the part and [Charles] Kean made me take them off, as their creaking annoyed him. Kean attended no rehearsals, Cathcart and Everett rehearsing for him. He was small of stature, but a good actor. He was not the great actor we had been led to expect, but, then—he was Kean.[36]

The Emergence of "American" Drama

Edwin Forrest is usually credited with launching the first significant era of indigenous drama written in the United States. In 1828, he personally funded a new play contest seeking a "Tragedy, in five acts, of which the hero or principal character shall be an aboriginal of this country, the sum of five hundred dollars, and half of the proceeds of the third representation, with my own gratuitous services on that occasion."[37] Fourteen playwrights responded, and Forrest's hand-selected committee of "literary and theatrical gentlemen" chose John Augustus Stone's *Metamora, or the Last of the Wampanoags* as the winner. Other actors soon followed Forrest's lead, either by hosting their own play competitions or commissioning playwrights to create star vehicles for them. Sometimes they even wrote their own featured roles. The result was an assortment of entertainments that captured elements of contemporary America: burlesques, variety skits, burlettas, melodramas, historical tableaux, military reenactments, and tragedies —all dramatizing distinct versions of the national character.

Pittsburgh saw its share of stage entertainments reflecting the complicated sociopolitical climate at midcentury, particularly in the ethnic skits that by then regularly targeted Irish, German, Jewish, and Native American characters, in addition to African American figures like Jump Jim Crow and Sambo. These skits reflected the growing anxiety over ethnic identity, since by 1850 a significant percentage (by some accounts nearly half) of Pittsburgh's white population had been born abroad. Another growing segment was made up of free blacks migrating to the city in search of industrial jobs and, until the passage of the Fugitive Slave Act in 1850, escaped slaves seeking asylum. As a result, Pittsburgh, like most large industrial cities, was rife with tensions over ethnic allegiances, the desire to become assimilated, and the urge to control both the emigration and assimilation of other, more recent immigrants.

The city's political situation reflected this growing complexity; by the 1854 election the two-party division of the early 1800s had splintered into the Democratic, Republican, and Know-Nothing parties. The anti-Catholic and xenophobic Know-Nothings were particularly successful in cities like Pittsburgh, where the recent influx of immigrants from Catholic Europe was seen as a threat to native-born Protestants. One notes in particular the large number of pejorative references to the Irish in titles of works produced on Pittsburgh stages in the first half of the century.

Although African Americans were regularly satirized on the minstrel stage, legitimate African American theater artists frequently made stops in the city and performed at the major downtown assembly halls. In 1848 the *Commercial Journal* reported that "Mr. Jones, the colored tragedian, is to give one of his unique and pleasant entertainments next Monday night. Other young colored men are to appear on this occasion, and new recitations are to be given by Mr. J." The *Pittsburgh Dispatch* also reported on Jones's week-long engagement, noting that the actor's "exhibitions have been well attended."[38] African American performers also appeared with whites on Pittsburgh stages as early as the 1830s, when the all-black Duquesne Band accompanied visiting minstrel troupes at Philo Hall. An 1868 playbill for the Pittsburgh Theatre boasts a new "extensive and talented Combination Troupe" that included white acts like the dancing Zucolo Sisters along with "Bob Hart, the funniest Negro Comedian and Johnny Campbell, the great Negro Wit" (*Pittsburgh Daily Post*, Apr. 16, 1968, 4). Without attendance records, it is hard to know the racial makeup of the audience at these events, but no doubt it was predominantly white, given the size of Old Drury and Philo Hall (1,500 seats) and the fact that advertisements appeared in white-owned newspapers. There is no record of black-owned playhouses during this period, although there was a classical music concert hall operated by a Louisiana-born Creole named John Julius.[39]

Certainly there was a predominantly white audience for the Pittsburgh premieres of several race-related dramas of the era. The antislavery cause was firmly supported in Pittsburgh by seven abolitionist societies and several abolitionist newspapers, including *The Albatross* and Martin Delaney's *The Mystery*, the first African American–owned newspaper west of the Alleghenies. In 1848 the abolitionist cause was taken up by Jane Grey Swisshelm, a reformer known for her acid commentaries and passionate positions on slavery and women's rights. Her *Pittsburgh Saturday Visiter* ran until 1857 and was instrumental in galvanizing local resistance to the Fugitive Slave Act of 1850. This heated political climate helped to attract the "immense audiences" for a stage version of *Uncle Tom's Cabin* in November 1853 at the Pittsburgh Theatre. (Musical numbers included in this production were among the first public performances of Foster's "Old Folks at Home," "My Old Kentucky Home," and "Massa's in de Cold, Cold Ground.")[40] Other plays with an abolitionist theme were also produced in antebellum Pittsburgh, as indicated by this notice from the *Post*: "We are to have on Monday evening next Mr. Jamieson's new play of 'The Fugitive Slave.'. . . Let everyone who has a desire to see American dramatic literature take a stand in our own country, rejoice the heart of the author-actor by their presence on Monday evening."[41] But less progressive views also held the stage in Pittsburgh. *The Octoroon*, Dion Boucicault's cautionary tale about the dangers of miscegenation, was produced at Old Drury to a crowd so large that some audience members were forced to find seating backstage. The theater manager became so concerned about an old woman wedged into the wings that he placed her chair on the stage "directly outside the picket fence which surrounded the home of Zoe, the octoroon, so that she would not be in the way of the wings, and she viewed the entire play from that point of vantage."[42]

Smoky City Dramas

In 1845 a programming strategy deliberately aimed at the tastes and allegiances of Pittsburgh's laboring class was initiated at the Pittsburgh Theatre under Charles C. Porter, who in that year took over the lease at Old Drury. To attract an audience, Porter promised "to tender to the Firemen of Pittsburgh the entire receipts of one night of each season . . . as a token of respect for their untiring and patriotic exertion to protect on all occasions, the lives and property of their fellow citizens" (*Pittsburgh Morning Post*, May 3, 1845, 2). The city was just recovering from a massive fire that had burned a third of the downtown and destroyed 1,200 buildings. Because volunteer firemen worked in the city's rolling mills, foundries, cotton and glass factories, and copper smelts, Porter hoped that these men would respond to a new kind of stage material that encouraged a sense of cultural ownership. This marketing savvy introduced the one true innovation of Porter's tenure: the creation of short plays with titles like *Blanche of Allegheny, Did You Ever Send Your Wife to East Liberty?* and *The Pittsburgh Fireman, Or the Penn Street Heiress,* evoking local neighborhoods and character types. None of these plays has survived, nor the names of the authors. It was common for an actor or actor-manager to take existing works and adapt them, so these short plays were most likely stock plots given a Pittsburgh veneer.

In January 1849 Porter caused a stir by producing *A Squint at Pittsburgh* and *1949, or Pittsburgh 100 Years Hence.* Both were billed as burlettas, short comic operas filled with topical references, comic songs, and broad, often licentious humor. "The Squint at Pittsburgh is a remarkable piece," noted the *Pittsburgh Morning Post* with considerable irony. "We hope the author's name may be made public soon, for he has certainly accomplished something unusual; he has exhibited more stupidity in one short act than any other author in this country is capable of doing" (Jan. 15, 2). The same reviewer was even less happy with the debut of Porter's second burletta, *Pittsburgh 100 Years Hence.* He acknowledged the audience's shouts of pleasure and the play's topical accuracy ("it is full of hits at the apparent tendencies of the present times"), but condemns the "filth that has been put into it" (Jan. 30, 2). Porter's indignant leading man, Charles Logan, fired back the next day in a letter entitled "To the Public." "The manuscript of *1949* is now lying in the box office," Logan announced, "and all who take any interest in the affair are invited to examine. If one word be found in it, that the most impure imagination can torture from the obvious innocent sense, the discoverer shall see the play instantly committed to the flames" (Jan. 31, 2).[43]

In 1859, William Henderson took over the lease of Old Drury just as the impending Civil War was turning Pittsburgh into the "arsenal of the nation," where "everything was turned out from the smallest arms to the great twenty-inch guns, monitors and gunboats."[44] Henderson focused on patriotic subject matter such as "Yankee" song and dance routines, dramas with titles like "The Land of Washington," and stage tableaux recreating recent events like the evacuation of Harper's Ferry, performed by a group called the Ellsworth Tableaux—most likely a local amateur company. After the war began, Henderson aggressively marketed his theater to bivouacking military personnel—literally thousands of soldiers arriving in Pittsburgh daily by train from all points. "As a result," notes a historian, "his establishment grew in popularity within the community; it became a gathering place for soldier and citizen to witness stirring, patriotic pantomimes, tableaux, and the popular dramas of the day. . . . The wily manager even went so far as to donate the proceeds from several performances to the local companies of volunteers."[45]

Henderson's most interesting programming innovation was to support new plays by Pittsburgh playwrights. Set in the city, they followed the structure of popular melodrama, evoking the image of the industrial laborer with titles like *The Story of a Coal Miner, The Workmen of Pittsburgh, The Boss, Our Boarding House,* and *The Iron City by Day and Night.* The last, by local poet W. Henry Lewis, starred Adah Menken and premiered on September 9, 1861, to a large and "fashionable audience." The critic for the *Post* noted that the new production was "well played and the scenery, new and appropriate, with the music, and the genuine merit of the piece, rendered it a complete success" (Sept. 10, 1861, 3). By producing Pittsburgh-themed plays, Henderson acknowledged the interests of his audience and began to encourage cultural exploration of the region. Managers at the other theaters followed his lead with *Pittsburgh by Gaslight* and *The Pittsburgh Firemen* (at Trimble's Variety) and *The Streets of Pittsburgh* (at the Theatre Comique). Though none of the scripts has survived, their titles suggest that they were attempts to capitalize on two of the most popular plays of the era, *The Streets of New York* and *Under the Gaslight.*

Smoky City drama reached its apotheosis, however, in the hands of Bartley Campbell—Pittsburgh's first native-born, nationally regarded playwright. Born in Allegheny City in 1843, Campbell began as a newspaper reporter who wrote occasional drama criticism for the *Pittsburgh Leader.* In the 1860s he became active in the local Democratic Party and founded a short-lived party organ called the *Pittsburgh Evening Mail.* After its failure he left the city for newspaper jobs in New Orleans, Cincinnati, and Louisville. His first play, *The Wilderness* (1870), never produced, dramatized General Braddock's defeat on a Western Pennsylvania battlefield during the French and Indian War. Campbell's first productions were *Peril; or Love at Long Branch* and *Through Fire*, both staged in 1871 at the Pittsburgh Opera House on Diamond Street. *Peril* soon caught the attention of producers outside of Pittsburgh, and Campbell's career as a full-time playwright was launched.[46] In 1878 he again focused on his native city with *The Lower Millions*, an account of the calamitous railroad riots of July 1877 when Pittsburgh's striking railroad workers and others battled the state militia for four days over a wage decrease. The Union Depot (the roundhouse) was burned to the ground and twenty-six men were killed.

The Pittsburgh Opera House's production of *The Lower Millions*, coming only a year after the riots, was much anticipated. According to one account, it featured 150 extras (playing the mob), some of whom reportedly had participated in the actual railroad strike. But though the reviews of the play's one-week run were generally positive, Campbell's dramatization disappointed many local workers by placing the strike in a steel mill instead of on the railroad—presumably to avoid any confrontation with the city's powerful managerial class.[47] According to the plot summary (the play has not survived), Campbell apparently deemphasized politics in favor of the love story.[48] Certainly the playbill for *The Lower Millions* reads more like an ad for a spectacle-extravaganza than for a work of political theater: "A Piece for the People. A Story of Our Recent Troubles. Bartley Campbell's Masterpiece . . . The Burning of the Round House! Pittsburg as seen from the Hills! Beautiful Scenery. A Star Company."[49]

Expanding Audiences

Just as the programming at Pittsburgh's playhouses grew more diverse between 1830 and 1870, so too did the clientele. When the Pittsburgh Theatre opened in 1833, the auditorium was distinctly partitioned: boxes and pit for the upper and professional classes and gallery seating (sometimes referred to as the "upper boxes") for the working class. Women from the upper classes regularly attended the Theatre on Third Street and the Pittsburgh Theatre, regarding the playhouse as both a community investment and a place to be seen—or even to appear on the stage, as noted in chapter 1. Working-class women probably did not frequent the Theatre on Third Street, however, since the pit and box seats were expensive and the gallery was masculine territory where no respectable woman would appear.

At midcentury, however, market competition among the playhouses of the Liberty-Penn corridor brought changes in the audience. The previously all-male clientele of the gallery was gradually replaced by a "family" audience that included women and children. A recollection from George Lowrie, a long-time door tender who worked for several different theaters, noted: "[When the] iron mills were running full and the men made big money, it was nearly impossible to handle the crowds on pay nights. I've seen puddlers and rollers and helpers and all the rest of them come and bring all their families, if the attraction was worth while, and there would be prison-bar shirts, red shirts, shirts sans collars, and the house would be filled to suffocation, largely with that class" (*Pittsburgh Dispatch*, Dec. 8, 1912). Most telling, however, are the theater ads themselves, which show a growing sensitivity to female tastes and opinion. In 1845 Elizabeth Clarendon, manager-lessee of the Pittsburgh Theatre, promised "to elevate and restore [the drama] to the high moral standing it originally possessed, and to accomplish this end, we are determined to banish everything of an obscene or profane nature, from the Stage; and nothing shall be done or said that could bring to the cheek of modesty a blush, or offend the most fastidious." In the same advertisement Clarendon sent a decidedly less subtle signal of her intentions to create a family environment: "A strong and efficient Police have been engaged, and will preserve order at all times" (*Pittsburgh Morning Post*, Mar. 10, 1845, 2). Clarendon was so bent on maintaining good behavior that she reportedly interrupted her own performance to horsewhip a male patron in the pit who would not stop catcalling. Draconian tactics aside, competing playhouses soon followed suit and the social transformation was under way. By the 1850s, most of the large downtown playhouses were selling tickets in three newly defined areas: the dress circle (with individual chairs), the gallery (still the most inexpensive bench seats), and the newly formed family circle. The appearance of the term *family* is clear evidence that women and children were welcome and theatergoing was no longer the sole province of laboring-class men and the elite, although the smaller variety houses continued to target an all-male clientele.[50] By the end of the 1860s the habit of theatergoing was well established among men, women, and children of all classes of Pittsburghers.

3

THEATER AS DESTINATION

1870 to 1897

Pittsburgh, January 30, 1868. Felix Brunot calls to order an emergency meeting of the shareholders of the Library Hall Corporation. "Gentlemen," Brunot yells as he holds up a copy of the *Atlantic Monthly*, "I direct your attention to Mr. Parton's recently published travel essay." The room rustles and shifts; a rumble begins to rise. "Mr. James Parton, who apparently visited us for a precious few days some months ago, writes of our city: 'What energy, what a fury of industry! All Pittsburg at work before the dawn of the day! The entire space lying between the hills was filled with blackest smoke, from out of which the hidden chimneys sent forth tongues of flame. If any one would enjoy a spectacle as striking as Niagara, he may do so by simply walking up along Cliff Street in Pittsburg, and looking over into—hell with the lid taken off.'" The room erupts in laughter as the phrase "hell with the lid taken off" rolls from mouth to mouth. Brunot bangs the table to get their attention. "I appreciate and share your amusement at Mr. Parton's purple prose,"

Fig. 5. Mercantile Library Hall on Penn Avenue, 1870. Source: Unknown (Curtis Theatre Collection, University of Pittsburgh Library).

he shouts. "But I beg you to consider the fact that the rest of the country will no doubt read this . . . assessment . . . of our city quite literally. We *must* build our new Library Hall as soon as possible—to show the nation that we are committed to more than industry here, that we care about the minds and morals of our young people, and we don't want them patronizing burlesque halls and variety saloons." A loud voice cuts Brunot off: "Never mind the preaching, Felix. We're all agreed that we need a decent concert hall." "Indeed," cries someone else, "I vowed last week I'd never again set foot in that disgusting Old Drury—the place reeks in the most appalling manner."[1]

The Lyceum Movement

By the time James Parton coined the infamous description of Pittsburgh as "hell with the lid taken off" in his 1868 *Atlantic Monthly* travel essay, the fact that the piece was overwhelmingly positive did little to boost the city's reputation. Pittsburgh was already being seen as a city of smokestacks, with work at the center of its collective personality. This view is demonstrated in *Peculiarities of American*

Cities (1883): "Work is the object of life with them. It occupies them from morning until night, from cradle to grave, only on Sundays, when, for the most part, the furnaces are idle, and forges are silent" (334). There was no question of the region's booming industrial capacity (from steel to aluminum) and the kind of work ethic required for such productivity. The city's infrastructure was also growing rapidly. From the 1860s to the end of the century, greater Pittsburgh welcomed a locomotive works, the Monongahela and Duquesne funicular railways (connecting the steep hills of the South Side with downtown), a cable and then an electric trolley system, two new train stations, a chamber of commerce, two waterworks, a sewage system, a gasworks, a paid fire department, a weather bureau, a banking clearing house association that included sixteen national banks and several local banks, a new city hall, a new courthouse, a massive new post office, hundreds of other new buildings (including the city's first skyscrapers), and more than a dozen bridges spanning the Allegheny, Monongahela, and Ohio rivers.

It goes without saying that late nineteenth-century Pittsburgh—a city of skyscrapers and modern technology and constantly increasing population—was hardly all work and no play, as shown by the growth of commercial theater and numerous civic and cultural organizations. In these years local philanthropists gave the city a zoo, a world-class equatorial telescope for the Allegheny Observatory, a splendid botanical conservatory, a parks system (eventually covering 900 acres), and several free libraries, concert halls, a natural history museum, and an art gallery donated by Andrew Carnegie. Most significant for a history of theater was the Library Hall Corporation, formed in 1866. This subscriber-based share company was an outgrowth of the Pittsburgh branch of the Young Men's Library Mercantile Association, a reading and lecture club founded in 1847 as part of the lyceum movement that began in New England in the 1830s. Lyceums—the name evokes the garden at Athens where Aristotle lectured—espoused the Jeffersonian ideal of popular enlightenment through community discourse. In many American cities and towns, the lyceum program sponsored adult education (in an era when few communities had public schools) and supported through its programming the sharing of ideas, opinions, and aesthetic expression. Pittsburgh participated in the movement by sponsoring discussion and debate groups, lectures, and library circles.[2] By the late 1840s the Young Men's Mercantile Library Association had amassed hundreds of volumes and was sponsoring a public lecture series.[3] This organization brought Ralph Waldo Emerson, Frederick Douglass, and Mark Twain to the city. All of this was accomplished in rented rooms and leased assembly halls, since the association did not own real estate.

In 1859 Felix R. Brunot and John R. McCune, former presidents of the library association, organized the Library Hall Company to buy land and erect a building to be perpetually leased to the association. The project stalled during the war years, when Brunot was imprisoned in Richmond, but after the war he resumed his philanthropic activities, and in 1866 he and other subscribers had raised enough money to purchase a plot fronting Penn Avenue, in the heart of the booming Penn-Liberty corridor. The goal was to build a hall sizable enough to combine lyceum-sponsored cultural activities with retail spaces, the rental income to provide the revenue to maintain the building. Brunot's mandate was, however, more philanthropic than entrepreneurial, as this 1866 mission statement demonstrates:

> The effect of such an institution is to increase the intelligence of the people among whom it is placed and to improve their morals, to draw them away from the haunts of vice, and especially to so form the habits and tastes of the young that they may not seek their enjoyment in dangerous and degrading associations. It makes men of business, also men of information and culture. It gives the mechanic and laborer the means of making their labor and skill more intelligent and useful, and in doing all this, it advances the cause of religion and the honor and prosperity of the community and of the nation. (*Daily Post Gazette,* Jan. 9, 1866, 4)

When Mercantile Library Hall (at 611 Penn Avenue) opened in the fall of 1870, the first floor was rented to a new "department" store called the Joseph Horne Company. The second floor housed the Mercantile Library's collection of over 10,000 volumes, the city's preeminent text collection. At the back of the library room was Library Hall, a concert space seating approximately 1,500 people.

The first performance in Library Hall featured the Pittsburgh Cantata Society, "the elite of vocalists of our city," in a gala evening. The *Post* pronounced it "a brilliant and successful affair" and predicted that the next performances featuring the English Opera Troupe would undoubtedly be "hailed with pleasure" (Oct. 14, 1870, 1). What the *Post* (and a few other dailies) were really hailing, however, was the creation of a new, class-restricted theater in the city:

The beautiful Mercantile Library Hall was opened last night to a large and brilliant house. . . . When the doors were opened for the first time to the public, and the tremulous sheen and flicker of the gaslight fell across and over its antique Moorish frescoes and oriental drapings of the stage, there was heard the rustle of silks, and the faint and half-imperceptible winnowing of dainty fans, while there was seen the glitter of jewelry and all the accompaniments that dance attendance upon a brilliant occasion; . . . the frescoing of the Hall is a reproduction from the grand Hall of the ancient Alhambra. The effect of the golden and emerald brackets, pendants and carved globes last night, had the same effect, as we suppose, upon the arabesques, quaint figures and drapery, as was thrown upon the original by the candelabra that came from the mines of Ormus, and were fashioned after devices that hailed from beyond the confines of Farther India. (*Pittsburgh Post*, Oct. 11, 1870, 4)

Here at last was a stage space where "brilliant" Pittsburghers could assemble without mingling with the rowdy gallery crowds at the Pittsburgh Theatre, the Academy of Music, and the other commercial playhouses along the Penn-Liberty corridor. Library Hall was intended to provide a safe haven for the elite and their creative efforts, both professional and amateur. The Symphonic Society (the genesis of the Pittsburgh Symphony), for example, was organized in 1878 as a group of local amateur musicians who gave public concerts at Library Hall and the opera house. Several professional or semiprofessional choral organizations also performed at Library Hall, including the aforementioned Cantata Society (1870), the Mozart Club (1878), and the Haydn Society (1888).[4]

Class-Oriented Playhouses

Not so well hidden beneath the democratic rhetoric of the lyceum movement and the Library Hall experiment was a different current, one less satisfied with the status quo at most of the city's theaters. Like other Americans of the period, Pittsburghers were struggling with how to establish a bona fide cultural climate in the Smoky City. Descriptions of the audiences' fashionable attire and glittering jewels were not so subtle codes signaling acceptance of a certain type of audience —that is, cultured Pittsburghers whose presence would elevate the social ranking of the new Library Hall. This gap between cultured and uncultured had always been present, of course; still, it was not economically feasible to emphasize this distinction—there simply weren't enough people to fill both kinds of halls. However, the flush economy and the rapidly expanding population enjoyed by post–Civil War Pittsburgh changed all that, and the trend toward separating people into sophisticated highbrows, as opposed to naive lowbrows, began in earnest. By the 1870s the local press, adopting this "high-low" rhetoric, had taken on the role of cultural arbiter, as the conservative *Pittsburgh Post* makes clear in the review just cited. Interestingly, the lower end of the social hierarchy also used the newspapers to signal class-based distinctions between entertainment emporiums. In the 1870s, for example, the *National Labor Tribune* (a locally produced union newspaper that was disseminated nationally) promoted the Pittsburgh Opera House as a "favorite resort of the workingman of this day, being a place where they can witness an intellectual performance, and where they may bring their families without fear of offending their most delicate sensibilities" (Aug. 25, 1877, 4).[5]

Cultural elitists like Felix Brunot were not satisfied with simply separating audiences, however. His lyceum initiative was rooted in a national effort to "raise the masses through culture," an extension of the long-standing belief among the nation's liberal thinkers, those who favored progress through reform, that participation in the correct kind of public amusements was necessary to a community's social health.[6] And though his Library Hall project quickly failed—in the 1880s the building was sold to a theatrical producer and became a commercial venue—the urge to remedy society's ills through culture did not disappear. Certainly Andrew Carnegie subscribed to this philosophy; his gift of a million dollars to fund a four-acre civic center housing a library, an art institute, a museum, and a music hall was a fulfillment of Brunot's original vision for Mercantile Library Hall. When the Carnegie Institute and Library was dedicated on November 5, 1895, Carnegie's speech to over 2,000 members of the city's elite called the complex the "noble quartet" (a reference to the four disciplines of natural history, art, music, and literature).[7] Carnegie believed that the gift of the institute demonstrated the city's change from a smoky hamlet to a modern, cosmopolitan center where art and culture were valued by everyone. This was the message in his 1897 letter to the board of directors:

> Not only our own country, but the civilized world will take note of the fact that our Dear Old Smoky Pittsburgh, no longer content to be celebrated only as one of the chief manufacturing centers, has entered upon the path

to higher things, and is before long, as we thoroughly believe, also to be noted for her preeminence in the Arts and Sciences. . . . I had not ventured to estimate at its value the mass of latent desire for the things of the spirit which lay inert in the hearts of our fellow citizens of the industrial hive, which needed only the awakening touch.[8]

The Second Penn-Liberty Playhouse Boom

Andrew Carnegie's "awakening touch" notwithstanding, most of the city's theater patrons were demonstrably more interested in another late nineteenth-century trend: the destination playhouse and the "New York theater" product. In the 1870s a new era began with the introduction of the combination company— road shows organized in large cities (usually New York) and sent out for touring seasons in towns connected by the nation's railways. Unlike the repertory-style touring companies of earlier eras, however, the combination company was not owned and managed by the actors but by professional impresarios. These businessmen chose a marketable play (or a small group of related plays) and a well-known stage performer and combined them with a full company of supporting players, a production crew, scenery and costumes, and a manager assigned to keep watch over the money box. The show was rehearsed (again, usually in New York) and then sent, via rail car, to rented theaters in cities all over the country. During the 1880s this largely self-sufficient business model became widespread, and by the 1890s it had effectively ended the era of the actor-centered traveling repertory company, since a long run of a single play was far more profitable. Not surprisingly, the advent of the combination company also damaged local stock companies. No longer needed as support for the traveling stars and no longer able to compete with the national combination company, they began going out of business. By the 1890s, most large cities hosted a greater percentage of traveling combination companies than local companies—and in some cities the resident professional theater completely disappeared.[9]

Pittsburgh was perfectly situated, both geographically and culturally, to play a key role in this late nineteenth-century phenomenon. The city had plenty of spending power, an established theatergoing culture, and excellent rail connections, making it attractive to combination company entrepreneurs. To accommodate the new business, a second playhouse construction boom began along the Penn-Liberty corridor. It included the Pittsburgh Opera House on Diamond Street directly behind the old opera house in the Odd Fellows' Hall (built in 1871, with a seating capacity of 2,300), the Exposition Hall Assembly Room (built in 1888, capacity 10,000), the Duquesne Theatre (built in 1890, capacity 2,112), and the Alvin Theatre (built in 1891, capacity 2,200). In addition, several theaters were expanded and refurbished: the Bijou (the rebuilt Library Hall, capacity 2,650), the Avenue Theater (the rebuilt old opera house, capacity 2,600), and the Harry Williams Academy of Music (the rebuilt Academy of Music, capacity 2,480). Like the construction boom of the 1840s and 1850s, most of these new and refurbished theaters attracted a diverse clientele and hosted a wide range of performance genres (drama, music, dance). But unlike earlier patrons, late nineteenth-century theatergoers were often more interested in the playhouse than the play. Theater buildings were entertainment destinations in themselves, as a notice for the opening of the Duquesne Theatre declared, "The theater itself will prove worthy of a long journey to see" (*Bulletin*, Nov. 22, 1890, 4).

In the last two decades of the century, the destination theater in one way fulfilled a role similar to that of the lyceum. Beginning in the 1880s, these beautifully appointed playhouses became de facto community centers where patrons could meet, discuss local events, relax in safe and luxurious surroundings, find entertainment and aesthetic pleasure, and enjoy the latest technology. Theaters were among the first buildings to install telephones, electricity, and "cooled air," among other amenities. But unlike the concert halls of the lyceum movement, they were commercial enterprises that could not afford to be elitist in their programming. Instead of attracting a "brilliant" audience adorned in silk and jewels, destination theaters targeted the well-paid members of the skilled laboring class and the emerging white-collar, professional sector.[10] As described in chapter 2, by midcentury Pittsburgh's skilled workers were economically powerful enough to cause several of the city's large auditoriums to include a "family circle." In the last decades of the century, these patrons were joined by professional workers, causing a significant shift in the theater industry. By that time, Pittsburgh's otherwise socially diverse audiences shared certain criteria by which they judged cultural experiences: they wished to enjoy visual splendor in comfort and safety, to admire sophisticated productions (if not always sophisticated plays), and, perhaps most important, to be assured of moral decorum in the playhouse.

Changing Audiences

The call to regularize the moral tone of the theater dates back to the puritanical bias of the colony's founders. The boards of directors and the manager-lessees of the Theatre on Third Street (1813) and the Pittsburgh Theatre (1833) had worked hard to establish a moral atmosphere acceptable to reputable citizens, including women and children. But gradually, as they fell on hard times, their programming and clientele seemed to follow suit. In the 1830s and 1840s, for example, the Pittsburgh Theatre was a first-rate building that drew full houses and a solid cross section of the population. By the late 1860s it had become the province of young laborers who associated theatergoing with heavy drinking and rowdy behavior. Perhaps only these young men, used to dealing with the harsh conditions of the mills and foundries, could tolerate the uncomfortable conditions of the dilapidated Old Drury. The place reeked, according to a vivid recollection:

> The theater was cleaned in a most remarkable manner . . . [the charwoman] would slush the floor of the parquet and afterward sweep the entire wash into the orchestra, from where it would run into the trap cellar below the stage and become absorbed by Mother Earth. . . . On the floor of the back aisle . . . were two or three hot air registers, which gave forth a pungent odor, that, in addition to the stray gas, stale sizing from the stage, and the exhalations of the audience, made quite an impressive odor that can never be forgot.[11]

It is hardly surprising that by the late 1850s the Pittsburgh Theatre and the other Penn-Liberty playhouses were considered unsuitable environments; for the most part, women attended only special events such as a lecture or concert or touring productions featuring star actors. And when they did attend, they were escorted by a husband, father, or brother, since unescorted women were assumed to be prostitutes bound for the third-tier gallery to conduct business. Given these circumstances, perhaps the most revolutionary shift brought by the destination playhouse was its transformation of the social contract inside the theater. By deliberately courting respectable women, the new theater managers effectively ended the reign of the masculinized playhouse (except, of course, for the concert saloon and burlesque theaters). In Pittsburgh, the success of the destination concept hinged on its ability to tip the gender scale and balance out the house on a daily basis. To accomplish this, theater owners began an aggressive marketing strategy aimed at an emerging audience: the matinee lady.

As the wife of a professional or small business owner, the typical matinee lady managed a household staff that included a cook, a nanny, and a housemaid and/or laundress. She was respectably educated and might even have graduated from a local institution such as the Pittsburgh Female College (founded in 1854) and the Pennsylvania Female College (founded in 1869, later renamed the Pennsylvania College for Women, now Chatham College). She belonged to several charitable organizations, giving both money and time for the care of orphans, destitute families, or recent immigrants. She might also have belonged to the Women's Club of Pittsburgh, founded in 1875 as the nation's second women's organization. And she might have joined the Monday Group, a loosely organized study and reading collective that began around 1885. Weekly discussions were held at the Penn Avenue home of Julia Warfield, a lady of considerable intellectual distinction, on topics ranging from the Italian Renaissance to the "Condition of Germany after the 30 Years War."[12]

A typical professional-class housewife would also have time to attend weekday cultural events. This habit may have been established during her girlhood years while visiting Major Burnell's—a two-room apartment set up for the display of "Works of Art and Great Natural Living Curiosities" on Fifth Street across from the Pittsburgh Theatre.[13] Like other midcentury "museums," Major Burnell's was a combination picture gallery, natural history exhibit space, and lecture hall devoted (at least for advertising purposes) to the lyceum ideal of a well-educated American public. It was also one of only a few public performance sites considered to be morally sound enough for unescorted women to assemble for conversation, instruction, and entertainment.[14] By the 1860s, Pittsburgh women were enthusiastic supporters of the museum ideal, as this notice from the *Pittsburgh Daily Post* illustrates: "Amusements: Major Burnell's Museum, at Franklin Hall on Fifth Street, is a most prosperous institution. Yesterday afternoon large numbers of ladies were present there" (May 23, 1868, 2). In the mid-1870s local theater managers, seeing the economic opportunity, began offering weekday matinees to attract this potential audience. They even appropriated the marketing rhetoric of the museums by signaling their intent to create a safe, clean, comfortable, and morally respectable environment:

The matinees at Library Hall will in all probability be largely attended—especially by ladies and children. Happily the performances are always of such a character that both ladies and children can attend them without the possible risk of encountering anything to give offense. The streetcars stop within a very short distance of this popular place of amusement, which makes it very convenient. The pavement leading from Sixth Street to the Hall, we understand, is to be thoroughly renovated by the authorities.[15]

The Destination Playhouses

Pittsburgh's second opera house, which opened in 1871, was located, not accidentally, directly behind the original opera house in the Odd Fellows' Hall on Fifth Avenue. The new manager, M. William Canning, was a sophisticated businessman who immediately established his theater as the city's principal rental site for the New York–based combination companies. Canning charged higher prices than other local theaters with the exception of Library Hall, but offered more. As one of his advertisements proudly announced, the "Pittsburgh Opera House plays only the higher-type New York theater." The gala opening week attraction, for example, starred the internationally acclaimed tragic actor Charles Fechter in *Hamlet, Ruy Blas,* and *Lady of Lyons.* Canning was equally attuned to the allure of the sensational. A few months after opening with *Hamlet,* he brought in a blockbuster touring production of *The Black Crook*—a controversial mixture of music, melodramatic sentiment, and female "ballet" dancers wearing tight-fitting leggings—the source of the evening's true sensation. Bringing the *Black Crook* touring company production to Pittsburgh in April 1871 was certainly a coup for Canning. Pittsburghers flocked to see it, effectively shutting out all competition. This caused complaints from the press, who warned that the public's taste for sensation would jeopardize the future of "the legitimate drama well produced" in the city (*Pittsburgh Chronicle,* Apr. 14, 1871).

Canning's booking coup may even have contributed to the quick demise of Felix Brunot's lyceum experiment at Library Hall in 1871. Unable to make the building pay for itself, the Library Hall Association's directors leased the theater space to none other than William Canning and his new partner, Harry Ellsler.[16] They quickly revamped Library Hall along the lines of a destination theater, expanding the auditorium and stage area to accommodate traveling productions, assembling a resident stock company to keep the space busy between bookings, and, perhaps most important, lowering prices. Within a year, Brunot's lyceum ideal of entertaining the elite and lifting the masses through cultural exposure had been supplanted by the destination playhouse strategy of entertaining the expanding working-class and professional audience.

Ellsler and Canning, like other savvy theatrical managers of the time, understood that the actual event—play, opera, variety act—was only a part of the experience sought by an audience. Patrons were equally interested in a theater's amenities, from fancy lounges ("the ladies reception room . . . is a vision") to technological wonders ("an Edison Telephone has been installed by the management for the benefit of our patrons"). Other nontheatrical "extras" came with the price of admission. During the tense election campaign of 1876, Library Hall sought to lure locals into the theater and away from the telegraph office, where it was the usual habit to await important news, with this inducement:

> It will be a great convenience and relief to the public to know the Mess. Ellsler and Canning have completed arrangements for reading the election returns from the stage as they are received. This will be very convenient, as you can have a comfortable seat, with plenty of room instead of being jammed and pushed about in a most unceremonious manner, and between acts, as it were, entertained with one of the best dramas ever placed on the stage, "Henry VIII."[17]

This strategy of co-opting compelling local events might have surpassed its logical conclusion in 1900, however, when the Avenue Theater (the old opera house) began offering the day's version of virtual baseball:

> While the Pittsburg Club is away the games played by them will be reproduced on the Stage of The Avenue Theater. Identically the same in every detail as they are played on the field. The diamond is there, perfect and complete, and dummy figures play the game precisely like the players themselves, their movements being controlled according to the detailed description of the game sent direct from the grounds where the club is playing, by wire to the stage of the Avenue Theater. Prices—10, 15, 25 cents.[18]

Perhaps no other Pittsburgh theater manager was more astute in the art of creating an event than Harry Williams, who leased the Academy of Music on

Liberty at Strawberry Way. Williams came to Pittsburgh just after the Civil War with a traveling stock company and stayed—acting around town, assembling a combination company, the H. W. Williams Own Combination Company, and taking over the management of the Old Drury in its final days. By the time he leased the Academy of Music in 1877, Williams was an established local actor-manager with solid New York connections. At the Academy of Music he presented legitimate plays, high-end touring musical acts (Adelina Patti, for instance), and New York–based burlesque and variety acts while maintaining his own stock company. He thus reinvented the old Academy of Music (which, like the Pittsburgh Theatre, had deteriorated badly in the 1860s) as a destination playhouse with popular appeal. Among his various gimmicks for attracting audiences was an exhibition of boxing kangaroos at no extra charge; the theater also provided the first outside display of electric light in the city. In 1877 Williams bought an electric dynamo and lamp that had been displayed at that year's Pittsburgh Exposition, set it up on a revolving stand in front of Academy of Music, and used it to promote his building by sweeping the arc light up and down Liberty Avenue.[19] Electricity inside Pittsburgh playhouses arrived five years later when Harry Ellsler began using incandescent lightbulbs onstage at the opera house (*Pittsburgh Commercial Gazette,* Sept. 27, 1882).

Another popular extra offered by the destination playhouses was a four-page newspaper-style program that listed the day's bill of fare, advertised upcoming attractions, and provided take-home entertainment. The Pittsburgh Opera House published a daily *Opera News* that contained the playbill for the performance and several columns—"Dramatic," "Opera Notes," and "Entr'acte" —filled with local and national arts industry gossip, silly stories, jokes and puns, and self-advertisement (couched as insider news). The weekly *Academy,* which featured a drawing of Harry Williams on the masthead, was similarly structured. *The Librarian*, published by Library Hall, was more idiosyncratic. In addition to the day's bill, a joke page, and upcoming attractions, it included a weekly column commenting on local events unrelated to the theater and often carrying a distinct editorial perspective. Items from the 1870s, for example, ranged from a request to station a policeman on a railroad bridge to an announcement that the "citizens of Pittsburgh and vicinity will no doubt be pleased to learn that Dr. Jackson has at last received a pension for his many useful services during two wars."[20]

Fig. 6. Academy of Music on Liberty, 1905. Source: *Pittsburgh Bulletin, 1905.*

The other use for these newsletter-programs was directly related to the expanding audience. In the drive to attract the city's high-paid laborers (and their
families), theater managers began mandating certain kinds of behavior and out-
lawing others in an effort to impose a higher standard of deportment. Many
men in the audience had been theatergoers in downtown playhouses like Old
Drury, Trimble's Variety, and O'Brien's Dime Museum, where male sovereignty
was understood and there were few restrictions on behavior. The newsletter-
programs instructed readers on how to behave in the new "temples of amusement." (The word "temple" was no accident, of course.) Catcalling, foot stomping,
rearranging the chairs, were forbidden. The long-established practice of entering
and departing during the performance proved harder to change. "The habit so
common in our places of amusement of people leaving their seats and pushing
for the doors before the closing of the last act of the play, is one that has been
often censured, but never with all the severity it deserves," stated *The Librarian*
in 1876. "The patrons of this establishment are of a class that know better, and
of whom a better style of behavior ought reasonably to be expected."[21] But the
problem persisted, and in 1887 the following testy and obviously pre–fire code notice appeared: "It is the height of ill breeding, causing annoyance to the audience

and the artists on the stage, to leave the house before the fall of the curtain on the final act of the play. The doors of the theater will remain closed to everyone until the play is finished."[22]

The Duquesne and the Alvin

In the midst of all this theatrical bounty, two "ground floor" destination theaters —the Duquesne (1890) and the Alvin (1891)—put Pittsburgh on the national map in terms of technical capacity and level of grandeur. A distinguishing feature of these large, state-of-the-art theaters was a street-level entrance. The Duquesne Theatre opened its magnificently oversized front doors on Penn Avenue near Sixth Street on December 1, 1890. City newspapers responded with long, glowing features replete with photographs, drawings, and testimonials. The *Bulletin* noted that it was "one of the few ground floor theaters in the State. The patron steps from the street to the lobby by one of four entrances, all guarded by wide double doors, half glass" (Nov. 13, 1890, 8). In keeping with current fashion, the interior of the theater was "Moorish" in décor and featured fourteen boxes flanking the proscenium and large, cushioned seats. The stage was among the city's widest, with a seventy-five-foot rigging loft and an asbestos fire curtain "by means of which the stage can be cut off completely from the auditorium." The building featured a grand, sweeping staircase leading to the balcony, a "handsomely furnished foyer" with mosaic tiling and beveled glass doors, a lavish ladies' sitting room, twenty dressing rooms (the better to attract the "finer-type" combination companies), and a new technology known as "iced air"—allowing the theater to remain open in the hot summer months. Most spectacularly, the Duquesne Theatre was Pittsburgh's first fully electric playhouse and featured over a thousand incandescent lights, with a state-of-the-art lighting board.

The Duquesne was managed by David Henderson, a playwright, designer, and businessman who wrote and produced "extravaganzas"—the spectacle-oriented blend of dance, song, and unlikely plot initiated by the success of *The Black Crook*. As with other destination playhouses, Henderson's programming was eclectic, offering a broad range of performance types. The new theater stood out, however, in its ability to attract the leading national and international actors. The gala opening featured the Emma Juch Grand English Opera Com-

Fig. 7. Duquesne Theatre on Penn Avenue, 1890 program cover.
Source: Unknown (Curtis Theatre Collection, University of Pittsburgh
Library).

pany in *Rigoletto, Lohengrin, Faust, Il Trovatore,* and *The Flying Dutchman.* Over the
next five years, the Duquesne hosted Joseph Jefferson as Rip Van Winkle, Rosina
Vokes and her London Comedy Company, James O'Neill in his signature role as
the count of Monte Cristo, the American Extravaganza Company in *Sinbad,*
Koster and Bial's Vaudeville Company, and Lawrence Barrett in *Romeo and Juliet.*
These were the day's leading actors and combination companies, and ticket prices

Fig. 8. Charles Davis transforms into Alvin Joslin, 1890. Source: Unknown (Curtis Theatre Collection, University of Pittsburgh Library).

at the Duquesne were accordingly high—about twice the cost of the seats down the street at Harry Williams's theater.

The excitement over the opening of the Duquesne Theatre was quickly surpassed by the opening of the Alvin Theatre on September 21, 1891. The Alvin, "America's Prettiest Theater," was built and managed by Charles L. Davis, star of the Alvin Joslin Comedy Company and, by most accounts, a very rich man. Davis had made his fortune during the 1880s by playing the character of Alvin Joslin, a crotchety New England farmer (a popular Yankee stage type). By the late 1880s, Davis was reportedly eager to build a home theater so that he could retire from the road and also provide other companies with the comfort he never found. A letter published some years later in *Billboard* explained his motivation:

> Davis had suffered the horrors of tanktown theaters for so many years that he announced his intention to give his brother actors one theater where they could enjoy every known comfort. Accordingly, he had built in the Alvin Theatre many large dressing rooms on the stage and on balconies overlooking it, all with outside ventilation. In all of these dressing rooms he laid expensive carpets, and he furnished them with the most handsome

Fig. 9. Green Room of the Alvin Theatre, 1891. Source: Unknown (Curtis Theatre Collection, University of Pittsburgh Library).

and costly pier mirrors, chairs, lounges, dressing tables and other furniture. Even the mangles were adorned with statuary and bric-a-brac and fine oil paintings . . . while the green room of the theater was as fine as the drawing room in any millionaire's palace.[23]

Why Davis chose Pittsburgh for this venture is a bit of a mystery. He had visited the city as an itinerant actor in the mid-1870s with his combination company. Davis's explanation, given to the packed opening night house, was that he chose Pittsburgh "above New York, Chicago, Cincinnati and Philadelphia [because it] badly needed a first-class theater. . . . Besides," he said, "I wanted to be among people who were all hustlers" (*Pittsburgh Post*, Sept. 22, 1891, 6). Hustlers maybe, but Davis's assessment of the city's needs was not accurate. Several of the city's newspapers noted the "organized opposition" to his new building, and the owners and lessees of the Pittsburgh Opera House, the Bijou, and the Duquesne were probably behind the effort to stop the appearance of yet another "temple" along the Penn-Liberty corridor. Whatever Davis's motives, he made Pittsburgh his home until his death in 1900.[24]

The Alvin playhouse was a relatively modest structure with a narrow street-level entry on Sixth Street (then called Federal Street), but on the inside it lived up to its "pretty" reputation. Both the *Post* and the *Commercial Gazette* were impressed by the enormous curtain painting, entitled "The Bridal Eve," depicting a bride preparing for her wedding day and apparently an entertainment in and of itself. Other special features of the Alvin included an open hallway (the "promenade") just behind the orchestra circle, "for stretching the legs." The promenade proved to be so popular with the patrons "that is was almost jammed" (*Post*, Sept. 22, 1891, 6). Davis's signature inspiration for the Alvin, however, was a "conservatory" on the ground floor just off the grand foyer with a large fountain at the center that sprayed Lily of the Nile perfume.

In the 1890s Davis became a colorful local character who used his flamboyant personal style as a marketing tool, wearing diamond studs on his dress shirts while sitting prominently in his private box to one side of the proscenium. This box was equipped with a silent call button to summon the ushers "for his real and fanciful errands," enabling Alvin patrons to watch him run his empire while they watched his shows.[25] Davis had a taste for Barnum-style "extras," such as a lobby display of his diamond collection touted to be worth $100,000. But he seemed to have a particular affinity for pleasing female patrons. The Alvin featured a ladies' reception room, described by the *Post* as a "vision of light," fitted out with a white piano, white satin pillows, and white upholstered chairs (Sept. 22, 1891, 6). He also made a practice of personally handing out silver spoons and photographs of male stars to unescorted women attending his ladies' matinees.

The Traveling Circuit

Like their forebears, late nineteenth-century combination companies traveled fixed touring circuits that took then through Pittsburgh on a regular basis. The variety-format companies regularly appeared at Harry Williams's Academy of Music, Harris's Family Museum, Harry Davis's Fifth Avenue, and World's Theater. The "legitimate" combination companies routinely included the Duquesne,

Fig. 10. "Bridal Eve" curtain painting at the Alvin, 1891. Source: Unknown (Curtis Theatre Collection, University of Pittsburgh Library).

the Pittsburgh Opera House, and the Alvin in all national tours. And solo stars (both national and international) moved from one playhouse to another in engagements lasting several weeks before moving on to another city. These stars also tended to return to Pittsburgh over and over again. When James O'Neill (father of Eugene O'Neill) began performing his signature role as the count of Monte Cristo during the 1883–84 season, for instance, he was billed as a "Popular Young Actor." Over the next decade O'Neill prospered in the role, and by the time he returned to play the count (this time at the Duquesne Theatre), his bill proudly declared him the "Eminent Romantic Actor." (The story behind those two billings is told in O'Neill's *Long Day's Journey into Night*.)

By the 1880s, Pittsburgh was roundly considered by managers and actors to be a good theater town with enthusiastic and unusually loyal audiences. In this heady theatrical climate, theater patrons were becoming sophisticated consumers with firsthand knowledge of international and national acting styles. A city historian wrote in 1908:

> Pittsburg has always patronized, quite liberally, the better talent on the stage. The favorite actor among the theater-goers, for many years, was Joseph Jefferson. Their manner of applauding his between-act-addresses, thoroughly demonstrated their affection for him. In one of his last appearances, he spoke of having played before the parents and grandparents of those who greeted him that night. But this great admiration for Rip Van Winkle did not prevent them from most thoroughly appreciating Edwin Booth. He undoubtedly drew the most cultured people of the city and fairly rivaled Jefferson in popular esteem. John McCullough as Virginius, and Lawrence Barrett as Hamlet or Cassius, stood next to these in the opinion of the people of Pittsburg, as manifested by their attendance. Salvini and Sir Henry Irving were also most highly appreciated. The latter never came to America without playing at least a week in Pittsburg, and neither of them were ever greeted by small audiences.[26]

The city's appreciation for traveling celebrity actors was not uncritical, however. When Henry Irving and Ellen Terry performed their Shakespeare repertoire, a local critic noted that although Terry

> was all that could be asked as to ease, grace and piquancy . . . she never loses thought of Ellen in her being Portia, and the fact that a large audience is watching her. Never for an instant. Every pose, every gesture is made with the audience in view, but the audience is quite well pleased to be there, so admirable are they all, and after a little time, in which to become accustomed to the consciousness, it is accepted as a sort of confidence with the lady, and they would not have it otherwise."[27]

Local critics were less gracious, however, about the steady influx of overproduced theatrical white elephants. When Augustus Daly's *Under the Gaslight* arrived at the Pittsburgh Opera House in 1890 for yet another week-long engagement (it first played the city in the late 1860s), the critic for the *Gazette* complained: "For two hours and a half the audience sat in momentary expectation of seeing the good part of the show. It came at the very last—the curtain. The play was lifeless, the scenery commonplace, and the express train, in which the plausible young man expatiated so strongly, was about the worst ever seen." And when the tired melodrama *A Dark Secret* appeared at the opera house, the *Post* called the production a "masterpiece of dry word rot—the deadly insidious dry rot that is sapping away the interest of playgoers."[28]

Neighborhood Playhouses

In the 1880s and 1890s most of the large destination playhouses were located along the Penn-Liberty corridor and within the city's expanding business district. Still, as Pittsburgh began annexing various boroughs, so did the theater industry. Beginning in 1872, formerly sovereign outlying communities such as Birmingham (now the South Side), Lawrenceville, Mount Washington, Oakland, and Shadyside were gradually absorbed into the city—a process facilitated by the rapidly growing mass transit system and the flight of the middle class from downtown. In the Oakland suburb salaried white-collar professionals began building new homes along newly gridded sections of old farmland. There they joined the city's founding elite, who had begun building mansions along the suburban extension of Fifth Avenue after the Civil War, and soon enough the neighborhood boasted exclusive hotels, such as the Schenley, athletic clubs, and several social societies. Given this potential audience, theater managers quickly responded. In the summer of 1891, the Hotel Kenmawr, an elegant residential hotel on Shady Avenue, hosted a "dramatic festival" on its lawn that included a professional production of *As You Like It*. The cast featured many local stock company professionals (perhaps unemployed during the summer hiatus) and was touted by the local press as the first "al fresco performance ever given in the United States." In 1896 the Casino Theatre opened in Schenley Park. Billed as the "only theater in the United States erected for the sole purpose of presenting . . . during the hot summer months," it had its own resident stock company and specialized in comic operas, including works by Gilbert and Sullivan.[29] A few blocks away on Craig Street, the 8,000-seat Duquesne Garden, a converted streetcar barn, featured yet another resident light opera company during the summer months. The area's most prominent new cultural destination, however, was the Carnegie Institute, located between Schenley Park (900 acres donated by the philanthropist Mary Schenley) and Fifth Avenue. The institute's beautifully dec-

Fig. 11. Casino Theatre in Schenley Park, 1896. Source: Unknown (Curtis Theatre Collection, University of Pittsburgh Library).

orated music hall became the first home of the Pittsburgh Symphony Orchestra and also hosted small-scale theatrical events.

The two largest playhouses outside the downtown area were in Allegheny City and East Liberty—thriving communities with distinct regional identities. Located just across the river, Allegheny was settled in the late eighteenth century and achieved city status in 1839. By the end of the century it was comprised of a number of ethnic neighborhoods (Deutschtown, at its center, was home to a large German population) and a variety of industries (notably the H. J. Heinz food processing plant). Allegheny City's largest playhouse was World's Theater on Federal Street, just over the Sixth Street bridge, with a seating capacity of 1,800. World's, with its continuous variety acts at low ticket prices, went through a number of owners and had various names, such as the New Palace Theater and the New World's Museum Theater. Other Allegheny City theaters of the period included a summer production company in Exposition Park (a baseball park at the mouth of the Ohio River) and Allegheny City's own Carnegie Music Hall, built in 1890, the first music hall built by Andrew Carnegie in the United States. It is now the New Hazlett Theater.

East Liberty, several miles to the east of downtown, was settled in the late eighteenth century and annexed to Pittsburgh in 1868. Several of the city's founding families owned large farms in the area, most notably Judge Thomas Mellon, whose sons launched the Mellon Bank empire. With a major rail depot and streetcar stop at its center, East Liberty flourished, attracting commuters who

worked downtown as well as professional-class residents. The area's first dedicated playhouse was the 2,200-seat East End Theatre. Built and managed by
Edward Wilt, a former lessee of the Pittsburgh Opera House, the East End was
designed along the destination playhouse guidelines—it was a palatial structure
housing a highly regarded resident professional company as well as high-end
touring shows. Under Wilt's management, the East End targeted the ladies' matinee crowd by featuring an in-house nursery staffed by "a maid to look after the
little ones."[30]

The Panic of 1893, an Industry Downturn

By 1892 Pittsburgh had become a key geographic link in the national theater industry and a major force in its growing economy, but two major crises interrupted this theatrical prosperity. In July 1892, 3,000 workers called a general strike
at the Homestead works of Carnegie Steel, owned by Andrew Carnegie and
Henry Clay Frick. When Frick called in three hundred heavily armed Pinkerton
guards, a bloody battle ensued, killing twelve.[31] The Homestead uprising inaugurated a new era of hostile labor relations in the city of Pittsburgh, but it was
only one of many workers' strikes across the country resulting from production
downturns and falling wages in the coal, copper, and steel industries. By 1893,
labor-management tensions and a generalized economic anxiety were climaxed
by a national bank panic and a serious, worldwide economic depression that
lasted through 1896. Like most American industrial cities, Pittsburgh experienced
high unemployment, a significant increase in homelessness (one story tells of a
dance hall in Allegheny City being converted into a men's dormitory), and many
business failures.

Not surprisingly, the city's leisure-time businesses were especially hard-hit.
The Pittsburgh Opera House struggled through the first year of the depression,
then closed its doors in 1894 and did not reopen until 1897. Harry Williams's
Academy of Music retreated to second-run touring acts in order to cut ticket
prices. The Bijou (the former Library Hall) drastically lowered its ticket prices to
match the "popular" priced houses like Harry Davis' Fifth Avenue Opera House,
Harry Davis's Eden Musee, Harris's Family Theater, and World's Theater. The
Alvin managed to stay open and to continue offering the "finer-type New York"

Fig. 12. The Bijou (formerly Library Hall) showing a melodrama, 1905. Source: *Pittsburgh Bulletin,* 1905.

theater, though under increasingly unprofitable circumstances. By 1896 Charles L. Davis, nearly bankrupt, was forced to lease the Alvin to Samuel F. Nixon and J. Fred Zimmerman, two Philadelphia businessmen who were just beginning to expand their territory by buying up playhouses and leases in other cities. The Duquesne underwent a similar fate when Henderson lost the lease to Charles Frohman and his New York–based theatrical empire. This was the start of the infamous "Syndicate," a theatrical monopoly operated out of Philadelphia and New York. Over the next decade, the Syndicate gradually took control of the theater industry in many geographically strategic cities. Pittsburgh was one of them.

4

THEATER AS BIG BUSINESS

1897 to 1915

Pittsburg, September 15, 1905. Harry Davis is not a drinking man or he'd probably have one now. He knows the minute he releases his men—carpenters, painters, machinists, carpet-layers—the whole lot of them will head next door to down as many boiler-makers as they can stomach before passing out for a few hours and beginning their next shift. He's working them hard, it's true, but no more than what he expects from himself. Twenty-hour days is what it takes to put up a new theater in four months. (Twenty hours a day and several hundred thousand dollars from the coffers of Harry Davis Enterprises, that is.) In two weeks and three days the new Grand Opera House will rise out of the ashes (practically still glowing) of the former Avenue Theater. Then he'll be the owner of the biggest legit theater in town, seating 3,000 plus standing room. And, because of his new deal with the Keith Vaudeville circuit, he'll be able to book the *real* headliners (and not those second-rate hacks that Harry Williams brings in down at the Academy).

Will Rogers, Bert Coote, Harry Davenport, Dan Daly—you name it, Keith's got them under contract and now they'll be coming to Grand. And he's still got his own Harry Davis Players to mount full-length plays for the swells that want to see legit stuff. You add that all together, and hometown Harry will finally be able to do what he's wanted to for ten years—compete with the syndicate-controlled theaters in Pittsburgh. Come October, the new Grand will be able to outseat and outsell the Nixon, Alvin, Belasco-Duquesne, and the Gayety. Just wait and see. Better yet, buy a ticket and see.[1]

The Theatrical Trusts

Pittsburgh made a dramatic recovery from the economic downturns of 1893 and 1897. As the *Bulletin* put it, "Considering the number of dark days we have had in Pittsburg this winter, it would be hard to understand the general cheerfulness of the community, were it not known that there has never been a more prosperous period in this city than that we have now" (Jan. 28, 1899, 1). The *Bulletin,* a "journal for the home" was really a cultural brokerage site for Pittsburgh society, providing a weekly assessment of the city's financial progress and social status. It also covered political opinion, national and international travel, "College News," focusing primarily on Princeton and Yale, "Suffrage News," and cultural events in Pittsburgh, New York, and Europe. Thus the magazine served as a kind of weathervane for the changing currents in the wider world. This was by design, since by the end of the nineteenth century Pittsburghers with money and social position saw themselves as part of a newly forming national upper class unconstrained by geography.[2]

Indeed, in fin de siècle Pittsburgh the issue of national identity had become very important as the city shed its nineteenth-century skin and shook off its frontier outpost label. In the 1890s Pittsburgh emerged as a corporate headquarters as well as an industrial giant, both the "world's workshop" and a cradle of modern big business practices. Many of the partnerships and corporate trusts that epitomize Gilded Age monopoly capitalism originated in Pittsburgh, notably the billion-dollar merger of Carnegie Steel with Federal Steel Company, American Steel and Wire Company, National Tube, National Steel, and American Tin

Fig. 13. Harry Davis in 1905. Source: *Pittsburgh Bulletin*, 1905.

Plate (among others), a conglomerate that provided a model for the modern national corporation. Other local companies also evolved into regional and national corporations, such as Jones and Laughlin Steel, the H. J. Heinz Corporation, Pittsburgh Glass, Mellon National Bank, Union Savings Bank, Gulf Oil, and Westinghouse Electric, and their founders and chief officers responded by building enormous homes and erecting ornate office towers in the downtown triangle. When the twenty-six-story First National Bank Building went up in 1912, it was only one of fifteen new skyscrapers dominating the Penn-Liberty corridor and the Fourth Avenue financial district. This gilded city skyline, lit by electric lights and filled with the hum of modern technology, represented a new Pittsburgh—"the very incandescence of human energy," as Willa Cather, freshly arrived from Nebraska, wrote in a letter home.[3]

The urge to build big and to nationalize an industry (and to monopolize its production components) was not confined to the industrial and banking sectors. Theatrical trusts of a sort can be traced to the combination companies of the 1870s and 1880s—when New York entrepreneurs began buying up many of the vital commodities of theatrical production, from the rights to produce hit plays to exclusive contracts with actors. Efforts to control the playhouses proved more difficult, however, since most were locally owned and managed. And though regional touring circuits linking key playhouses did exist—such as the Ellsler Brothers' circuit between Cleveland and Pittsburgh in the 1870s—they often relied on family and personal business partnerships and were generally short-lived.

The modern theatrical trust was initiated by the union of three theatrical partnerships, two in New York (Marc Klaw and Abe Erlanger; Charles Frohman and Al Hayman) and one in Philadelphia (Samuel F. Nixon and J. Fred Zimmerman). In 1896 these formerly independent operations combined their leased or wholly owned theaters to form routes that stretched from New York and Philadelphia to points due west, aligning about three dozen directly controlled theaters and affiliations. Like other big business trusts, the goal of the new partnership, soon dubbed the "Syndicate," was to monopolize the industry in a broad geographical market through the use of clever leasing and performance contracts. By 1900 the Syndicate controlled the booking contracts in more than 700 legitimate playhouses.

As noted, because of its strategic position, excellent rail service, an abundance of playhouses, and established audiences, Pittsburgh was among the first targets of Syndicate expansionism. Colonization began in 1896, at the height of the depression, when Charles Davis leased the Alvin to Sam Nixon and Fred Zimmerman.[4] The two Philadelphians began their takeover in true imperialist fashion, by pretending to bolster local pride: "The advent of Nixon & Zimmerman's management in Pittsburgh is an important event in the theatricals of this city," they announced in their first glossy playbill program. "It means that the local theater-goers are to have better attractions, more attractions—in fact everything of interest and in the way novelty that is offered. . . . From the time of the announcement that Nixon & Zimmerman had secured the Alvin it has been a matter of congratulation that this city was to be included in the list of those cities that have already profited by their presence and constant personal direction."[5] About the same time, John Henderson lost his lease at the Duquesne to Charles Frohman, another syndicate partner. Within a year the new management team, led by Nelson Roberts and John Dons, had turned the Duquesne into a continuous vaudeville house offering a string of variety acts beginning at eleven in the morning and running without interruption until evening. These acts all came from the Frohman-controlled theaters in New York, primarily Hammerstein's Entertainment Emporium and Koster and Bial's vaudeville palace. By the end of the century, the city's two major theaters, destination playhouse jewels of the early nineties, were owned and operated by the syndicate.

Theaters for the Carriage Trade and Low-Priced Theaters

In 1903 Pittsburgh became a key syndicate stronghold when Nixon and Zimmerman built the Nixon, "The World's Perfect Playhouse." Located on Sixth Avenue above the mass of playhouses along the crowded Penn-Liberty corridor, the Nixon was intended to appeal to the carriage trade, those who arrived in their own vehicles rather than by streetcar or on foot. Its stately carriage entrance mimicked the portico outside the Carnegie Music Hall in Oakland, allowing well-off patrons to enter directly into the theater, avoiding the dirty street and sidewalk. At a reported cost of $1,200,000, the Nixon was undoubtedly Pittsburgh's perfect playhouse—an elaborate French beaux-arts style brick and terra-cotta façade mounted on a steel frame that was much touted for its fireproof construction. Inside the 2,183-seat house, the walls were of marble, the first balcony was cantilevered in a way that drastically improved the sight lines in the dress circle, and the boxes overlooking the orchestra seats were decorated in royal crimson, white, and gold—colors suitable for a Gilded Age audience. Perhaps the most talked-about feature of the Nixon was its innovative "rising promenade," an inclined floor that connected the orchestra seats to the first balcony dress circle without a staircase. The less expensive seats in the second balcony could be reached only by a separate entrance on William Penn Way. This allowed for a type of racial segregation, since African Americans were expected to use the second balcony.[6]

Fig. 14. Nixon Theatre opening program, 1903. Source: Unknown (Curtis Theatre Collection, University of Pittsburgh Library).

A year later a second syndicate-controlled playhouse was built for a more "popular-priced" crowd. The Gayety (now the Byham Theater) was built in 1904 by the Hyde and Behman Amusement Company of Brooklyn under the booking direction of Klaw and Erlanger, the most aggressive members of the Syndicate. The Gayety promised to provide Pittsburghers with "family burlesque" and the "finest plays in the best décor for a third of the cost of any other theater in town." The concept of an inexpensive theater for respectable (that is, not exclusively male) patrons was not new, as we have seen. Still, by 1904 the burlesque stage, though not yet the strip show it later became, was securely the province of a laboring-class, all-male audience. In that respect, the Gayety was something of an innovation, having made "wonderful strides in the commendable effort to elevate burlesque, . . . lifting it from the rut it so long occupied."[7]

Theater as Big Business

Fig. 15. First floor of the Nixon Theatre in 1905, the "world's perfect playhouse."
Source: *Pittsburgh Bulletin*, 1905.

Both the Nixon and the Gayety were beautifully decorated and fitted out with the latest lighting and stage machinery. And both theaters were successful from the start, bolstered by Syndicate operating money and good ticket revenues. The Nixon's programming was more traditionally legitimate, featuring touring productions of recent Broadway successes in addition to international ballet and opera companies. In its first ten years, the grand playhouse hosted Ethel Barrymore, Maude Adams, Henry Irving, Richard Mansfield, and Ellen Terry in sophisticated dramas such as *Man and Superman* and *Peer Gynt* and more popular fare like *Alice Sit by the Fire* and *Ben Hur*. In contrast, the Gayety marketed itself as both high-class and inexpensive, an appealing combination that attracted an economically diverse audience. Its version of "family burlesque" amounted to a constantly changing mixture of full-length plays, satirical sketches, and variety-style music and dance productions (usually featuring a chorus of female "leg" dancers). As with most theaters named "Gayety," the programming was overtly populist and tended toward extravagant spectacle, as this playbill illustrates:

Fig. 16. The Gayety Theater on Sixth Avenue, 1905. Source: *Pittsburgh Bulletin*, 1905.

"This Week Only! Siberia by Bartley Campbell. Introducing the Kishineff Massacre with Destruction of the Jewish Quarter" (*Bulletin*, Nov. 19, 1905, 13). It was also decidedly lowbrow at times. When the Extravaganza Company appeared in 1905, for example, Gayety advertisements invited local audiences to witness a "troupe of international champion women wrestlers" and to take up an offer of a hundred dollars "to any local woman who can stand up ten minutes with any of them, Miss Bradford, the English champion, offering five hundred" (*Bulletin*, Dec. 9, 1905, 14).

Harry Davis Enterprises

Not all entertainment moguls of the big business era were syndicate members. Pittsburgh's most successful theatrical entrepreneur of that time was the home-grown Harry Davis, manager or owner of a dozen local theaters and movie houses between 1890 and 1928. Davis, born in London, emigrated to Pittsburgh with his millwright father in 1870. After a few years in a public school in the Twelfth Ward (now the Strip District), he became a traveling carnival barker, then tried to assemble a barnstorming company before running out of money. Davis made his first significant profits in the late 1880s by selling ten-cent tickets to a walking match—a competitive event then in vogue. He took his $900 profit and bought the lease on the old O'Brien Dime Museum at 72 Fifth Avenue. Using his carnival barker skills and an instinct for identifying popular fads, Davis quickly turned the musty old variety house into the Eden Musee, an exotic wonderland with a Hall of Wonders freak show, a cabinet of curios (containing an Indian ar-rowhead and Confederate money), and a come-on-in lobby display featuring Old Rube—a "monster snake" supposedly caught by Harry Davis's "men" while on an African safari. The stellar attraction was the Theatorium, where a thirty-minute variety bill was led by the Lecturer, a minstrel-style interlocutor figure (probably Davis) who introduced the acts, including an exotic dancer named Little Egypt. The ticket seller was Johnny Harris, who soon became Davis's business partner, then brother-in-law, and in later years a state senator and the head of his own local amusement business.[8]

By 1891 Davis was netting $20,000 a year from the Eden Musee, and he used that income to expand in several different directions. In 1892 he leased the Pitts-burgh Opera House (located directly behind the old opera house and fronting Diamond Street) with the intention of offering full-length plays, but the panic of 1893 and the subsequent depression postponed that venture for several years. In the meantime he became the manager of the Casino, a converted ice skating rink located in Schenley Park, and for a few summers produced comic operas with his own Casino Comic Opera Company. But Davis's biggest success in these years was the Avenue Theater. In the early 1890s he took the lease on the decrepit Fifth Avenue Lyceum (the original opera house), refurbished the auditorium, and assembled his own professional stock troupe, the Harry Davis Musical and Travesty Company. Davis's entrepreneurial instincts also led him to sniff out a brand-new technology. In the fall of 1896, just a few months after the Lumière brothers first exhibited their "cinematograph" in New York City, he and Johnny Harris, his erstwhile ticket boy turned general manager, brought the invention back to Pittsburgh and installed it at their Avenue Theater. As the first public show-ing of film in the city of Pittsburgh, the event generated much public curiosity:

> The marvelous Lumière Cinematograph will be seen for the first time in Pittsburgh . . . Among the many views which will be exhibited at the Av-enue to-morrow is "Babies Quarrel," which is said to be wonderfully nat-

ural. A list of other views are "The Children at Play," "Drawing a Coke Oven in France," "The Swans at the Botanical Gardens in Paris," and "Arabian Cortege at Geneva Exhibition." . . . It seems like witchery to look at the life-sized figures of stage dancers, whirling, kicking, and bowing, while the drapery floats about their nimble forms, and know they are not actually living. (*Pittsburgh Dispatch*, Sept. 6, 1896, 5)[9]

Davis's success gave him even bigger ideas. Since he still held the lease on the larger Pittsburgh Opera House that abutted the Avenue Theater, he soon struck on the plan of building a single underground entrance to both theaters. For one price a patron could visit the Avenue, the Pittsburgh Opera House, and a brand new Children's Miniature Theater in the basement, where mothers could "check" their babies in the charge of a nurse.[10] But another economic depression in 1897 caused a dip in theater attendance, and the "three-in-one idea" never caught on. Soon after, Davis closed the Avenue and moved his stock company into the larger opera house space, where he produced melodramas and standard plays. As the economy recovered around 1899, Davis quickly expanded his operations again. He created a second stock troupe, the Avenue Dramatic Company, to perform at the newly renamed Avenue Family Theater, producing "wholesome" melodramas such as *Ten Nights in a Bar-Room*, and old standards such as *Rip Van Winkle*.

After 1900, both the Family Avenue Theater and the Pittsburgh Opera House drew large audiences. Harry Davis Enterprises was the most prominent locally based amusement company in Pittsburgh, with holdings that included several penny arcades and small dime museums scattered around the downtown. In June 1905 Davis and Harris opened the city's first stand-alone movie house (one of the earliest in the United States) at 433–435 Smithfield Street. The purpose of the Nickelodeon, reportedly the brainchild of Harris, seems to have been to make some money from the large number of Lumière movie shorts (called "flicker films") that had been stored at the Avenue Theater since Davis began showing them in 1896. Using one of Davis's vacant storefronts, they set up ninety-six opera chairs, a sheet for a projection screen, and an old phonograph to accompany the silent photoplays. With an admission price of a nickel, it opened for business on June 19, 1905.[11] This inauspicious beginning suggests that neither Davis nor Harris had any grand notions at the start. Davis did not publicize the new venture, even though he advertised his playhouses every week in

Fig. 17. Chorus girls in Christmas pantomime at the Grand Opera House, 1903. Source:
Pittsburgh Bulletin, 1903.

the leading journals. Perhaps this is because by 1905 moving pictures were not a
novelty in Pittsburgh; they were a regular feature at most of the city's playhouses.
Even the stately Carnegie Music Hall showed travelogues.[12]

Despite Davis's modest intentions for the Nickelodeon, the novelty clearly
had mass appeal. Within a few weeks the little space was showing the roughly
fifteen-minute program continuously (from 8 A.M. to midnight) to thousands of
people a day.[13] Most customers were likely members of the working class, including the ever-increasing number of immigrants attracted by the cheap entrance
fee and the fact that a knowledge of English was not necessary to fully enjoy
the films. The real innovation of the Nickelodeon, then, was the inversion of
status implied by its independence from the playhouse stage. Instead of being a
novelty attached to a live theater, the moving picture was now the only feature.
This foreshadowed the moviegoing phenomenon that eventually led to the end
of popular theatergoing and permanently reshaped the role of live drama in
American culture.

Also in June 1905 the Avenue Theater and part of the Pittsburgh Opera
House burned to the ground. Davis immediately saw an opportunity to compete
more effectively with the city's larger syndicate-controlled playhouses by building a 3,000-seat auditorium on the site of the destroyed theaters. Between June
and October 1905, he built a new, much grander entry on Fifth Avenue on the site
of the burnt-out Avenue and thoroughly remodeled the auditorium of the opera
house to make the largest legitimate playhouse in town. At the same time, he
also signed a booking agreement with Benjamin Keith's Vaudeville Management

Fig. 18. Interior of the Grand Opera House, ca. 1905. Source: *Pittsburgh Bulletin, 1917.*

Association to host national headliners ranging from Eddie Foy and George M. Cohan to Harry Houdini, Ruth St. Denis, and Bert Williams.[14] With the new Grand Opera House, Davis finally had the best of all worlds. He was both a big-time producer as part of the Keith-Albee empire and a trusted local businessman who pledged to his fellow Pittsburghers, "Performances in the Grand will always be artistic and refined and . . . nothing will be permitted upon the stage which, by spoken word or mute action, should offend the most circumspect patron."[15]

By 1906, Davis's various theatrical enterprises had become so far-reaching that he began publishing a weekly journal, *The Harry Davis News.* He needed eight tabloid-size pages just to cover the playbills for his playhouses and movie theaters and to advertise his other ventures, including a restaurant in the Grand Opera House—one of the first cafeterias in the city, advertised as a "new idea in dining." Over the next decade Davis continued to expand his business, sometimes in partnership with John Harris and sometimes independently. In 1909 the partners launched a circus production company, the Hippodrome, at Forbes Field—the city's brand-new ballpark in the rapidly growing Oakland neighborhood. And in 1914 they opened the Schenley Theater, near the University of Pittsburgh campus, which had recently been relocated to Oakland. The Schenley, like the Nixon a decade earlier, was intended to appeal to the elite. The opening gala featured the chancellor of the university, who gave a welcoming address from the new stage. The Schenley Players, billed as a "Company of Dramatic Artists, Presenting the Highest Class of Comedy and Drama in the Best Possible Manner," featured Nance O'Neil, a celebrated actress known especially for her interpretations of Ibsen's women.[16] Other members of the company, including George Alison, Louis Kimball, Roxanne Lansing, and Alfred Hickman, seem to have been imported from Davis's downtown stock companies. Perhaps because of its location in a wealthy neighborhood, the Schenley was also a favorite among touring ballet companies. Anna Pavlova appeared there several times beginning in January 1915.[17]

The last playhouses built and operated by Harry Davis were the Davis Theater on Smithfield and William Penn Place (now Mellon Square Park), built in 1915, and the Million Dollar Grand, built in 1918 to replace the Grand Opera House after it was destroyed in a spectacular downtown fire. A block from the Nixon Theatre, the Davis clearly catered to patrons interested in legitimate theater and high-end variety entertainment. Davis's growing list of stock companies (the Harry Davis Musical and Travesty Company, the Harry Davis Stock Company, the Harry Davis Players, and Davis' Famous Players) were by then nationally known. In 1904, Alice Kauser included Davis's enterprises in her list of the nation's "most successful stock managements."[18]

Davis was both versatile and eclectic in his programming, moving between continuous vaudeville, popular melodramas, and, on occasion, the headier repertoire of the art theater movement. "Henrik Ibsen's most famous drama, 'A Doll's House,'" the Bulletin noted in 1913, "is to be the powerful and unique attraction offered by the Harry Davis Stock Players at the Duquesne Theatre next week. Ibsen in stock is a striking novelty in itself and will mark one more signal achievement in the history of Pittsburg's favorite local organization of players" (Jan. 11, 1913, 10). Probably this versatility was due to Davis's ability to attract notable actors, including (besides Nance O'Neil) Mary Hall (known for dramatic roles like Camille), Pittsburgh-born William Powell (whom Davis trained), Thomas Meighan, Leah Winslow, Corliss Giles, Robert Gleckler, H'al De Forest, the McHugh family (including two child actors), Thurston Hall, and Dennis Harris (brother of John Harris). Like most professional stock actors, these men and women came and went over the years, regularly performing in New York and

Fig. 19. Harry Davis Players stock troupe at the Grand Opera House, 1898. Source: Unknown (Curtis Theatre Collection, University of Pittsburgh Library).

abroad as well as in Pittsburgh. Quite a few of them, including Powell, De Forest, and Hall, were among the first generation of successful Hollywood actors.[19]

The Art Theater Movement

By the early 1910s, variety-style theater in the form of elaborate vaudeville shows and family burlesque accounted for 50 percent of Pittsburgh's theatrical output; most new playhouse construction was motivated by the large profits of the vaudeville stage.[20] Some Pittsburghers were not pleased by this development. When the new Harris Theatre was going up in the fall of 1911, with an announced program of continuous vaudeville, the *Pittsburgh Dispatch* called it "a painful blow. . . . What an ideal home for a permanent repertory or stock company—one that could be built up, developed and placed within the reach of every playgoer in town! But such is life. Vaudeville happens to be a gold mine at any time and in any place, and stock isn't" (Dec. 24, 1911).

This fear of a decline in legitimate theater was not unique to Pittsburgh; the success of popular-priced playhouses and variety formats was cause for alarm in cities all over the United States. Even when full-length plays were produced, they were often seen as "warmed-over Broadway entertainment." By the early 1910s, a theatrical counterculture began to emerge in support of serious drama. Known as the art theater movement, it was the first sustained effort to launch an alternative business model that could rival commercial theater by actively supporting indigenous work. As Sheldon Cheney wrote in *Theatre Arts Magazine* in 1916, the art theater was to be "free alike from the will of the businessman, from the demands of movie-minded audiences, and from the fetters of superstitious traditionalism."[21]

Pittsburgh's indigenous art theater began in a flurry of activity in the early teens. In January 1913 a flood damaged the Kenyon Opera House at 711 Penn Avenue, an elegant playhouse that had been opened only a year earlier by Thomas Kenyon, owner of a successful North Side vaudeville house, the Kenyon Theater. After the flood waters receded, Kenyon shut his opera house down. William Moore Patch, a local actor-manager, took over, giving the space a new name and a new purpose. The Pitt Theatre Company of Pittsburgh opened in 1913 as a "High-Class Repertoire Organization" with "The Most Expensive and Evenly

Fig. 20. The Pitt Theatre (formerly the Kenyon) with inset photo of William Moore Patch (lower right corner), 1913. Source: *Pittsburgh Bulletin, 1913.*

Balanced Stock Company in America" (*Bulletin*, Sept. 20, 16). Patch declared his aim to be "the production of new and original plays, as well as the encourage-ment of native, and, above all, Pittsburgh Playwrights."[22]

Patch lived up to his ambitious agenda for a time. He organized a resident repertory company that included a group of seasoned professionals (Clara Whip-ple, Lois Miller, Robert Gleckler, Louis Kimball, Maurice Schoenfield, and Richard Dix) as well as a local celebrity, Mary Hall, who had joined after working with Harry Davis for three years.[23] Patch launched his first season with Maurice Maeterlinck's *Sister Beatrice* (1900), a poetic drama that had become a favorite of the alternative theater. In keeping with his intention to feature Pittsburgh play-wrights, Moore next produced *The Leper: A New Drama on the Burning Question of Eugenics* by George Seibel, a local librarian, newspaper reporter, and by 1913 a successful playwright. In 1906 he had been commissioned by Richard Mans-field, a well-known classical actor, to write a play about the poet Omar Khayyam.

(It was never produced, however, owing to Mansfield's death.) Seibel had also written two plays, *Christopher Columbus* and *Oedipus*, for Robert B. Mantell, the Scottish-born tragic actor who first came to Pittsburgh with Helena Modjeska's company in 1878.[24]

The Leper, which told the story of a villainous suitor who hides his disease, was a critical success and became a cause célèbre. Charles Bregg of the *Gazette-Times* compared the play to the work of Ibsen and Shakespeare and found in it "a ringing message of moral uplift" (Oct. 12, 1913, 6). The demand for tickets was so great that "many people were turned away. . . . The Pittsburgh newspaperman's remarkable play has created a veritable sensation. Several ministers are going to discuss it in their pulpits this Sunday. Doctors, educators and others are using it as the staple topic of conversation" (*Bulletin*, Oct. 18, 13). Patch continued to produce socially conscious dramas, including *The Second Mrs. Tanqueray*, Arthur Wing Pinero's drama about a woman with a "past." But the producer's ambitious vision of an art theater for downtown Pittsburgh must not have paid the bills. By May 1914 the Pitt was showing "photo-dramas," and soon after Patch gave up his lease.[25]

The Drama League

The most influential organization of the early art theater movement in Pittsburgh was the Drama League of Pittsburgh, organized around 1912 under Lincoln R. Gibbs, a University of Pittsburgh history professor.[26] It began as an affiliate of the Drama League of America, an audience-centered organization launched in Chicago in 1909 to "awaken the public to the importance of the theater as a social force" and to "stimulate interest in the best drama."[27] The very existence of the Drama League reflects the sense of sovereignty assumed by arts patrons of this era. Whether it was vaudeville or Shakespeare, many American theatergoers felt empowered to express their opinions. Certainly this was true of the league's Pittsburgh branch. In 1914 the league's new president, Elmer Kenyon (son of Thomas Kenyon) began publishing a weekly newsletter to encourage attendance at "good drama." "The fact that a bulletin is issued on a play indicates that, because of its artistic merit or the timely and vital nature of its appeal, the Committee deem it worthy of support."[28] Each issue described an upcoming production based on theme, technique, acting, plot, and social value. About *The Blindness of Virtue* by Cosmo Hamilton at the Pitt Theatre, for example, the newsletter stated: "Theme: The danger to children of ignorance of the facts of sex. Technique: A thesis play and consequently in frequent danger of being 'talky'" (*Bulletin,* Jan. 30, 1914). The league sometimes took on the role of moral arbiter, as in this comment on Oscar Wilde's *Lady Windermere's Fan* in 1915: "The author sets forth with shrewdness and considerable humor the development of independence in a likeable young couple about to be married. The comedy, which is wholesome throughout, abounds in natural and ingratiating fun." The Drama League of Pittsburgh also sponsored a weekly play-reading discussion group and various get-togethers, like the tea party held in 1921 for the members of the Provincetown Players, in town for a short season at the Nixon. Over the next several decades the Drama League gradually expanded its role and function, evolving into a kind of nerve center for local theater production, and in later years the *Bulletin* (subsequently renamed the *Review* and later the *Digest*) became the leading disseminator of vital information about auditions, meetings, lectures, contests, discussion groups, and classes.

A Technical School for Stagecraft

Perhaps the most revolutionary impact of the art theater movement in Pittsburgh was the establishment of the nation's first degree-granting program in theater production. In 1900 Andrew Carnegie offered the city a million dollars to establish a polytechnic school for training working-class citizens in technical crafts. By 1906 the School of Applied Industries and a related women's college, Margaret Morrison (named for Carnegie's mother), were in operation. In 1912 the School of Applied Design opened with departments in painting and decoration, music, and architecture.[29] In that year, the institution was renamed Carnegie Institute of Technology and was chartered by the state. Two years later, Carnegie Tech began offering the nation's first bachelor of arts degree in theater.[30] The dramatic arts program enabled both men and women to pursue a rigorous apprenticeship in all aspects of the field, from acting to costume construction, fulfilling Andrew Carnegie's vision of providing technical education to the masses.[31]

To run the new department President Arthur Hamershlag brought in Thomas Wood Stevens, a playwright, director, artist, and lecturer at the University of Wisconsin. In 1912, all eighteen applicants, nine women and nine men, were accepted. (Entry auditions were mandated for the following year.) The new Kresge Theater was inaugurated with a student production of *Two Gentlemen of Verona* in April (on Shakespeare's birthday). During his tenure Stevens designed an innovative curriculum that combined practical experience with liberal arts course work.[32] Stevens hired two English stage directors, Ben Iden Payne and William Poel, as instructors. Payne had turned the Gaiety Theater in Manchester, England, into a leading regional repertory theater producing serious new works by Bernard Shaw and John Galsworthy. In 1913 he came to the United States, where he worked in Chicago, New York, and Philadelphia, helping to establish a model for noncommercial regional theaters.[33] While directing in Chicago, Payne was surprised when Tech's President Hamerschlag invited him to work with his institute's new drama department. Payne recalled, "He was well aware that a drama department at the university was a daring innovation but, he said with unnecessary truculence, he was determined to carry it out. He wondered whether I might be able to give him any advice as to how it should be constituted. It was such a new idea to me that I could do very little besides wish him good luck."[34]

Despite his initial skepticism, Payne came to Carnegie Tech in March 1915. His first task was to direct Bernard Shaw's *You Never Can Tell* for what was then billed as the "Carnegie Institute of Technology Theater of the School of Applied Design."[35] In 1916 Payne persuaded Stevens to hire William Poel, founder of the Elizabethan Stage Society of London and a leading proponent of a movement to reconstruct the performance conditions of the Elizabethan stage. Poel's first production was a staged reading of a seventeenth-century masterpiece, Calderon's *Life is a Dream*. He then introduced the "Elizabethan manner" of production in his staging of Ben Jonson's *The Poetaster*. Poel soon moved on, but Ben Payne became the co-head of the School of Drama and over the next eighteen years refined Poel's ideas about Shakespearean performance.[36] Between them, Payne and Stevens established a high standard for Carnegie Tech's School of Drama, a continuing legacy that influenced both local and national theater pedagogy for the rest of the century.

Theater Journalism

Coverage of local theater may be found in the first editions of the *Pittsburgh Gazette*. The first signed reviews did not appear until the end of the nineteenth century, however. This reflected a shift away from political party journalism to news-centered journalism. Beginning with the first penny presses of the 1830s, newspapers became more like entertainment, and the political tracts and long editorials of the eighteenth century were replaced with reporting on everything from crime to sports to the arts. During this era some theater commentary was written by anonymous staff writers, though a significant portion came from press agents who placed stories (in the guise of reviews) in exchange for advertising dollars. Small paragraphs that appeared in the amusement columns of several local papers, for example, are strikingly similar in subject matter and wording, revealing that editors reprinted verbatim the press materials distributed by theater managers. Indeed, these columns appeared on the same page as paid advertisements for the local playhouses, suggesting a close correspondence between an advertisement and a mention in the amusement column. This form of theatrical payola was commonplace and was not, for the most part, considered unethical.[37]

Despite this inauspicious start, press coverage of theatrical events began to play an important, and mostly legitimate, role in the evolution of the Pittsburgh's rapidly expanding theater culture by the turn of the twentieth century. The city's numerous English-language daily and weekly newspapers hosted a half dozen full-time drama critics and many more who wrote on a freelance basis.[38] Among them was Willa Cather, who in 1896 became the drama critic for the *Pittsburgh Leader*, the largest newspaper in Pennsylvania. Unlike the day's mostly anonymous theater writers, Cather frequently signed her reviews, using either "Willa" or "Sibert," a family name. She also stood out for the intensity of her remarks, often in first person and in an unabashedly candid style. Her opinion of the renowned Maude Adams, for example, pulled no punches: "To me she is merely a clever ingénue, very unattractive to look at. Her perpetual 'girlishness' bores me to extinction, and the nasal twang in her voice is unpardonable." She was equally intense in her praise, as in her passionate assessment of Richard Mansfield's performance in *Cyrano de Bergerac*: "Each night you seem to wear the livery of a new master to make your body the receptacle of a different soul.

Fig. 21. Logo for "Plays and Players" column in the *Pittsburgh Bulletin*. Source: *Pittsburgh Bulletin*, 1890.

Each night your limbs seem molded, your cheek seared, your eyes burned by the despotic usage of the particular passion you assume, as a house, long occupied, seems as last to conform to and even share the caprices of its tenant."[39]

While some theater reviews appeared under their own headlines, most critical analysis was couched within long, newsy columns with titles like "The Passing Show" and "Plays and Players" (in the *Bulletin*), "Impressions of the Play" and "Stage News and Gossip" (in the *Gazette-Times*), and simply "Stage" (in the *Commercial Journal* and the *Post*). These columns were the relatives of the amusement sections of early eighteenth-century newspapers, combining information from press releases with critical commentary and, inevitably, some puffery. They also reflected the European practice, since they tended to mimic the French feuilleton, then in vogue. They were written in a loose, gossipy style, fueled by press agent propaganda, that sold newspapers and contributed to the growing cult of celebrity that surrounded the most famous stage actors.[40] When Sarah Bernhardt performed a short season at the Alvin in 1901, for instance, several theater columns were devoted entirely to a discussion of her shoes, including her size (two) and the extent of her collection (four trunks full).

By the early twentieth century, the city's seven dailies all had full-time drama editors and reviewers, including C. K. Lancaster at the *Chronicle Telegraph*, John K. Enge at the *Press*, Jackson Haag at the *Post*, Harry S. Silver at the *Leader*, and James Edward Leslie at the *Dispatch*. Charles M. Bregg of the *Gazette-Times* was considered the dean of local critics, however. By the time he came to Pittsburgh in 1900 he was already nationally known for his erudition and his distaste for the "prurient" side of theater. (He reportedly refused to print words or phrases from play titles that he found offensive.) Bregg was famous for his unwavering opinions and stubbornness. When the Nixon management, annoyed by a bad review, withdrew its advertising from the *Gazette-Times* and refused to provide the customary complimentary tickets, Breggs simply bought cheap gallery seats and continued to write his weekly reviews. Even after Henry Vaughn Moody's melodrama, *The Great Divide*, became the toast of Broadway despite a negative review during its tryout run in Pittsburgh, Breggs would not reconsider his opinion. When the touring version of the play came to Pittsburgh, he turned in another scathing assessment, noting without rancor that the "prestige of a long New York run has been added to the inherent virtues and vices of the Moody play. This does not alter fundamental truths."[41]

Big Business Trends

Early twentieth-century Pittsburgh was clearly a land of theatrical plenty. The *Bulletin* noted in 1905:

> Theatrical managers say there are few better towns in the country than Pittsburg, and the wealth of play houses, with their diversified amusements to satisfy every taste, is an admirable proof of the assertion. The people are good theater-goers; they like to "laugh and grow fat"; and they can afford it, too. Metropolitan in taste, the managers know it is no use to offer Pittsburg anything but the best in the several lines of theatrical productions; and each season invariably shows agreeable improvement in the attractions offered. Pittsburghers are furthermore benefited by all that can be derived by wholesome competition in the theatrical world. (September 30, 1905, 1)

Certainly this spirit of competition, "wholesome" or otherwise, was at the root of the city's newfound cultural self-confidence and its robust theatrical economy. The syndicate had taken an early position in the city, but around 1905 the rival Shubert organization, with famed David Belasco—playwright, director, and impresario—bought the lease on the Duquesne Theatre on Penn Avenue and renamed it the Belasco.[42] With stars like Sarah Bernhardt "under the Direction of Sam S. and Lee Shubert," the Belasco-Duquesne became the base of Shubert operations in Pittsburgh and a serious rival of the Syndicate-controlled Nixon, Alvin, and Gayety.[43] The third national player in the battle for Pittsburgh was Benjamin Keith's Vaudeville Managers Association, a New York theatrical trust launched in 1901 to centralize (and monopolize) vaudeville house bookings. Keith first entered the Pittsburgh market in 1900 when he bought the Alvin Theater for his touring vaudeville acts. Around that time, Keith also began renting to Harry Davis, who brought in his local stock company for seasons at the Alvin. In 1905 Keith and Davis expanded their Pittsburgh partnership at the new Grand Opera House.[44] By the early teens the Syndicate had overplayed its hand and was on the decline, nationally and locally. The Shuberts, on the other hand, continued to build theaters and contractual monopolies. In Pittsburgh Shubert theaters thrived through the twenties and, at one time or another, included affiliations with the Alvin, Duquesne, Pitt, Davis, and Grand Opera House.

Because of the industry warfare and the thriving local economy, the number of playhouses producing full-length dramas increased significantly in the first decades of the century. In 1916, local patrons could see plays at the Nixon, Alvin, Duquesne, Schenley, American, Carnegie Music Hall, Syria Temple, Grand Opera House, Kenyon, Pitt, Gayety, Lyceum, Liberty, Sheridan Square, Simon, Triangle, Hippodrome, Exposition Hall, Empire, and Davis.[45] In addition, several new playhouses, including the Victoria and the Academy, were devoted exclusively to "refined," that is, family-oriented, burlesque. New vaudeville houses included the Liberty, Rowland, and, most notably, the 1,800-seat Harris Theatre on Diamond Street near Smithfield. Built by John Harris in 1911, this luxurious playhouse first presented continuous vaudeville but gradually developed a national reputation for high-quality imported variety acts.

By the 1920s, Pittsburgh was developing a reputation as the "city of theaters," with a daily attendance of 25,000–30,000 at downtown houses clearly affecting trends in the entertainment industry.[46] The *Press* observed, "Your Pitts-

Fig. 22. Full house at the Alvin Theatre, 1908. Source: Unknown (Curtis Theatre Collection, University of Pittsburgh Library).

burgh theatergoer's opinion seems to go a great way with your producer" (Dec. 18, 1922, 3). How could this all-work-no-play iron-fisted Presbyterian outpost have evolved into the "city of theaters"? There are several explanations. First, by 1910, the city had about 550,000 residents, providing a ready market for regular (sometimes daily) theater consumption. And because theatergoing had become an affordable activity, the antitheatrical bias of the past had all but faded from memory. Second, the reemergence of class-based segregation of audiences expanded the industry's reach, and carriage trade playhouses like the Nixon and the Schenley served a clientele that had ceased to attend plays during the destination playhouse craze of the 1880s and 1890s. At the same time, popular-priced theaters like the Gayety and the Harris continued the destination playhouse's mandate to entertain working-class audiences. Perhaps most important, Pittsburghers had more spending power, and were more inclined toward leisure, than at any other time in the city's history.[47]

The diversity of this rapidly expanding Pittsburgh audience is demonstrated in the range of advertisements in theater programs, ranging from durable goods like automobiles and refrigerators (in the Nixon, Schenley, and Carnegie Music Hall programs) to insurance, restaurants, catering services, furniture, and sewing machines (in programs for the Belasco, Gayety, Grand Opera House, Alvin, and Davis). Many were targeted at women, a testimony to their growing economic power. An ad in the Nixon program for the Western National Bank was obviously meant to appeal to housewives with money to spend, promoting the benefits of a checking account and noting that the bank maintained "a well appointed room for the exclusive use of women patrons."[48] Other ads directed to middle- and lower-income women and displaying ready-made clothing, hats, and cosmetics appeared in programs for the Gayety, Alvin, Duquesne-Belasco, and Lyceum. Another emerging economic class were the pink-collar workers, young, single women employed downtown as typists, stenographers, telephone operators, and store clerks.[49] They were economically independent, with free time and at least enough disposable income to buy a fifty-cent theater ticket and a new hat. And unlike the matinee ladies of the 1880s, these young women could attend evening performances unescorted. As Harry Davis wrote in 1915 in advertisements for his new theater: "None but refined and wholesome plays will be placed on view—in other words a theater where mothers and daughters may go without being accompanied by their men folks, if they so desire."[50]

Young men were also appealed to in advertisements for the latest trends in "collegiate" attire—possibly even the teenage George S. Kaufman, who regularly attended the Alvin, Duquesne, Gayety, and Nixon between 1905 and 1909.[51] Political candidates also advertised in playbills and programs from the 1910s. The Duquesne Theatre program book from September 1911 touted the "Republican Candidate for County Controller for Re-Election R. J. Cunningham" on one page and the "People's Candidate William Conner of Braddock Borough for Register of Wills" on the facing page. Seen daily or weekly by so many city residents, theater programs were good vehicles for campaign messages. A Liberty Theater program book contained this appeal: "To the Voters of Pittsburgh. In presenting my candidacy for re-election I take this method to direct your attention to my pledge for a businesslike, non-partisan administration and offer my record in Council as confirmation."[52] Seven years before women could vote, such messages were obviously targeted at male theater patrons.

5

THEATER AS DISTRACTION

1915 to 1931

Pittsburgh, October 31, 1931. Who'd have thought that the talkies could have come so far in just a few years? Not George Sharp, that's for sure. After all, the first ones to play were nearly inaudible. But the quality soon improved and within a year all the theater owners around Pittsburgh were busy installing state-of-the-art audio equipment. And then, of course, they wanted a good return on their investments, so they began booking more and more movies. Leaving less and less stage time for legit theater. Meaning less and less work for the George Sharp Players. Like every other stock company manager across the country, Sharp has been bleeding his best pro actors to Hollywood. Between the growing economic crisis—the local papers are reporting that a third of Pittsburgh residents are now unemployed—and the growing popularity of movie palaces like Loew's Penn, the theater business in town just plain tanked. Seems like nowadays people don't need (and can't afford) anything but a cheap movie and a box of candy to make a night out.[1]

Fig. 23. Loew's Penn auditorium, 1930. Source: Library and Archives Division, Historical Society of Western Pennsylvania.

Wartime Theater

When the first military draft lists were published in July 1917, thousands of Pittsburgh men entered the Great War as soldiers. But the Pittsburgh steel industry had already been at war for several years, fulfilling its responsibility "of furnishing the bulk of war material for army use."[2] As early as 1914 Pittsburgh was sending munitions, missiles, and other war-related steel products to the Allies. By 1915, orders from abroad had increased so significantly that most of the city's steel mills were operating on a twenty-four-hour schedule. Extra shifts necessitated a larger workforce; the Carnegie Steel Company added 8,000 workers in February. The increase in production and employment was good for the city's economy, making the depression of 1914–15 somewhat less problematic for Pittsburghers than for other Americans. And because the manufacturing economy was healthy, other local industries continued to grow, including commercial theater.

But as soon as the United States entered the war and American troops saw actual combat in the fall of 1917, leisure time all but disappeared. Men not serving in the armed forces worked double shifts in the mills or long hours in offices, and women volunteered at canteens and Red Cross centers or went to work in the temporary munitions factories erected inside the manufacturing plants.[3] As a result, Pittsburgh's theaters, especially those presenting full-length plays, saw significant slowdowns at the box office, forcing producers to find other uses for their stages. Both Harry Davis and the Erlanger chain (the former Nixon-Erlanger partnership) offered their playhouses for a variety of wartime events throughout the eighteen months of U.S. involvement, from fund-raising efforts to lectures on patriotism to recruitment rallies led by celebrities. There was a Lillian Russell Recruiting Day in Pittsburgh and another in McKeesport, with the latter event netting 259 new recruits.[4] Other special wartime events included lectures on patriotic themes and presentations, usually before the show, by the Four-Minute Men—volunteers who went around the city in revolutionary-era costumes encouraging the sale of war bonds and savings stamps to help finance the war. Pittsburghers contributed over a billion dollars to the purchase of Liberty Bonds and put many millions into war savings stamps.[5] In addition, all the downtown theaters ran recruitment ads for the armed forces. A full-page color photograph in the Shubert-Alvin program displayed two handsome, smiling sailors in crisp white uniforms, with the caption: "Your country needs more of them—why don't you join?"[6]

Interest in the war became fodder for new plays, particularly melodramatic spectacles. *Seven Days' Leave*, a popular English potboiler, was a hit at the Alvin in November 1918 and again in 1919 at the Duquesne Theatre.[7] Its success was based on vivid spectacle that allowed audiences to "see the U-boat attack at midnight and the destruction of the Pirate" while at the same time assuring the squeamish, "No trench scene—no war horrors—just solid, substantial entertainment, and lots of it!"[8] Theatrical performances were also used for fund-raising. The Nixon raised a record amount for the Red Cross by hosting a touring production of *Out There*, which featured an all-star cast led by George M. Cohan and Laurette Taylor. The *Pittsburgh Sun* reported that the June 1, 1918, benefit performance netted "$135,000 for the matinee and evening performances. The same show, given in the same way and for the same purpose in New York, brought in $70,000; in Chicago, which ranked second of the cities visited, it had netted $80,000."[9] When the Armistice was declared in November 1918, Harry Davis—ever ready to exploit the news—turned a scheduled appearance by Lillian Russell into a celebration. The celebrated star had been set to headline a Keith bill with a wartime theme ("Miss Russell will be flanked by a squad of soldiers from the Marine Corps"), but after victory was declared Davis reorganized the show and renamed Russell's appearance "Pittsburgh Victory Week" (*Bulletin*, Nov. 9, 1918, 10).

Something for Everyone: Vaudeville

Pittsburgh's roaring twenties was a time of stunning economic growth and loud, boisterous cultural expansion. In 1920 the population of Allegheny County exceeded one million for the first time, and over the next decade the region's prosperity continued to rise along with its population. A Chamber of Commerce report announced: "The value of our industrial production was almost tripled between 1910 and 1926, and multiplied almost ten times since 1880 . . . an almost phenomenal increase."[10] The Eighteenth Amendment stimulated yet another profitable leisure-time industry; Pittsburgh was reputedly the "wettest" city in America. Sixth Street, home to the Gayety and the Alvin, was known as "the Great Wet Way" where whiskey was readily available and "booze barons riding in flashing cars were pointed out as celebrities."[11] All of this material well-being, legitimate or otherwise, engendered a newfound self-awareness among the city's leaders, who launched a public relations campaign known as "Pittsburgh First." The objective was to promote Pittsburgh as "more than just the nation's workshop" and to escape the Smoky City image.

The Pittsburgh First campaign naturally included the cultural sector, since Pittsburgh's commercial theater industry was already first. Bolstered by the booking power of several national and local companies, Pittsburghers of the twenties enjoyed an abundant range of stage attractions. But nothing succeeded so well as vaudeville, the variety-style format "invented" by B. F. Keith in the 1880s when he updated (and sanitized) popular acts for a family audience. By the twenties, vaudeville had evolved into a true cultural phenomenon—a social experience that obliterated the gap between high and low entertainment by merging song and dance (with stars such as Eddie Cantor, Sophie Tucker, and

Al Jolson), comedy, short plays, moving pictures, gimmicks, wonders like Harry Houdini's escape acts, and even social commentary like that of Will Rogers.[12] Edward Albee, B. F. Keith's business partner, famously explained it in this way: "In vaudeville, there is always something for everybody, just as in every state and city, in every county and town in our democratic country, there is opportunity for everybody, a chance for all."

For Harry Davis, the success of vaudeville lay in its ability to evolve along with rapidly changing popular tastes and habits. In his words: "No branch of the show business . . . has been so completely revolutionized as vaudeville. . . . It is the one amusement, too, that has constantly grown better and constantly developed along ever advancing artistic levels. It has never taken a step backward for, from the day it emerged from what was vulgarly known as 'variety' to the present time, the aim of vaudeville managers has been to consistently improve its tone and raise its standard" (*Bulletin*, Sept. 2, 1916, 11). Davis's assessment, while self-serving, was accurate. Vaudeville had improved upon the aesthetic and social functions of variety-style theater, and theatergoers responded positively. With tickets at fifty cents, a vaudeville house offering continuous performances throughout the afternoon and evening was immensely appealing. As noted, in 1923 total attendance at the ten leading vaudeville houses was 25,000–30,000 a day, and certain individual theaters played to 25,000–50,000 per week (*Pittsburgh Sun*, Dec. 1, 1923, 3).

The appeal of vaudeville also crossed racial lines. Because of the color line in many of the downtown playhouses, variety theaters and night club derivatives began dotting the thriving Hill District neighborhood around 1910.[13] The area encompassing Centre and Wylie avenues was a busy, culturally mixed neighborhood with a large number of professional and laboring-class blacks. Perhaps the first vaudeville house to feature black artists for a black audience was the Star Theater at 1417 Wylie Avenue. The Star booked its talent through the Dudley circuit in the early teens, became part of the Southern Consolidated Circuit between 1916 and 1921, and finally joined the powerful Theater Owners' Booking Association (TOBA) circuit after 1921.[14] TOBA controlled leading acts like Bessie Smith, who appeared at the Star in 1924. By the time the Star went out of business in the mid-twenties, black vaudeville acts were also featured at other Hill District theaters, including the Elmore, presenting the Dusty Murray Chocolate Town Revue, and the Roosevelt, with its Club Arabian Revue, featuring twenty-five "Colored Jazzmanians." Black-owned social halls like the Pythian Temple, built in 1927 at 2007 Centre Avenue and later renamed the Granada Theater, also hosted touring and local vaudeville performers as well as musical revues, bands, and local talent shows.[15]

The Oakland Cultural District

As the downtown theaters became increasingly devoted to vaudeville and mov-ing pictures, other types of stage performance moved to Oakland, two miles to the east. Here the Carnegie Institute Music Hall, Syria Temple, and Masonic Hall all shared green lawns and acres of parkland with some of the city's wealth-iest neighborhoods. Many Oakland residents were consumers of high culture in-terested in symphonic music, opera, and full-length dramas, especially when presented at theaters in their own calmer, cleaner vicinity. Oakland's most promi-nent cultural institution was the Pittsburgh Symphony Orchestra, founded in 1895 as the resident orchestra of the Carnegie Music Hall. The PSO disbanded in 1910, then was reorganized in 1926 by its own musicians and an executive board made up of local business leaders.[16] After 1926 the orchestra performed in the 3,800-seat Syria Temple, a few blocks from its former home. There the PSO quickly became the city's leading cultural force. On April 24, 1927, for example, the orchestra defied Pennsylvania's antiquated blue laws by playing a Sunday concert for a standing-room-only crowd of nearly 4,000. Nine members of its ex-ecutive committee were arrested for defying state law, including Richard S. Rauh, who later helped to found the Pittsburgh Playhouse.

During the 1920s, the Carnegie Music Hall hosted smaller-scale events such as touring productions of Shakespeare and dramatic recitations like those of the character monologist Ruth Draper, a "favorite with the prominent women of the city" (*Bulletin*, Jan. 13, 1923, 9). The Syria Temple hosted large touring produc-tions imported by May Beegle, a theatrical and music promoter who called her-self "Pittsburgh's impresario." During the twenties Beegle presented Anna Pavlova and Mickail Mordkin, the renowned flamenco artist La Argentina, mod-ern dance "music visualizations" by Ruth St. Denis and Ted Shawn, Eleonora Duse in a repertoire of classic drama, the French Army Band, the Chicago Grand Opera, the New York Philharmonic, the Metropolitan Opera, the Provincetown

Players, and soprano Rosa Ponselle. Attendance at these events was de rigueur for the city's blue book; each September the *Bulletin* published the names of local Pittsburghers who had taken a box at the Syria Temple and would be attending the season's most fashionable events.

Oakland was also home to several of the city's earliest independent, or non-commercial, theater companies. As noted in chapter 4, Pittsburgh's art theater movement originated in the early teens, with a few local artists and managers calling for a new era of "aesthetic" theater and indigenous dramas. But its real birth came with the Stage and Play Society, founded in 1915.[17] The group, with 500 participants by 1929, mounted an annual season at Carnegie Hall that frequently included plays written by its own members. One was Chester Wallace, an officer of the society, whose one-act play, *The Wasp,* was produced in 1929.[18] In 1930 the group moved to the Twentieth Century Club, a prominent women's organization located nearby on Bigelow Boulevard. The Stage and Play Society flourished for many years. In addition to producing challenging and original works, it offered lectures, playwriting labs, workshop production opportunities, and acting classes for an increasingly female membership.

Another influential little theater, the Guild Players of Pittsburgh, founded in 1919 by Carnegie Tech's Theodore Viehman, performed at the Conservatory of Music on Dithridge Street. Viehman was joined by several other Carnegie Tech faculty members, including Chester Wallace, and drama students from Tech and the University of Pittsburgh. The fledgling company had considerable community support and boasted a list of subscribers and benefactors that reads like a who's who for 1919. Its ambitious first season included Shaw's *You Never Can Tell* and Susan Glaspell's little miracle of social observation, the one-act play entitled *Trifles.*[19]

In 1925, Lane Thompson launched the Community Theater of Pittsburgh, the first attempt to organize the city's many amateur theater groups then working mostly in church basements and school auditoriums. Pressure from such organizations fueled a campaign to build a new playhouse. A 1926 press release noted, "The Community theater of Pittsburgh intends to have a playhouse that will afford all the fifty or more amateur producing groups of the city a workshop where their dramatic efforts may be staged adequately and effectively."[20] The *Gazette-Times* had already noted the need for a playhouse in 1925: "We have in Pittsburgh . . . a large and intelligent group of people already interested in the

Community Theater movement. For years the city has needed, not so much encouragement to develop its talent, but simply an adequate theater in which that talent may reveal itself" (Nov. 29, 1925). Although the playhouse was never built, the Community Theater supported a number of Oakland theater groups at work in the Oakland area during the mid-twenties.

Little Theater Lane

By the late twenties, independent, noncommercial theater companies sponsored by churches, colleges, Bohemian-inspired clubs, and civic organizations could be found across the United States. In Pittsburgh, a list of little theaters published in 1928 included the People's Playhouse of the North Side, the Suburban Theater of the South Hills, the Tarkington Theater, the Saturday's Children's Playhouse, the Modern Mummers, the Sunday Night Players, the Community Players of Pittsburgh, the Pittsburgh Musical Comedy Club, the Pitt Players, the Duquesne University Red Masquers, Carnegie Tech Drama, the Y Playhouse, and the IKS Players (*Pittsburgh Press,* Oct. 29, 1928, 6). This odd mix of theater groups shared a desire to bring stage modernism "to the smaller towns that would otherwise never see the changes that are being wrought in stage decoration as well as in the content of modern plays."[21] They also tended to be populated by the city's white, politically progressive, Protestant and Jewish middle class.[22]

The vitality of Pittsburgh's little theater movement was noted by local drama critics. By 1928 there were regular weekly columns in the *Pittsburgh Sun* ("At the Little Theaters"), *Pittsburgh Press* ("Little Theater Activities"), *Pittsburgh Mirror* ("Our Non-Professional Play Producing Groups"), and *Pittsburgh Gazette-Times* ("In the Little Theater World").[23] Columnists reported on theater activities and productions and regarded little theater as a breeding ground for new professionals "on the road to significant careers on the professional stage"*(Pittsburgh Press,* Oct. 29, 1928). Journalists on the little theater beat promoted the aesthetic value of these activities and encouraged an emphasis on "drama" as opposed to mere "stage attractions." A columnist for the *Pittsburgh Sun* wrote, "A community theater will give local patrons of the drama an opportunity to prove conclusively to the world that Pittsburgh's interest in things dramatic is on a par with that manifested in most other American cities" (Apr. 29, 1925, 6).

The most ambitious effort along this line was the Little Theater Lane initiative of 1929, a privately funded project to create a "little Greenwich Village" in downtown Pittsburgh. The officers of the organization (all local theater people) marketed the idea of a "lane" of buildings devoted to theater arts.[24] Work on Little Theater Lane began in 1930 with the purchase of four dilapidated cottages on Watson Street (later demolished), to be converted into an "art and culture center." One would house the Pittsburgh Radio Artists' Bureau, another the Pen and Ink Club for playwrights and journalists ("furnishings will be Bohemian"). There would be a bookshop, a circulating library, an official headquarters for Pittsburgh's little theater artists, with a stage and fifty-seat auditorium in the basement. A larger theater and "Bohemian tea room" were hopes for the future. "Dreams of the sponsors of the little theater movement know no limit," observed the *Pittsburgh Press;* the project would be "the physical manifestation of all that is artistic in Pittsburgh" (Jan. 5, 1930, 2).

At first the Little Theater Lane project moved along quickly, opening an "intimate theater space" in February 1930 and announcing the formation of "a citizen's committee to include 100 prominent Pittsburghers" and a membership drive with the ambitious goal of raising $50,000 (*Pittsburgh Press,* Feb. 16, 1930, 2). But these plans were evidently slowed by the Depression.

By 1931, most board members and officers had resigned. Despite another attempt at fund-raising, no more was heard about Little Theater Lane.

Movie Playhouses

The advent of cinema brought irreversible changes. While by the mid-teens all of Pittsburgh's commercial playhouses were showing some combination of live stage entertainment and film, the "photoplay" was still largely a novelty and secondary to the live stage show. By 1923, however, there were roughly 100 stand-alone moving picture theaters in the city proper and 223 in the greater Pittsburgh area. According to the *Pittsburgh Sun,* more than 100,000 people a day visited these theaters (only New York, Chicago, and Philadelphia had a larger seating capacity).[25] Most of the new movie-only theaters were located in outlying neighborhoods like the Hill (with twelve), East Liberty (ten), and the North Side (three). Among the most elegant were the Garden on the North Side, the Liberty at Penn and Shady, and the Regent in East Liberty. The most exotic of all was the Cinema Theater on Liberty Avenue (now the Harris), Pittsburgh's first foreign movie house; it showed "real honest to goodness German talkies" and appealed to those interested in "something entirely different in the way of motion pictures."[26]

By 1920, the definition of a *theater* had effectively changed. No longer just a playhouse, the modern theater offered both live entertainment and moving pictures. In Pittsburgh this conversion from destination playhouse to movie palace began when Harry Davis's Grand Opera House (built in 1905) burned to the ground in 1917. Davis quickly erected the Million Dollar Grand, a 2,000-seat theater with entrances on both Fifth Avenue and Diamond Street (now Forbes). The large stage was suitable for plays and large vaudeville productions accompanied by a full orchestra. Its spectacular amenities included a bowling alley, a billiard room, a restaurant, and a ladies' lounge called Marie Antoinette's Bedchamber, "furnished with that exquisite taste which was a predominating characteristic of the French queen."[27] Cages of singing canaries hung in the mezzanine.

What really set the Million Dollar Grand apart was a large screen at center stage and the promise of "continuous movies" in addition to vaudeville acts and stock plays. An organist and "symphony orchestra" (often only a band) accompanied the silent films until Davis installed sound equipment in the late 1920s. And while the Million Dollar Grand was not yet called a "movie palace," it offered many features that characterized the great movie palaces of the twenties, including first-run Hollywood films and live music and performances modeled on the Broadway revue. A 1924 advertisement reads: "On the stage, Gilda Gray, the original exponent of the Shimmy, and famous Ziegfeld Follies star, makes her first appearance in a motion picture theater, with her Hollywood Beauties" (*Bulletin*, Dec. 30, 1924, 14).[28]

The city's first bona fide movie palace was Loew's Aldine, which opened in 1923 in the Victoria, a former male-only burlesque house on Liberty Avenue. The Loew's chain combined moving pictures on the big screen with national stage acts—a recipe Marcus Loew had perfected in other cities by adapting some destination playhouse practices, such as distributing a gossipy newsletter and hosting weekly special events. The first Aldine special event was Jazz Week, "with a jazz program of song and dances, a jazzy prologue and in fact everything will be jazz and humor, not excepting the film feature, which is Buster Keaton, in his second and latest full length comedy 'Our Hospitality.' The jazz part of the program for the most part will be supplied by the Versatile Sextette Orchestra which comes here from the smart Rendezvous of New York." The Aldine continued to offer stage novelties to accompany its feature films, from a burlesque-inspired dance act called "Silk Stockings" to the Kiaros, who specialized in "Japanese Dexterity."[29]

In 1926 Marcus Loew announced his plan to erect the largest theater in Pennsylvania on the site of the old Hotel Anderson at Sixth and Penn. The 3,486-seat Loew's Penn opened on September 6, 1927, in a gala event attended by state and local officials and a standing-room crowd.[30] Designed by the Rapp brothers of Chicago, it was promoted as the most ornate theater ever erected in the city. Loew's Penn featured a three-story grand lobby with a fifty-foot vaulted ceiling, ornamental columns, a marble staircase, crystal chandeliers, marble wall panels, and silk draperies—significantly outdoing the lobbies of the largest destination playhouses of the 1890s. At a cost of $5 million, the project exceeded all previous theater construction in Pittsburgh (with $3 million raised by selling public stock, much as subscribers participated in funding theaters in 1813 and 1833).[31] The opening program was a silent movie entitled *Adam and Evil* and a stage show featuring the "Loew's and United Artists' Symphony Orchestra in the disappearing pit, with Don Albert at the podium and Ted Lewis and his band on stage."[32] The Penn hosted a rotating mix of national acts, including Paul Whiteman and the Rhythm Boys (featuring a young Bing Crosby), Perry Como, Buster Keaton, Jimmy Durante, Fred Waring, and many others.

Loew's Penn was soon rivaled by another "temple of the cinema" owned by the rival Stanley Corporation and promoter James Bly Clark.[33] The 3,749-seat Stanley, on Seventh Street, reportedly cost $3 million and boasted a giant marquee illuminated by 10,948 lightbulbs. The opening gala on February 27, 1928, featured a silent version of *Gentlemen Prefer Blondes* and a lavish stage show with a forty-piece orchestra, a male chorus, and a "joyous frolic of twenty beautiful showgirls."[34] On July 16, the Stanley showed Pittsburgh's first "talkie," entitled *Tenderloin*, although the sound was, according to newspaper accounts, mostly inaudible.[35]

The last of Pittsburgh's great movie palaces was the Enright, another Stanley chain theater, that opened in East Liberty on December 28, 1928. It was named for Thomas F. Enright, a Pittsburgher who was the first American soldier killed in the Great War. For the opening, Stanley executives imported from their Indianapolis movie palace a young singer named Dick Powell to become the resident master of ceremonies. Because the acoustics in the Enright were terrible, Powell's light tenor voice could not be heard. He began using a megaphone—a necessity that soon became his signature. With "a knack for crooning soft ballads," Powell was an immediate success (*Gazette,* June 2, 1929). In 1929 he was transferred to the Stanley Theatre downtown, where he added to his success. One reviewer remarked, "We've seen M.C.'s and M.C.'s but to us there is none as clever as Dick. The boy can do anything and do it well. Sings better than Crosby, Columbo and Valee together. And plays darned near every instrument in the band."[36]

Dick Powell's success illustrates the great innovation of the movie palace era: the marriage of high-end vaudeville and moving pictures under the careful management of a charismatic master of ceremonies. By combining the familiarity of live stage acts with the new technology of film, and by offering both in glamorous surroundings, movie palaces provided pleasures both old and new. As with all cultural shifts, however, there were detractors. Elmer Kenyon for one saw the Penn and the Stanley as threats to live theater. Writing in a local journal, the *Storegram,* Kenyon noted:

> Of late, as the public finds increasing diversion in music that assaults nerves with jazzy rhythms, pictures that move on the silver screen, cars that carry families to the country roads, and richly embellished mahogany boxes that draw forth sounds from every quarter of a radio-conscious world, there have been signs that the art of Thespis exerts less and less of its magic lure. And now Pittsburgh is about to be impressed with the most certain seal of modernity—the "Roxy" type of motion picture cathedral—and with two "cathedrals" at that. The actor, who with the brush of speech paints human passions, may become for a time a thing of memory.[37]

The George Sharp Players

When the Million Dollar Grand was sold to Warner Brothers in 1928, the Harry Davis Famous Players permanently disbanded after thirty-five years of continuous production. The Davis troupe's longevity was astonishing, since local professional companies had been steadily going out of business since the 1880s—victims of the New York touring companies. But the combination of vaudeville and movies proved to be a knock-out punch for professional stock in Pittsburgh, as it was elsewhere. By the late twenties there were only a few professional stock companies in residence at the large destination playhouses. The two largest and most successful—the Al Smith Players and the George Sharp Players—were summer stock companies assembled in the spring and disbanded in the autumn, thus allowing the actors to maintain winter contracts in larger cities such as New York and Chicago. Al Smith ran a number of "floating" stock companies that traveled from Brooklyn to Erie to Pittsburgh (and many towns in between). In Pittsburgh Smith was based at the old East End Theatre in East Liberty, which by 1926 had gone through several different names and as many stock companies. In 1927 Smith rejuvenated the space and began producing his special mix of light vaudeville and full-length comedy (*Charley's Aunt* was part of the 1927 season). A showman in the Harry Davis mold, he published a newsletter, *Al's Applesauce*, that featured gossip and news about his star actors and pages of jokes, riddles, and other take-away entertainments.

George Sharp created and managed the city's most successful and accomplished summer stock troupe after the Harry Davis Famous Players disbanded. Sharp first came to Pittsburgh in 1926 as the national tour manager of *Abie's Irish Rose*, which ran for twenty-six weeks at the Pitt Theatre on Penn Avenue. He returned to the city the following winter, rented the Pitt, formed his own company (by hiring many of Davis's best-known players, including Thurston Hall and Anne Forrest), and began producing a rotating mix of contemporary hits, melodramas, mysteries, and musical comedy revues—all under the slogan "Spoken Plays at Picture Prices." The first season was so successful that Sharp told the *Sun-Telegraph* he planned to "make this company a Pittsburgh institution. People want the drama in three dimensions, not merely flickers and shadows. They want to hear the human voice, not merely echoes and static. But the average man cannot afford to pay two days' wages for two hours' entertainment. A stock company saves the railroad's share of the admission price . . . and it gives good actors a chance to get out of the ruts of long runs."[38]

Sharp's analysis was smart and aggressive, as was his management style. The company continued to prosper in seasons at the Pitt and Alvin (where he also mounted occasional runs). As Sharp's reputation grew over the next three years, so did his ambitions. He began importing actors from New York—notably Ann Harding, Alexander Kirkland, Harry Banister, Paul McGrath, and Shirley Booth—and producing recent New York hits during a long summer season that ran from May through October. The company mounted *Rain, The Constant Wife, Death Takes a Holiday, The Show Off, The Play's the Thing,* and Eugene O'Neill's *Strange Interlude.* This sprawling nine-act play was an odd choice for a stock company, but it was successful nonetheless. In the *Sun-Telegraph,* William Lewis noted that Sharp's company "went about the work of presenting the nine acts of psychology, biology and pathology as casually as if it were the merest light and frothy comedy."[39] Sharp balanced O'Neill's experimentalism with productions of *Daddy Dumplins* and *The Cat and the Canary.*

Over his five-year tenure in Pittsburgh, Sharp was a favorite with drama critics, who reviewed his shows respectfully and chronicled the activities of his company. George Seibel of the *Sun-Telegraph,* for example, outlined the intellectual demands of working in Sharp's stock company:

> While these people are memorizing one role they are rehearsing another and playing a third. . . . They work hard, these people who play—and the good folks who think an actor's life is an easy one, full of dissipation and luxury, ought to be made to serve a few weeks in a stock company. It is a strenuous existence that requires all the energy and brains the player has at command. But there are compensations in the good fellowship behind the curtain—which prevails among Mr. Sharp's happy group—and in the satisfaction every one feels in the success of one another. There doesn't seem to be a bit of professional jealousy in evidence.[40]

Sharp also nurtured local talent, notably Helen Wayne, a Carnegie Tech drama student who later became the leading lady of the Pittsburgh Playhouse. Finally, Sharp had a genuine respect for local audiences. His newsletter, *Sharp Points,* was an interesting four-page publication that discussed the theme of the week's play and the actors' impressions of their characters. Compared to similar publications, it was notably more substantive.[41]

Perhaps owing to the Sharp Company's success, a few rival professional groups were formed in 1928. The Nixon Players, started by Ann Harding and Harry Bannister, formerly with Sharp's company, lasted only one summer season before the husband and wife team went to Hollywood in 1929.[42] The Gayety Players emerged in 1928 during a Sharp hiatus, but even though Siebel gave them a good launch, this company also lost most of its stars to Hollywood. Sharp endured a little longer by finding interesting actors, like Shirley Booth, to replace those heading west and by hiring more and more local people, many of them recent graduates of Carnegie Tech. Nevertheless, after 1931 he too closed down and headed for Hollywood. (Edwin Vail, Sharp's stage manager and a sometimes actor, tried to reorganize the company under his own name in 1932, but it operated only sporadically.) Success in California must have been elusive, however, and in November 1934 Sharp returned to Pittsburgh to direct the temperance melodrama *The Drunkard* in the English Room at the Fort Pitt Hotel. The show was mounted under the George Sharp Players' banner, but the group's heyday had clearly come and gone, since the production disappointed his formerly loyal audience. It was also obsolete. As George Siebel noted, the postprohibition audience "drained bottles of Pilsener while cheering the hero and booing the villain" (*Pittsburgh Leader,* Nov. 1934). This appears to have been Sharp's final effort in Pittsburgh.[43]

The Theatre Guild in Pittsburgh

A different version of the modern stock company came to Pittsburgh in 1928 when New York City's renowned Theatre Guild began an annual five-week residency at the Nixon Theatre. Founded in 1914 as the Washington Square Players, the Theatre Guild reorganized in 1919 as a subscription theater with a loyal audience eager to see adventurous drama—new plays by emerging American playwrights and works from the European avant-garde. By 1925 the Theatre Guild had 25,000 subscribers in New York (an extraordinary number even by today's standards), and three years later the company expanded further by launching seasons in regional cities.[44] When it was announced that Pittsburgh was to be included in this outreach effort, some local theater patrons and professionals feared that the city would fail to appreciate its sudden bounty and thus chase the Theater Guild away. Elmer Kenyon, former president of the Drama League and head of the Drama Department at Carnegie Tech, made that position clear in a letter published in the Nixon Theatre programs in 1928:

The Theatre Guild season of five weeks beginning September 24 at the Nixon Theatre seems to us so important that we are venturing to call it to your attention in the hope that you will devote part of the first meeting of your organization to a discussion of the civic and cultural importance of keeping Pittsburgh in the itinerary of this finest of art theaters so far developed in America. Many of us for years have wished that we might have the advantages enjoyed in New York by almost thirty thousand appreciative subscribers, but now that the wish is about to be realized there is, in the light of past experience, grave doubt as to whether Pittsburgh has enough intelligent playgoers to encourage an organization like the Guild to return.[45]

Whether Kenyon was deliberately overstating his case or just fretting, his "grave doubt" proved unnecessary. The Theatre Guild mounted an annual subscription season at the Nixon Theatre for the next twelve years, staging an interesting array of plays by Eugene O'Neill, Bernard Shaw, Philip Barry, Henrik Ibsen, Maxwell Anderson, Lillian Hellman, Shakespeare, Molière, and many others.

The Decline of the Legitimate Stage

Even with the Theatre Guild's annual residency and the good efforts of the little theaters and resident stock companies, straight dramatic fare in Pittsburgh was clearly on the steady decline during the twenties. The range of full-length plays being offered during this period was not nearly as varied as in previous decades. Some theaters, such as the Pitt and the Lyceum, could not compete with the big-time variety acts at the Million Dollar Grand, the Shubert-Alvin, and the Davis and began staying dark for weeks at a time. Fewer and fewer theaters produced full-length plays, and then only for limited runs or special engagements, such as the appearance of the Moscow Art Theatre at the Pitt in 1923. Even the Nixon—the city's best-known legitimate house—began offering a rotating mix of touring productions in a variety of genres and styles, with only about half being full-length plays. The rest of the venerable theater's rental weeks were booked with Hollywood blockbuster movies, vaudeville shows, special events (not always theatrical), and, most prominently, Broadway-style musical revues such as George White's *Scandals*, Raymond Hitchcock's *Hitchy-Koo* series, Irving Berlin's *Music Box Revue*, and the enormously successful Ziegfeld Follies. The last proved so popular with Nixon audiences, in fact, that in 1916 Ziegfeld began using the theater as a tryout house for his annual installments of the Follies—a pattern that lasted long after the heyday of vaudeville had passed.

Pittsburgh's loss of status as the "city of theaters" is illustrated by the tone of the media sensation following the death of Eleonora Duse, at the age of sixty-four, at the Schenley Hotel in 1924. The actual facts of Duse's final days in Pittsburgh are hard to ascertain, since the publicity machinery surrounding her farewell tour was substantial, involving glamorous misinformation designed to sell tickets while also protecting the star's reputation from her own increasingly erratic behavior. What is known is that by the time Eleonora Duse arrived in Pittsburgh on April 1, 1924, on her latest "farewell" tour of the United States, she was so ill with respiratory disease and travel fatigue that she required up to a week of rest between each performance. As part of this schedule, Duse spent four quiet days at local hotels before appearing in *La Porta Chiusa* in front of an appreciative full house of more than 3,800 at the Syria Mosque, "possibly . . . the largest audience that ever attended the presentation of a dramatic production in this city" *(Gazette-Times,* Apr. 6, 1924).

Illness prevented Duse from leaving as scheduled, however, and by the next week conflicting reports began to appear in the city's dailies about her status. Her manager told reporters, "Mme. Duse gave her performance of 'The Closed Door' in a chilly theater. Going to and from the Mosque she passed through the rain and returned to her hotel quite chilled. From this time on she was indisposed, and in several days influenza began to develop." But immediately upon her death on April 21, media reports began to enhance Duse's death with the addition of the "tragic circumstance" involving a closed stage door, echoing the title of the drama she had just starred in, *La Porta Chiusa.* According to this version, Eleonora Duse was locked out of the stage entrance to the Syria Mosque on the evening of April 5 and was forced to stand in the cold rain long enough to become chilled and drenched. By the time she returned to her hotel after the performance, she was gravely ill.

The next step in the process, vilifying the city of Pittsburgh, was secured in book form in 1930 by E. A. Rheinhart in *The Life of Eleonora Duse:*

> But she had to go on to Pittsburgh, she, who loved so many towns and yet
> so often spoke of cities with hatred and loathing, as if in doing so she had

The SELWYNS
and FORTUNE GALLO
in Association with
EDITH TAYLOR THOMSON
have the great honor of
presenting the World's
Greatest Tragedienne,

ELEONORA
DUSE

Syria Mosque
Pittsburgh, Pa.

Saturday
Evening
April 5, 1924

DUSE'S ACTING
IS A TRIUMPH
OF MIND OVER
MATTER

Fig. 24. Syria Mosque program for Eleonora Duse's last performance, 1924. Source: Unknown (Curtis Theatre Collection, University of Pittsburgh Library).

had some prescience of the city for which she was bound now: "the most horrible city in the world," with its confusion of climbing sky-scrapers jutting up from its inferno of fog, its smoke-grimed angular erections of iron and cement. . . . She shut herself into her room in the hotel. She passed four days here. On the evening of the 5th of April she had to leave it at last and act once more. An icy rain was falling, mingled with sleet. She must lose no time in getting from her car into the theater! But the stage door was closed and the attendant was not there. She had to stand and wait outside in the cold and wet. When the door was opened at last she was shivering with cold. In desperation lest she should miss a single performance now that she was so near the end of her engagements, she compelled her feverish body to obey her. And she acted so marvelously and with such uncanny power to her last audience that few people in the theater who knew her divined that this was her farewell. She was driven back to the strange hotel already burning with a fever which quickly inflamed her worn-out lungs. She soon knew herself that the end of her labours and her wanderings had come. . . . Pittsburg would not even leave her corpse in peace. While the news of her death flew to all the countries in the world, her body was removed from the custody of her friends and laid in the mortuary: it was in the early hours of Easter Monday, the 21st of April, 1924, the morning after the night in which she died."[46]

It was a good story. A great actress of international renown travels to a smoky industrial city in the heart of a crass nation, because, even at her advanced age, she must earn a living. And what more proof can there be of her transcendent status as *artiste* than the ironic fact that the horrible weather and the careless door attendants in this smoky *ville hideuse* should be the cause of her untimely demise. As in all good stories, the power of the narrative is dependent on the vividly drawn contrast between protagonist La Dusa, and villain—the cold, unfeeling, ugly industrial city of Pittsburgh.

6

THEATER AS SOCIAL CHANGE

1931 to 1940

Pittsburgh, April 9, 1937. Way in the back of the gymnasium at the Centre Avenue YMCA, Armithine Latimer tries to relax for a minute. It's seven o'clock—one hour until the official debut of the Negro Y Playhouse. By looking over the top of the folding chairs Latimer can see through to the temporary stage she and her crew of volunteers have constructed at the other end of the room. It looks good. It looks like a real theater. She takes a deep breath, trying to absorb all that has been accomplished here over the last four months. Latimer believes passionately in Mr. W. E. B. DuBois's call for the creation of a black theater of, by, and for the people. She also believes in the power of the independent theater movement (she was trained, after all, at the famed Hedgerow Theater in Philadelphia). That's why she decided to organize her own troupe, the Latimer Players, made up of young men and women from the Hill District eager to work hard and willing to learn what it means to be an actor. In just an hour, she will take the stage to welcome the black community to their own theater under their own roof in their own neighborhood. A new era has begun. She can feel it stirring in this once empty gymnasium.[1]

Pittsburgh's Great Depression

Pittsburgh's success as the nation's and the world's leading supplier of war and building materials in the early twentieth century is offset by a much darker narrative defined by steadily increasing poverty among the city's working poor, including the waves of immigrants from across the Atlantic and migrants from the South. For these Pittsburghers, the postwar economic boom so proudly reported in the "Pittsburgh First" campaign meant very little. Jobs were scarce for unskilled, non–English-speaking immigrants and were constricted by a color bar for migrant African Americans. Housing for the poor was crowded and dangerous. The city's public health infrastructure—from sewage removal and water filtration to medical care—was minimal to begin with and could not keep pace with the exponential growth of the population after 1900.[2] Hence the Great Depression took the heaviest toll on Pittsburgh's poor and laboring classses. By the end of 1932, steel production in some Western Pennsylvania mills had decreased by as much as 50 percent, and the city's unemployment rate rose to close to 40 percent. Unemployed workers stood in long bread lines at the Emergency Relief Bureau and various soup kitchens around town. Homeless people began squatting in abandoned buildings and in Pittsburgh's largest shantytown, which extended past the vacant Pennsylvania Railroad property north of Liberty Avenue and into today's Strip District. "Managed" by Father James R. Cox, the pastor at Old Saint Patrick's, Shantytown was home to hundreds of unemployed men— mostly day laborers let go after the downturns in the mills. In the fall of 1932 Cox told a reporter, "We are facing the worst winter in the history of the world. . . . This is a nation of big business and big farming. When either one breaks down, we are lost. Where we should come from the soil, subsist on the soil, and return to the soil, we seem to be born through steel, live on steel and meet our death through steel."[3]

Relief efforts came from a wide range of sources. In 1930 Allegheny County voters provided a $5 million unemployment relief bond to sponsor a welfare agency for the unemployed. In 1931 local philanthropists, including the Henry

Fig. 25. Armithine Latimer
of the Negro Playhouse,
1937. Source: *Bulletin-Index*,
1937.

Clay Frick estate and the Mellon family, began distributing tens of millions to charitable agencies, many of which had gone bankrupt during the first year of the Depression. Between 1932 and 1934, city-funded building projects like the new Mount Washington roadway and the federal government's Civil Works Administration and Works Progress Administration began supplying money and jobs to the unemployed. Even Pittsburgh's commercial theater industry sponsored a series of fund raisers that began on November 25, 1930, with a midnight benefit at the Stanley Theatre. "All-Star Benefit Show for Needy of City Attracts Capacity Audience" trumpeted the *Post-Gazette* the next morning, noting that the standing-room-only crowd had come "generously to the support of a worthy movement," as had the Stanley Corporation, Loew's, Warner Brothers, and the Erlanger chain, with headliners ranging from Dick Powell, a local favorite, to Phil Baker and Fred Stone.[4]

Depression-era Pittsburghers also found a kind of relief by participating in a new era of theater defined by a commitment to social progress through the arts. During the 1930s, noncommercial theater was the city's most vibrant and productive creative sector. A cultural renaissance of sorts was under way in the work of a new brand of community theater in which social responsibility and service became guiding aesthetic principles. Pittsburghers in general were moving leftward during the 1930s, like the rest of the nation. In 1932, when Father Cox formed the "Jobless Party" during a rally for the unemployed at Pitt Stadium, the city voted Democratic after nearly sixty-five years of Republican dominance, electing Franklin Roosevelt largely on the promise of his New Deal. During this time, Communist Party activity in Pittsburgh increased significantly, especially after the Popular Front officially abandoned its opposition to Roosevelt's New Deal and began focusing on other issues such as citizenship, the definition of censorship, and the rise of fascist regimes in Europe.[5] In the midst of this new cultural climate, approximately sixty community-serving theaters began operating in and around the city between 1935 and 1939. Although they varied in philosophy and demographic base, they fell into three community-serving categories: those with a political orientation; those identified with religious or ethnic groups; and those devoted to civic causes.

Political Theater

Drama concerned with political issues had its origins among factory trade unions and political organizations during the nineteenth century and was mostly performed by the workers themselves for other workers. By the late 1920s, however, politically based performance had expanded beyond the factory and was being organized and promoted by networking groups like the Workers' Dramatic Council and publicized in journals like *Workers' Theater* (which began in 1931) and *New Theater* (1935). *New Theater,* which was sold on Pittsburgh newsstands, called on stage artists to build a "strong new theater of definite social basis and direction" with this strongly worded appeal: "If you have been thinking seriously about it, you know beyond the possibility of self-deception that in the United States, as well as in other parts of the world, fascist tendencies are growing. They threaten, here as elsewhere, not only the work of radical artists, but all the cultural achievements that humanity has so slowly and laboriously built up throughout the centuries."[6] Given Pittsburgh's formative role in the organization of labor, workers' performance groups were likely present in the mills and foundries from the mid-nineteenth century on.[7] Evidence of such activity dates at least to 1904, when a group from the Workmen's Circle was producing agitprop theater at Arnfeld's Hall, an informal meeting place on Penn Avenue popular with members of the Federation of Organized Trades and Labor Unions. Other references suggest that workers' theater events, from meetings to community performances, were held at two Hill District sites: the Union Labor Temple, the former Syria Temple at the corner of Washington and Webster streets in 1910, and the Labor Lyceum, built in 1916 on Miller Street. The Union Labor Temple was the city's first building erected to serve a wide range of unionized workers. The Labor Lyceum was more specifically linked to the socialist movement and hosted various workmen's circles, or labor fraternities, as well as the Third Ward Branch of the Allegheny County Socialist Party (also called the Jewish Socialists) and the Jewish Communists. (The seal on the front of the Labor Lyceum contains the phrase "Workers of the world unite.")[8]

The most active political theater performed at the Labor Lyceum was the New Theater of Pittsburgh, organized in 1935. Made up of the remnants of several earlier workers' theater groups, the New Theater was headed by J. Ernest Wright, a University of Pittsburgh English professor who was "let out" during a period of layoffs in 1932. Wright, an activist with a clear leftist agenda, believed that the "theater belongs to the great masses of the people . . . those whose Depression never ends." In addition to Wright, the New Theater was led by two Carnegie Tech drama teachers and an advisory board that included the city's leading black political activists, notably Assemblyman Homer S. Brown and Grace Lowndes of the Urban League.[9] They offered classes in eurhythmics, stagecraft, tap dancing, fencing, diction, and acting to their working-class neighbors. The theater's chief agenda was to produce new plays with overt political messages, beginning with Clifford Odets's Waiting for Lefty in 1936. It was an enormous success, playing to standing-room-only audiences and winning the Samuel French trophy, awarded by the Drama League of Pittsburgh for best play in the annual competition. This was a notable achievement for a prounion play, given the generally conservative membership of the Drama League.[10]

The New Theater produced other prolabor plays in 1936 at the Labor Lyceum and at various clubs and fraternal organizations in Western Pennsylvania and Youngstown, Ohio, including Alice Ware's Mighty Wind a'Blowin' and Union Label. Soon Wright was being called a "Communist leader" in the local press.

Fig. 26. J. Ernest Wright of the New Theater, 1937. Source: *Bulletin-Index*, 1937.

An anonymous writer to the *Bulletin-Index* accused the New Theater of being "a camouflage by the Community Party in Pittsburgh to raise money for propaganda purposes." The author knew "for a fact that Wright was the leader of the Communist Party in Pittsburgh and dared him to deny it." Wright responded that he was not a party member, noting that anyone interested in "the facts" could easily obtain the "names and official titles of the actual leaders of the Communist party in this district." He went on to assert, "I am not averse to standing, and neither is New Theater, with those men and women whom I know to be Communists, in the rapidly growing American People's Front of all progressive, Socialist, Democrat, Republican, or Farmer laborite . . . against all manifestations of Fascism, and for the defense of culture" (*Bulletin-Index*, June 19, 1937, 4).

In 1936 Wright and company joined the New Theater League, a national consortium of noncommercial companies dedicated to progressive political action. The Pittsburgh branch of the New Theater League operated as an umbrella organization representing the New Theater as well as two African American companies—the Olympians and the Emco Art Players. Wright clearly started the new league as a protest alternative to the Federation of Non-Commercial

Theaters, a whites-only umbrella group organized in 1935 "for the common interest and advantage" of the burgeoning independent theater community.[11] Its
segregationist practices were consistent with the long-standing policy of the
Drama League, which had excluded Pittsburgh's largest and oldest African
American troupe, the Olympian Players, since its founding in 1923.[12] This policy
reflected the racism that had long characterized Pittsburgh's cultural sector. As
one commentator wrote in 1940: "Unwritten rules in musical, literary, art, and
historical societies, and unexpressed but understood disfavor among their memberships have kept doors closed to Negroes in some of the most highly developed of the white community."[13] Given this context, the New Theater League
was evidently the first racially integrated noncommercial theater organization
in Pittsburgh. In turn, it engendered the city's first truly integrated theater audiences: "An audience made up equally of Negroes and whites sat spellbound
and silent in the moldering auditorium of the Hill District's ramshackle Labor
Lyceum," reported the *Bulletin-Index* in 1937. "If the audience was a cross-section
of the Hill, no less so were the players. Both actors and watchers were so used
to the neighborly juxtaposition of members of the opposite races that such an
incongruity as a white doughboy having a colored mother never once shattered
the illusion" (May 27, 1937, 27).

　　There are no records of the New Theater League and New Theater productions after 1938, possibly because in 1937 Wright took a position with the
WPA-sponsored Ethnic Survey Project to write "The Negro in Pittsburgh." This
was a study of the social history of African Americans in Western Pennsylvania
under the Federal Writers' Project. Wright served as chief editor and coordinator
of the project until the federal funding was cut and it was abandoned in 1939.[14]
At this time, Wright might also have been involved with the apparently short-
lived Pittsburgh unit of the Federal Theater. Like the Federal Writers' Project,
the FTP was a WPA program intended to provide employment opportunities for
theater artists and craftsmen charged with producing a wide range of stage entertainment. With home bases in forty states, the FTP employed over 12,000
people nationwide. About 50 percent of its personnel were actors; the rest were
writers, designers, theater musicians, dancers, stage hands, and theater staff.
Though histories of the FTP do not mention a Pittsburgh connection, one may
find a few local references to a Pittsburgh unit. The *Pittsburgh Sun-Telegraph* reported in 1937: "The Pittsburgh unit of the Federal Theater under auspices of the
Works Progress Administration will give four performances next week: Monday

at Woods Run Settlement, Tuesday at Improvement of the Poor, Webster Avenue, Thursday at the Friendly Inn and Friday at the Poke Run Presbyterian Church in Mamont, Pa." (Jan. 17, 1937, 2).

Black Theater

Despite, or perhaps as a result of segregationist practices, African Americans developed a vibrant cultural life in several neighborhoods. In the Hill District, African American professional societies, learned organizations, sports teams, civic leadership organizations, and political groups thrived. The *Pittsburgh Courier* (the nation's leading African American newspaper), the Pittsburgh chapter of the National Association for Colored People, founded in 1915, and the Pittsburgh Urban League, founded in 1918, led many local battles for civil rights.[15] Along Centre and Wylie avenues, scores of black-run businesses (restaurants, drugstores, barbershops, banks, jewelers, and doctors' offices) stood side by side with Jewish delicatessens, Italian markets, a wide range of churches, from Syrian Orthodox to Baptist to Roman Catholic, and thousands of row homes. Scattered throughout and ascending the hill were a number of celebrated nightclubs— the Crawford Grill, the Granada, the Savoy, the Roosevelt, and the Harlem Casino—which attracted an integrated audience of music lovers from the area and from elsewhere. Pittsburgh's Hill District became known as the "jazz crossroads of the world," to quote Harlem Renaissance poet Claude McKay. The success of these black-owned nightclubs is partly explained by the astonishing number of Pittsburgh-born jazz and blues artists of the era, among them Errol Garner, Ethel Waters, Billy Eckstine, Maxine Sullivan, Earl Hines, Mary Lou Williams, Billy Strayhorn, Lena Horne, and Dakota Staton. Their success was also owing to the vibrancy and range of the live theater and dance presented in those clubs, which along with the music featured everything from floor shows to musical reviews to dramatic readings.

Pittsburgh's black-run theater companies date back to the late 1870s, when George Gross organized a dramatic group in a hall in old Germantown in Allegheny City and presented *Ten Nights in a Bar-Room* and other popular melodramas. There are also records of an all-black *Macbeth* produced by the Lend-a-hand Club of Allegheny City in 1898 (some forty years before Orson Welles's Haitian-inspired production for the Federal Theater Project). In addition, Pittsburgh's African American community boasted a number of highly regarded elocutionists, from Thomas Ewell, who opened the School of Elocution and Dramatic Arts in the East End in the 1890s, to E. Marie Coleman and Suzie Lee Venzuella, who taught private elocution lessons in the 1920s. Venzuella also directed and produced several all-black productions, including an outdoor *Midsummer Night's Dream*. This complemented the work of Richard B. Harrison (later the star of Broadway's *Green Pastures*), who spent the better part of 1925 teaching and coaching in Pittsburgh. Harrison produced *Damon and Pythias* at the Pershing Theater in East Liberty and *The Merchant of Venice*, with himself as Shylock, in the stately auditorium of Schenley High School.[16]

Many African American theater companies rehearsed and performed in churches.[17] The best known were the Olympian Players, which began as the Metropolitan Baptist Church Dramatic Club in the early 1920s. In its first decade the club gave a tithe of its box office receipts to church-related African American charities. By the thirties, the Olympians had evolved into a largely secular organization producing "plays dealing with Negro life, written by Negro authors." Other African American companies were associated with civic and political organizations, such as the Kay Dramatic Players, who were members of the Women's Progressive Club. The Kay Players were given to cautionary melodramas like *The Perils of a Great City*, produced in 1935. The Urban Players, the dramatic wing of the local Urban League, also promoted progressive causes. In 1935 the organization's industrial secretary, a Mr. Lett, wrote and produced a play about "the difficulties facing Negro youth when they get out into the white world and look for jobs." It was repeated for a national audience at the annual Urban League convention.[18] A few years later, the company produced a radio version of Paul Green's *The No 'Count Boy*, a "Negro play for Negro players" and a first in broadcasting.[19]

The North Side Civic League Dramatic Division was founded and led by activist politician Walter Worthington, whose vision was to dramatize political causes. He wrote in a 1933 manifesto: "The Afra-American stands in a strategic position the parallel of which cannot be recalled. He stands to profit by the mistakes of his teachers. He is the largest and the most powerful minority in America." Worthington's play, *Independent Hamilton*, was presented at Allegheny High School on April 26, 1932, making Worthington the first Pittsburgh-based African American playwright of record.[20]

In 1932 several Olympians petitioned to be admitted to the Drama League of Pittsburgh. Walter Worthington, as chairman of the group's Drama Extension Committee, wrote a letter asking that the group be permitted to make an appeal for membership in the Drama League. A meeting did occur, but the Olympians were not allowed to join the league. Worthington and his supporters then decided to create a separate Negro Drama League for "the stimulation of intelligent dramatic appreciation, with the hopes that the same may lead ultimately to the presentation of plays conceived, written, acted and produced by their own membership."[21] Over the next five years the Negro Drama League supported a dozen African American theater companies: the North Side Civic League Dramatic Division, the Kay Dramatic Players, the Little Theater off Court Square, Entre Nous, Nightingale Arts, Imperial Art Players, Blue Ribbon, Pen and Masque, Emco Art Players, the Collegiate Dramatics Club, Talley Amateurians, and the Urban League Players. Between 1932 and 1936 the Negro Drama League also sponsored a range of activities, including classes in stagecraft, acting workshops, lectures, social events, and its own independent annual best play competition.

The Olympians won the first competition in 1932 with *The Slave*, produced at the Fifth Avenue High School for the benefit of the Davis Home for Colored Children. This one-act play was a departure for the Olympian, since plays directly addressing social problems were generally regarded as "inappropriate" because of their "too great realism."[22] *The Slave* stirred up controversy. An anonymous letter to the *Pittsburgh Courier* expressed fear that the content would offend white people in the audience: "It is the club's very poor choice of a play I am criticizing, knowing that it was to be a public affair thus assuring them there would be white people in the audience, since a few of the judges were white. Perhaps they were broad-minded white people, but who really knows? . . . The broken English constantly used and that 'lazy nigger' phrase surely did wring my heartstrings. When, Oh, Race, will you ever awaken to your ignorance in doing such things as this?" Olympian member Edward W. Brown wrote in the next week's *Courier*:

> Of course, we knew it was to be a public affair and yes we expected white people to be present. But what of it? Are we as a race, to allow the likes and dislikes of white people to determine our actions? Whether they were broad-minded or not should not make any differences to us. If it made them color and feel uncomfortable to see themselves portrayed as cruel and unsympathetic toward the Negro why should you worry? . . . You are only wasting your words and emotional energy when you raise a cry to

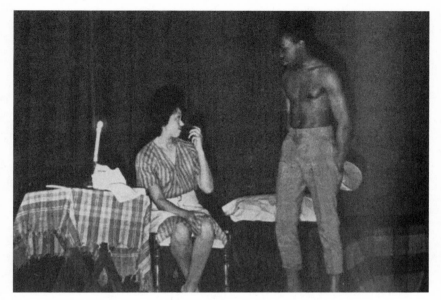

Fig. 27. The Olympian Players in *Breeders*, 1937. Source: *Bulletin-Index*, 1937.

God pleading to HIM to awaken your Race. Why not set the example by first awakening yourself?[23]

Despite the controversy, the 1933 competition featured more race-themed plays, notably Ridgely Torrance's *Rider of Dreams* and a local script depicting racial injustice displayed by a southern jury. In 1934, all submissions to the Negro Drama League's annual play contest were by white authors. This was a deliberate decision made in response to differing philosophies among the group, according to founding member Lynn V. Hooe, who noted that some members wanted to include the white perspective.[24] In 1935 the Olympians won their ongoing petition to participate in the Drama League of Pittsburgh's annual best production competition, not only breaking the color bar in that respect but also winning popular acclaim with their production of Randolph Edmonds's *Breeders*. After that time the Olympians, sometimes under the New Theater League umbrella and sometimes independently, regularly entered local drama competitions and made joint presentations with white theater groups.

The Negro Drama League disbanded in 1936, but its function was soon replaced by a "long-needed centralized playhouse for colored actors. . . . The Center Avenue Branch of the YMCA has taken over the task of bringing together, under one organization, the many fine Negro players that this city can boast" (*Pittsburgh Press,* Mar. 29, 1937, 17). Under the financial stewardship of the YMCA, this "long-needed" theater space was the brainchild of Armithine Latimer, an actress and director trained at Philadelphia's Hedgerow Theater under the famed Jasper Deeter. While organizing her own theater company in Pittsburgh in 1936, Latimer contacted Howard McKinney at the Centre Avenue YMCA (the "Colored Y"), who had earlier tried to launch a playhouse for the Negro Drama League, but was hampered by Depression-era budget cuts. By 1937, however, McKinney's budget had been restored and he was ready to build a performance space for all of the city's African American theater troupes in the Y gymnasium. The Negro Playhouse of Pittsburgh opened on April 9, 1937, attracting the attention of the press. Even the Drama League's conservative *Drama Review* expressed support, noting (apparently without irony) that the "independent Negro groups that have been having quite a struggle will be united under a single organization. This fills a gap that had been a sore spot in the local little theater front for some time" (Apr. 1937, 1).

For the next two years, the Centre Avenue Y served both the independent African American companies and a consolidation of those companies into the Negro Playhouse of Pittsburgh. Most productions were evenings of one-act plays ranging from boulevard fare (*Not Today, Madam!*) to social progress plays (*Breeders*) to musical reviews (*African Aria*). A modern dance company sponsored by the Emco Art Players also performed at the Negro Playhouse. By 1940 the concept of a centralized company seems to have been abandoned; still, many independent black companies continued to perform under the auspices of the YMCA for several more years.[25]

Jewish Theater

The earliest commercial Jewish theater groups in Pittsburgh were the Yiddish traveling companies of the late nineteenth century that performed at Hill District union halls. European Yiddish theater, an offspring of the European variety entertainment industry, was popularized in the 1870s by a Rumanian writer and performer named Abraham Goldfadden, who coined the melodramatic style associated with the entertainment branch of Yiddish performance—the *shund*.

The other branch—the art branch—can be traced to a group of young Russian actors working in Odessa in the early 1910s and to Jacob Gordin, an American playwright who modeled his new Jewish dramas on the social realism of Henrik Ibsen. This work gave rise to serious Yiddish theater companies in America, most notably Maurice Schwartz's Yiddish Art Theater of New York. By 1905 Yiddish stars like Keni Liptzen were appearing in Pittsburgh at the Belasco, on Penn Avenue, and the Nixon. Other companies performed at the smaller playhouses on Centre Avenue in the Hill District, notably the Lando Theatre, where Schwartz's Yiddish Arts Theater frequently appeared. The Simon Theater, on the other hand, was known for showing the *shund* type of Yiddish theater, including melodramas, musicals, and sketch comedy.

Pittsburgh's first indigenous Jewish theater group seems to have been the dramatic division of the Columbia Council School's Self-Culture Club. The Council of Jewish Women—made up of middle- and upper-class German Jews— founded the Columbia Council School in 1895 in order to serve the waves of Jewish immigrants from Eastern Europe.[26] Most of these impoverished newcomers settled in the Lower Hill in slum housing that had been abandoned by earlier immigrant groups, including the Irish and the Italians. With little money and no English, they confronted significant barriers after arriving in Pittsburgh. The aim of the Self-Culture Club was to promote Americanization through a variety of activities, first at the Columbian Council School and, after 1909, at the Irene Kaufmann Settlement House at 1835 Centre Avenue. Over the next two decades the IKS provided Hill District residents, including non-Jews, with a "better-baby clinic," public baths, a "milk well" for schoolchildren, English language instruction for all ages, immigration services, citizenship classes, a "people's college" staffed by volunteer professors from the University of Pittsburgh, and sports. The organization's creative expression branch gave classes in oral expression, acting, and stagecraft and sponsored the Yiddish dramatic studio, a children's theater, a Young Players' Guild, and a little theater company called the Irene Kaufmann Settlement Players.[27]

The IKS Players began in 1922 with a regular season of plays in the settlement house's 350-seat theater (admission thirty-five cents). The plays were usually comedies and mysteries—light fare chosen to entertain a diverse audience filled with many non-English speakers. During the thirties, however, the IKS Players evolved into a semiprofessional company with a paid director, Louis Isaacs, and a new auditorium, the Theresa L. Kaufmann Theater, adjoining the

Fig. 28. A Yiddish play performed at the Irene Kaufmann Settlement House, 1926. Source: Irene Kaufmann Settlement Collection, Archives Service Center, University of Pittsburgh.

settlement house. The group's mission had also evolved, offering a hope that its activities might "lead ultimately to the presentation of plays conceived, written, acted, and produced by their own membership." To that end, the organization sponsored playwriting workshops, including one specializing in social themes, and conducted a touring schedule that included performances throughout the city and in West Virginia.[28]

The other semiprofessional Jewish theater company was the Y Playhouse, founded in 1927 at the Young Men and Women's Hebrew Association in Oakland. Headed by Helen R. Stout, the Y Playhouse billed itself as an art theater with a mandate to "produce plays with a social conscience." In 1930 the company produced *The Golem*, written and directed by Boris Glagolin, a world premiere of the play in English. Glagolin, a veteran of Stanislavski's Moscow Art Theatre and the author of *New Ideas in Theatrical Art*, announced on his arrival that he was staging the city's first "constructivist" work, meaning a style of theatrical production focused on the expressive potential of the actor's body rather than on elaborate stage sets. "Life, not a picture of Life," he told the *Pittsburgh Press*, "is the credo of the modern Russian theater and its founders" (May 20, 1930, 25).

In the thirties the Y Playhouse attained semiprofessional status under the direction of Alfred Golden. In addition to ambitious productions such as Ibsen's *Ghosts*, Paul Green's *The Field God*, Clifford Odets's *Golden Boy*, and Solomon Anski's *The Dybbuk*, the Y also produced works by local playwrights, including *A Job for Joe* by Madeline Skelly Foust, a "social drama" about unemployment. (Foust was appointed dean of the drama department at Duquesne University in 1936.) The Y players—performing in the stately Morris Kaufmann Memorial Auditorium with sets and costumes built in the Y scene shops—became known for the high quality of the acting and sophisticated production values. Shows at the Y Playhouse often featured guest appearances by well-known actors, such as former Carnegie Tech innovator Ben Iden Payne, who played in *The Queen's Husband* in 1930, and the Provincetown Players' Sheba Strunsky, who appeared in *The Golem*. By the 1930s the group had grown more secular; while most of the players remained Jewish, ethnic plays had all but disappeared from the repertoire.

German Theater

Foreign-language theater was part of the community-based cultural activity of many immigrant groups settling in Pittsburgh. The practice was especially prominent among the city's large and financially well-established German community. Beginning in the early 1840s, an amateur thespian group called the Theatrical Amusement Society (Theatralischer Unterhaltungsverein) produced short seasons at the Atheneum on Liberty Avenue featuring the popular melodramas of August von Kotzebue. By the 1850s other German-language thespian organizations were mounting performances organized at holiday times and for special occasions. These included Thalia Clubs, inspired by the Greek muse of comedy, and several Turner Societies, dedicated to promoting German culture in America. As with the thespian societies founded by the Scots-Irish earlier in the century, the German-language repertoire consisted primarily of light entertainment—short-form comedies and variety acts. On occasion, however, full-length classics such as Goethe's *Faust* and Schiller's *The Robbers* were staged.[29]

In 1863 a theatrical manager named A. Charles founded the Pittsburgh Stadttheater, the city's first professional German-language theater company modeled after the Stadttheater in New York City. Over the next five years, this stock company performed at the Atheneum, the Academy of Music, and the Pittsburgh Theatre and featured visiting stars from other professional German-language theater companies around the country. Despite strong support from the city's German-language newspapers (including regular production reviews in *Freiheits Freund),* the Stadttheater disbanded in 1868 and was not replaced—perhaps because second-generation Germans were not as interested in native-language traditions as their elders.[30] Still, amateur theater organizations continued to stage German-language theater in the Deutschtown section of Allegheny City and at the German Club in Oakland. The Deutscher Theaterverein Thalia, for example, was an active part of the little theater movement during the 1920s and 1930s and was dedicated to staging performances of the "best works of German literature."[31] There is no record of the club after 1937; anti-German sentiment may have discouraged further activity.

Catholic Theater

A century ago Catholic theatrical presentations based on the liturgy—from living nativities to Easter dramas—were regular features in Pittsburgh. The longest-running and most recognized worship drama is a depiction of the Easter story, *Veronica's Veil,* written and first produced in 1913 by Father Bernardine Dusch, pastor at St. Michael Parish on the city's South Side. Staged annually by church members during Lent, *Veronica's Veil* was revised in 1919 and eventually spawned a company known as the Veronica's Veil Players, who continue to produce the play each Easter.[32] Another kind of Catholic drama that was associated with the little theater movement began in the 1930s when Catholic theater groups started producing plays outside the sanctuary. The Newman Players met at St. Paul's Cathedral High School to "create a Theater which shall be artistic, cultural, educational and entertaining; to produce clean plays of high literary standard." The group's mission was to use the stage to support "Catholic standards of morality."[33]

In 1936 the Catholic Theater Guild of Pittsburgh was founded and headed by Mary Clancy to "produce and to encourage the production of first-rate

Catholic plays . . . truly Catholic drama in the complete sense."[34] Clancy had worked with the Drama League and the Pitt Summer Players before founding the Catholic Theater Guild. The guild's first production was *A Saint in a Hurry* by José Maria Peman. Clancy also wrote a theater column for the *Pittsburgh Catholic* and edited the guild's newsletter. Though Clancy left the city in the mid-1940s, the Catholic Theater Guild continued its mission for the next two decades and evolved into an interracial, nonsectarian amateur group by the 1950s.

Civic Theaters

The growth of identity-based independent theaters in Pittsburgh during the early 1930s reflected the impact of the little theater and art theater movements on noncommercial theater and the increase in socially conscious community activity during the Depression. Likewise, the civic theater movement shared a similar sense of community mission and was also supported by local efforts. "Civic" theaters were not overtly associated with ethnic, religious, or political groups but were motivated by civic pride and a desire to free the Smoky City from its working-class reputation by raising the aesthetic standard of theatrical production. These groups disdained the Depression-era fluff (à la Ziegfeld) favored by the commercial playhouses in favor of "serious" drama. Moreover, they differentiated their professionalism from the work of unabashedly amateur companies, no matter how serious those companies were. For example, the mission statement of the Experimental Theater in Shadyside, issued by Freeman Hammon and Fernand Fillion in 1933, explained that it was "not a community theater, but a cosmopolitan project intended to function on a larger and more efficient scale than any community endeavor could sustain." The Experimental Theater's one main purpose was "to find and develop Pittsburgh talent, to act as a dramatic laboratory where Pittsburgh-written plays may be produced, staged, and acted by Pittsburghers" (*This Week in Pittsburgh*, June 8, 1934, 1). Though the Experimental Theater did not survive past its first season, the company produced four locally written scripts, including several by George Baird, a University of Pittsburgh professor and director of the Cap and Gown drama club.[35]

Another short-lived venture was the Stage Guild of Pittsburgh, founded in 1933 by Chester Story, the former president of the Drama League. The Stage Guild billed itself as "Pittsburgh's Professional Acting Company" and noted that all of the actors "had appeared or are now appearing on the professional stage." The group's intention was "to form the basis of a real civic theater." The company mounted a summer season (including a production of *Symphony in Two Flats*) in nearby Oakmont before moving to St. Francis Hospital auditorium in September 1933.[36]

Several other theaters also resisted taking on the amateur, community-serving mandate. The most prominent was the Kilbuck Players, founded in 1933 by Robert Alan Green, an actor and director. Green's company performed in a forty-four-seat playhouse (touted as the "world's smallest theater") set up in the basement of his wife's home, the Bain mansion on the North Side. The Kilbuck Players briefly achieved national recognition in 1934 when *Theater Arts Monthly* praised its production of *Ghosts* and in 1937 when it was named "one of the ten foremost little theaters in the United States" by the *New York Times*. Other professionally inclined civic theaters from the late thirties included the Laboratory Theatre of the International Institute in Oakland (1938) and the South Park Playhouse, created in 1937 by the Allegheny County Board of Commissioners and touted as the "first municipally owned summer theater in the United States."[37]

The Pittsburgh Playhouse

The city's most influential and enduring civic theater—the Pittsburgh Playhouse —also got its start in 1933. The organization began modestly as the Pittsburgh Summer Playhouse, a stock company in residence at a suburban preparatory school under Morris Edgar Fierst and two partners, Mrs. Evan Jones and George Lobingier. When fall arrived, some company members, including Helen Sisenwain, who had just graduated from Carnegie Tech, regrouped and took a new name: the Pittsburgh Civic Playhouse. Like the Stage Guild and the Experimental Theater, the new troupe had professional aspirations. However, the Civic Playhouse adopted an unusual nonprofit fiscal strategy, vowing to devote all income to enrichment and enlargement of the project. The mission stated:

> In the purely business theater an individual production may prove the measure of success or failure of the dramatic company. A Civic Playhouse can afford to speculate on the basis of a play's intrinsic merits rather than on its

box office potentialities. . . . If the sustenance of the theater is to be considered a vital element in society, then its growth should come more from within. We have reached the condition where, if the people of America want good plays, they must learn to create and support theaters of their own.[38]

With a clear mission and a group of well-trained volunteer performers, the Pittsburgh Civic Playhouse produced a full season in 1934 while moving between auditoriums at the Schenley Hotel, the Catholic Boys' High School, and the Arnold School on Braddock Avenue. The repertoire included recent New York successes such as *The Silver Wedding, Up Pops the Devil, Mourning Becomes Electra,* and *The Green Bay Tree.* The notable exception was the world premiere of *The Female of the Species,* an original play by Alfred Golden of the Y Playhouse starring Judith Anderson. (The play later moved to Broadway.) In 1934, and faced with a deficit, founders Fierst and Jones approached Richard S. Rauh, a businessman, for financial guidance. Rauh, long a key player on Pittsburgh's arts scene, was an officer of the Pittsburgh Symphony Society and a board member of the Mendelssohn Choir.[39] He agreed to help on condition that he could assemble a seven-member executive board that included Mrs. J. Frank Drake, Elizabeth Heinz, and Mrs. Charles Rosenbloom.[40] The board consulted local theater experts such as Harvey Gaul, theater critic for the *Post-Gazette,* and they hired Helen Stout, former head of the Y Playhouse, as the company's part-time director. On November 17, 1934, the Pittsburgh Playhouse was incorporated as a nonprofit educational institution chartered by the commonwealth of Pennsylvania.

Thus reconfigured and renamed the Pittsburgh Playhouse, the company debuted on December 10, 1934, with *Art and Mrs. Bottle,* a recent Broadway hit, at the Frick School auditorium. The marketing rhetoric for the 1935–36 season indicates that the well-heeled board of directors sought to rescue Pittsburgh from its industrial image and to establish a new level of cultural sophistication. Anxiety about the city's loss of reputation in a depressed time is reflected in a statement that appeared in the season's final program in May 1936:

There was a time when Pittsburgh was a "key city," but if today we have anything to do with a key in the vast Odeon of Thespis, it's a bent, broken, back-door key. In other words, we're in the sticks. . . . Sometimes we think

Pittsburgh is a town of immaturity and arrested development, living on its past, remembering the days when mushroom millionaires were spawned over-night, a city doing little for the present, and having precious few men caring anything for the future. But we have the beginning of one resource, the Pittsburgh Playhouse. Will we develop that resource or just go Pittsburghian and let it drag along till finally it dies of anemia?[41]

Attempts to bolster the city's image were partly based on the ever-present tension between Pittsburgh's working-class and professional-class cultural identity. The Playhouse board hinged the company's future success on its association with affluent patrons and the construction of a "sophisticated" audience eager for this new breed of civic theater. Hopes that this audience would not dare go "Pittsburghian" and would support the Playhouse in the future reflected an urge for the kind of civic theater that could rival the touring shows at the Nixon and help to rescue the city from its rapidly declining theatrical reputation.

That proved to be the case. The Playhouse quickly became the city's largest noncommercial theater, outlasting all other such efforts and collecting a loyal group of subscribers. In 1936 the organization leased the former German Club on Craft Avenue in South Oakland and began to use the refurbished auditorium, which they called the Hamlet Theater. Herbert Gellendre, who had worked with Richard Boleslavski's American Laboratory Theater and the Neighborhood Playhouse in New York City, was appointed director. Under Gellendre's leadership the company became increasingly professional, and in 1937 several union actors were recruited from New York City. Gellendre's tenure was stormy, however. His ambitious repertoire, including plays like Maeterlink's *Pelleas and Melisande,* Kaiser's *From Morn to Midnight,* and J. B. Priestley's *Laburnum Grove,* launched an art-versus-box-office argument with and within the board, as did his continuing deficits and arrogant management style. In April 1937 Gellendre was fired.

Frederick Burleigh, a director at the Indianapolis Playhouse, replaced Gellendre as the full-time managing director.[42] From the start Burleigh's management style and aesthetic philosophy seemed more compatible with the goals of both the board and the community. He immediately ended the practice of hiring professional actors and instead put this notice in the local papers: "If you have talent and are interested in working exceedingly hard, putting in long hours under professional direction, just for the sake of the game and without hope of

Fig. 29. Fred Burleigh and cast at the Pittsburgh Playhouse, 1940. Source: Unknown (Curtis Theatre Collection, University of Pittsburgh Library). Courtesy of Point Park University.

monetary reward, you should have your name in the Pittsburgh Playhouse casting file.”[43] By the close of the 1937–38 season, there were 640 applications, including forty people interested strictly in backstage work. Burleigh's repertoire included a number of Broadway hits and musicals (*Children of Darkness, Hold Your Hats, The Pursuit of Happiness, Accent on Youth*), though he also produced international texts and socially conscious dramas from the American stage—notably Leonid Andreyev's *He Who Gets Slapped* and Sinclair Lewis's antifascist melodrama, *It Can't Happen Here*. By the end of 1939, after Burleigh's second season as managing director, the Playhouse had settled into a pattern that would continue for the next twenty-five years: it was a semiprofessional civic theater with a professionally trained staff and non-Equity actors, using "the best local talent available." It had found a way to remain commercially viable while defining a new era of civic theater.

Changing Audiences

By the end of the 1920s vaudeville had been dethroned. The decline began in mid-decade when the "talkies" proved to be far more popular than the combination of silent movie and floor show, and theater owners and managers quickly realigned their priorities. In 1928, when Harry Davis sold his Million Dollar Grand to Warner Brothers, the live shows immediately ended and the large auditorium became a movie-only house. Soon after, the Gayety (renamed the Fulton), the Harris, the Davis, the Shubert-Pitt (renamed the Barry), and the Shubert-Alvin (renamed the New Harris-Alvin) became movie houses. For just as full-length drama could not compete with vaudeville in the teens and early twenties, vaudeville could not compete with the talkie. A snappy marketing brochure called *Show Places, Know Places, Go Places in Pittsburgh*, makes this vividly clear:

> Remember when it was the smart thing to go to the Davis? . . . Remember seeing us in the lobby? And such headliners as Sophie Tucker, Belle Baker, Fanny Brice, and others? We'll say you do! Them was the happy days! And then along came the talkies. And the big headliners took a bee line out to the coast . . . the haven for actors. And things were in a turmoil. But progress must go on. The Davis had to meet the requirements of a new day and age in the show business. The theater had to be remodeled—new equipment for talking pictures installed, etc. And now—the Davis is a picture house showing high class talkies at low prices.[44]

Or, as Samuel Reevin, the treasurer of the Theater Owners' Booking Association, explained to the *Pittsburgh Courier:* "Hard times, combined with the popularity of automobiles and talking pictures and other advanced types of pleasure-giving devices, have dulled the interest of the theater-going public" (Jan. 4, 1930, 12).

In Depression-era Pittsburgh the number of theatergoers patronizing full-length plays steadily declined. This was a widespread phenomenon across the country, of course, the result of tight budgets and competition from newer forms of mass entertainment: big-budget Hollywood movies, spectacle-oriented touring musical revues, radio dramas, and even the burlesque show. Formerly the exclusive province, as one commentator archly stated, of "scrubbed mill hands, cheap shysters, college boys, jittery-eyed perverts and tawdry tarts" who routinely spent a portion of their wages at venues like the Academy and George

Jaffe's Variety Theater (at Sixth and Penn),[45] by 1933 a new era of marquee-level burlesque had become a destination for upper-class slumming:

> It's the smart thing to go to a Burlesque show these days. Burlesque is all the rage in New York and as Broadway goes, so goes the rest of the world. Pittsburgh has literally gone Burlesque crazy. It used to be that very few women went to Burlesque, but you ought to see them flock, whole parties of them, to the Academy for the new type of Burlesque. You'll find girls as beautiful as the best Ziegfeld presents. Girls with figures that make Earl Carrol's beauties look just mediocre. The prices are very reasonable, so if you want a fast stepping show, with plenty of good dancing, a lot of comedy and good looking girls, we suggest the Academy.[46]

This "new type" of burlesque was so popular with mainstream audiences that when George Jaffe's Variety Theater on Penn Avenue brought Minsky's Revue to Pittsburgh for the first time in 1934, the razzle-dazzle strip show played to steady full houses twice a day, "while vacant weeks lay dust in the galleries of the Nixon, Pittsburgh's only legitimate theater."[47]

Yet there continued to be a committed audience for some genres of serious drama. The Theatre Guild's annual six-week Pittsburgh season at the Nixon played undisrupted throughout the lean years of the Depression and featured serious plays performed by the day's leading stage actors, including Alfred Lunt and Lynn Fontanne in *Amphitryon 38*, Katherine Cornell in *Saint Joan*, Helen Hayes in *Victoria Regina*, and Tallulah Bankhead in *Antony and Cleopatra*. And of course the astonishing proliferation of noncommercial independent theaters, which by 1938 had peaked at over one hundred local companies operating in the city and suburbs, bespeaks a loyal audience. Many were local theater practitioners who supported the work of indigenous companies out of friendship and community activism. Another group were so-called cultural mavens who believed that theater could enhance the quality of civic life and were willing to support it financially. And another segment was made up of well-educated rank-and-file Pittsburghers who supported and participated in the community-serving theater movement.[48] During the 1930s Pittsburgh's noncommercial theater audience represented a true cross section of the city's population: laborers, professionals, whites, blacks, recent immigrants, Jews, Catholics, third- and fourth-generation Scots-Irish Protestants, radicals, conservatives, aesthetes, and passionate amateurs. Collectively they sustained a wide range of noncommercial theater companies.

7

THEATER AS REGIONAL RENAISSANCE

1940 to 1968

Pittsburgh, January 8, 1965. "Listen to this," his wife says to him as he maneuvers the sedan through the Liberty Tunnel. "'Washington should invoke the Sherman Anti-Trust law against Lincoln Maazel on the grounds of being a monopoly. . . . There are three shows current at the Playhouse . . . and Mr. Maazel is in every one of them.'" She goes on to read the rest of *Post-Gazette* critic Harold Cohen's amusing account of the actor running madly between three stages and three plays all in the course of three hours (while also applying and removing several moustaches and a pair of sideburns). It's an amusing story and he laughs along with his wife as they head toward their six-thirty dinner reservation at the Playhouse restaurant. They're meeting friends—one of the other lawyers at the firm and his wife—so it should be an enjoyable evening. Maybe they'll even stop in downstairs at the Stage Door Club cocktail lounge for a nightcap if the play isn't too long.[1]

Fig. 30. Helen Wayne Rauh and Lincoln Maazel at the Pittsburgh
Playhouse, 1965. Source: Unknown (Curtis Theatre Collection, University of Pittsburgh Library). Courtesy of Point Park University.

Wartime Culture

By the end of the 1930s Pittsburgh's economy had almost fully recovered from
the industry downturns of the Depression—the result of defense contracts pour-
ing in from wartorn Europe. By 1939, two years before the United States entered
the war, the city's steel mills were already operating at full capacity. Employment
rose, as did the population. The day after the attack on Pearl Harbor, 1,200 Pittsburghers entered the armed services, and by 1942 more than 115,000 had enlisted
or been drafted. Women entered the workforce in record numbers in the

mills and at the newly constructed munitions factories. Labor unions called what was described as a "peace truce," agreeing not to strike for the duration of the war.

The outspoken progressive views that had characterized noncommercial theater during the 1930s gave way, at least on the surface, to concerns over maintaining the home front. So many men from the independent theater community were called up that theater newsletters began featuring special columns listing which company members joined what branch of the armed forces. "Michael Sakach—He's in the Navy now," noted the Crafton Players newsletter in February 1942. "Jack Garvin—Helping the Coast Guard rout submarines. Campbell McRae—He's A-1 in the Army and he's 1-A in our hearts. Ream Lazaro—By now he should be getting his first flying lesson, as taught by the Air Corps."[2] Other local actors began appearing in variety acts at the USO–Variety Club Canteen at the Pennsylvania Station, where thousands of soldiers from all over the United States saw them perform. One local variety act even made it to the big time. In 1942 the Four Evans, a family dance team, became an official USO act and toured Europe and the Far East, including the besieged city of Bastogne during the Battle of the Bulge.[3] By the end of 1943, fewer than half of the hundred-odd members of the Federation of Non-Commercial Theaters, the New Theater League, and the Negro Playhouse were still working. When the war ended, the heady era of community-serving theater was over.

Postwar Culture

Pittsburgh emerged from World War II prosperous (war-related revenue reportedly totaled more than a billion dollars) yet troubled by a host of urban ills. Within a week of victory in Europe, local industries began laying off thousands of workers as contracts were canceled. The labor peace pledged by the CIO and the AFL ended in January 1946 when 70,000 U.S. Steel workers walked off their jobs, launching a twenty-seven-day shutdown. The city's long-standing air pollution problem, exacerbated by expanded industrial production during the war years, had truly turned Pittsburgh into hell with the lid off—a place darkened by coal smoke, automobile fumes, and particulates from unregulated industry emissions. Many still recall when downtown streets were sometimes so dark that streetlights came on at noon and the air was so filthy that office workers changed their shirts at lunchtime. In the forties there were several life-threatening smog alerts. In January 1944, smog trapped thousands of war workers in their factories when a "zero ceiling" air quality alarm forced a curfew. And for four days in 1948 an inversion blanketed the town of Donora, Pennsylvania, south of Pittsburgh, with a lethal mixture of fog and toxic emissions from the Donora Zinc Works and a U.S. Steel plant. Twenty people died and thousands were hospitalized.

Other postwar problems included a decline in downtown property values resulting from years of neglect. By 1945 most of the destination playhouses that had once lined the Penn-Liberty corridor had either been torn down or fallen into disuse. The decline of Felix Brunot's original Library Hall is an example. After nearly forty years as The Bijou, one of the city's leading playhouses, in 1910 it was sold and turned into a second-run stock house called the Lyceum. In the 1920s it was known as the Academy, a classy burlesque theater. And by the early 1930s it became the Variety, a live-action adult theater offering "Real Burlesk" and "20 Hot Shot Cuties on the Runway" at the midnight shows. In 1934, under new management and again under the Lyceum banner, the theater made a brief attempt to return to a legitimate repertoire. But the St. Patrick's Day flood of 1936, when the building stood in ten feet of water for several days, finally ended its sixty-six-year run. Similar fates befell the Duquesne Theatre (razed for a parking lot in 1930), the Davis (shut down in the mid-thirties and later razed for Mellon Square), and the Pitt-Shubert–Pitt-Barry (razed for a parking lot in 1950).[4]

The greatest postwar blow to the once famed city of theaters, however, was the loss of the Nixon—the only remaining downtown playhouse offering live professional theater. During the lean war years the Nixon had continued as Pittsburgh's premiere booking house. But that too came to an end in 1950 when the Alcoa Corporation erected a new office tower on the site. The final show at the old Nixon, Mae West's revival tour of *Diamond Lil*, played to a capacity audience of 2,256 people. Last-nighters mourned the loss with a special farewell dinner in the Nixon Restaurant, a popular spot among the upscale theater crowd. And even though the New Nixon opened soon after in a refurbished movie palace on Liberty Avenue, it could hardly compete with the "world's perfect playhouse."

By the early 1950s even the city's two grand movie palaces, the Stanley and the Penn, were struggling to fill their enormous auditoriums.

There were several reasons for the decline in commercial stage activity. Because of economic shifts in the theatrical road industry, Pittsburgh had lost its status as an important tryout booking town to cities like Baltimore, Washington, D.C., and New Haven—all much closer to New York City and therefore offering lower production costs. As a result, fewer new plays, musicals, and revues came to the city. At the same time, commercial air travel made weekending in New York possible for upper-class residents, which hurt local ticket sales. (An advertisement for Trans-World Airlines referred to Pittsburgh as an "air suburb" of New York City.) Perhaps most significant, in these years professional- and working-class Pittsburghers stopped frequenting the downtown theaters at night, since their suburban neighborhoods had their own movie houses, social halls, night clubs, and dinner theaters.

Pittsburgh's traditional conservatism also played a role in the decline of commercial theater. This was less a product of the alleged Scots-Irish resistance to pleasure as a habit of emotional restraint and skepticism. In the heyday of vaudeville, Pittsburgh theatergoers gained a national reputation for "sitting on their hands" and being prudish. Local residents saw themselves quite differently, however. To Pittsburghers this restraint was a mark of being "select and discriminating," as Beatrice Lewis wrote in the *New York Herald Tribune* in 1941. But while Lewis's analysis defied the customary stereotype of a "working-class city with working-class tastes," she noted that the city government "does almost nothing to promote the cause of its legitimate theater. It means little to business men that out-of-towners come in for a show and remain to shop." Lewis also made it clear that government regulations were a handicap. When the New York City Theater Guild offered to send a lecturer to Pittsburgh schools to discuss their upcoming touring production of *Twelfth Night*, the Board of Education prohibited it "under a blanket regulation forbidding any advertising in the schools," although such presentations had been allowed in every other city on the show's itinerary (*New York Herald Tribune*, July 6, 1941). This attitude was consistent with the hands-off policy of city government. One mayor told the *Pittsburgh Press*, "I agree with Thomas Jefferson. The best government is the least government. . . . The theater is not properly a government concern. Let the people do such things for themselves."[5]

Renaissance I

Efforts to lift Pittsburgh out of its industrial rut, to reverse its decline in national status—the city had slipped from sixth to twelfth largest in the nation—and to address a lingering cultural malaise, were left largely to the private sector. The Allegheny Conference on Community Development, incorporated in 1944, was a nonprofit organization that set out to fulfill Robert Moses's "golden triangle" redevelopment plan of 1939 by rebuilding large sections of the downtown, including the Point and the Lower Hill. Renaissance I, a twenty-year effort, entailed the demolition of hundreds of acres of buildings, new construction, reengineering the city's flood control efforts, and implementing smoke control and emissions regulations that began to clean the air for the first time since industrialization.

Critical to this postwar renaissance was a strategic plan to use the arts to dispel, as Allegheny Conference leader Henry John Heinz II put it, the "lingering conception of Pittsburgh as a 'mill town' that is bereft of any beauty and grace" and replace it "with a bright new image of progress and cultural enlightenment for Pittsburgh."[6] In 1947 the conference announced plans for the Pittsburgh Center, a mammoth arts and sports complex to be located on a hundred acres in the Lower Hill, the area now occupied by the Mellon Arena. The design included concert halls and auditoriums, a sports arena, offices, and luxury apartments connected by gardens and covered walks and accessible by underground entries. This ambitious plan, involving the demolition of a significant portion of the Hill District, reflected the belief that to restore Pittsburgh to its former preeminence the region would need to "have major league ball teams, major league symphonies, major league government; and to have that we have to have major league stadiums and major league symphony halls."[7] After several false starts, the design for the Pittsburgh Center became two separate projects, a stand-alone sports arena and The Center for the Arts, with two playhouses, a grand opera and symphony hall, and an art museum that would house the collection at the Carnegie Institute. It was soon dubbed Pittsburgh's "Cultural Acropolis" because the architect's rendering placed it in stately grandeur on a hill overlooking the city.

The site for the arena project became available after the implementation of the 1949 Federal Housing Act, the first urban renewal legislation allowing for the destruction of dwellings and attendant relocation of residents out of "blighted" communities. In 1956 the demolition of the Lower Hill began, uprooting approximately 10,000 people and 416 businesses. And in 1961 the Civic Arena, with its massive dome, became home to a variety of sporting events, conventions, touring spectacles like the circus, and the Civic Light Opera.[8] The Center for the Arts never materialized, however, even with a million-dollar gift from the A.W. Mellon Foundation to purchase the land and encouragement from the Howard Heinz Endowment, which offered $8 million for the new symphony hall.

The arts center was abandoned for many reasons. The black community, which had not systematically resisted the first phase of the Lower Hill demolition, began to mobilize strong opposition to further redevelopment in what had been the city's largest and most politically powerful black neighborhood.[9] On the other side, many funders and civic leaders insisted that unless about fifty blocks to the east of the Civic Arena (still a blighted area) were cleared, "not a nickel would go toward a symphony hall or anything else."[10] As a result, by the mid-sixties the arts center plan reached a stalemate. A comment in the *Pittsburgh Press* blamed the problem on the city's "split personality" where the "loudest hurrahs go . . . to those who produce steel, brick, and glass. Knowing their place, artists don't push too hard. Like the disillusioned J. Alfred Prufrock in T. S. Eliot's poem, they ask favors with a timid and hushed: 'Do I dare? . . . Do I dare?'" (Dec. 4, 1967, 21).

In fact, many Pittsburgh artists of the postwar era did indeed dare. Despite the decline of commercial theater and the city's failure to build an arts center, cultural life was not nearly as bleak as has been claimed. There was a world-class symphony orchestra, three ballet companies, a modern dance troupe, several choral groups, two operas (including Mary Dawson's Negro Opera Company, the nation's first black professional troupe), several chamber orchestras, many folk ensembles (led by Duquesne University's Tamburitzans), and a contemporary music society. Some were well established, like the Mendelssohn Choir, while others were new, like the Center for the Arts in Shadyside, which had housed various performing arts groups since 1941. Some were traditionally structured, like the Pittsburgh Ballet Theatre, which provided the corps de ballet for the opera, and some were experimental, like the Contemporary Dance Group, a cooperative of local dancers modeled on the Martha Graham and Doris Humphrey collectives, which gave independent dance concerts and appeared jointly with local theater companies.[11] Most important for this study, the activity of a handful of independent theaters, a dozen or so strawhat troupes, several dinner theaters, and three university student companies prove that postwar Pittsburgh was not a two-theater town with only one professional road house—the Nixon—and only one community-based theater—the Pittsburgh Playhouse.

The Green Pastures and the Curtaineers

In 1941, actor, playwright, and community activist Walter Worthington left the Olympians to form his own company, the Green Pastures Community Theater. Named for the Broadway success by Pittsburgh area native Marc Connelly, the company was formed after his play *The Green Pastures* was mounted at the Pittsburgh Playhouse with an all-black cast (a Playhouse first). The production, with Worthington as "De Lawd," not only was a success with the white subscription audience, but also brought large numbers of African Americans into the Hamlet Street theater. With the support of a group of influential civic leaders, including the wife of Robert L. Vann, publisher of the *Pittsburgh Courier*, Worthington announced that the Green Pastures Community Theater would be "modeled after other famous Negro theater groups." The fall 1941 season was to include *Porgy and Bess, Mamba's Daughters,* and *Jubilee. Porgy* opened according to plan in December at Wadsworth Hall in the Hill District's Terrace Village, a large WPA-sponsored public housing project. But this was the last show ever mounted by the Green Pastures company, allegedly because the production of *Porgy* bankrupted the fledgling group.[12] Moreover, five members of the company were called to military service at the end of the first season.[13]

Another Hill District theater began in 1941, the result of a study on inter-racial relations commissioned by the Irene Kaufmann Settlement House on Centre Avenue to examine the growing tension between the settlement's traditional white clientele and the increasing numbers of African Americans seeking its services. The study produced a plan to "bring about better understanding, attitudes, and relationships between all peoples and groups in the Hill" through various community initiatives, including a new drama group "encompassing all phases of the theater and open to interested adults and young people in greater Pittsburgh, regardless of race or creed."[14] The new company, the Curtaineers, was first led by Lynn V. Hooe, former director of the Olympians, and featured Willis Walker, Leona Worthington, James Davis, and Lorraine Ball, among others. In 1945 the

Fig. 31. The Curtaineers in *Zombie*, 1944. Source: *Pittsburgh Bulletin-Index*, 1944.

IKS hired a white director, Simon Gerson, a graduate of Carnegie Tech and a long-time resident of the Hill, to run the company. The rationale behind this change was that a true "interracial group would not be achieved unless a white, competent director could be secured."[15] After Gerson's appointment, the company changed from being essentially all black to roughly half black and half white.

Over the next fifteen years the Curtaineers played in the Kaufmann auditorium to audiences that reflected the demographics of its location—African Americans, Syrians, Italians, Germans, and East Europeans, many of them Jewish. As the programs stated, one goal of the organization was to advance "the cause of democratic understanding." Productions ranged from standard commercial fare like *Gaslight, Room Service,* and *Ten Little Indians,* to odd relics such as *Gammer Gurton's Needle* (an early Renaissance drama) and contemporary works, among them *A Streetcar Named Desire, On Whitman Avenue, The Time of*

Your Life, and *The Glass Menagerie.* During the forties Gerson consistently followed what was at that time a radical notion: a color-blind casting system:

> Giving Negro members roles which would have the effect of strengthening the prevalent stereotypes was assiduously avoided. . . . What followed from this was the pattern of placing Negroes in the dominant roles. In the play "Blind Alley," a psychological melodrama, the plot revolves around the conflict between a gangster-killer and a college professor. Negroes were cast as the professor and his family. The gangster and his girl friend, unsympathetically depicted by the playwright, were white. . . . Moral and sympathetic roles may be played by white or Negro members—but are usually played by the latter. Immoral and unsympathetic parts are usually reserved for the whites, though Negroes may be employed in conjunction with whites. . . . Use was made of those situations in which a sense of community rather than dissimilarity could be conveyed. In the play "The World We Make," the workers in the laundry scene, occupying the same positions and sharing the same problems, were both white and Negro. Similarly, choral work and choruses presented an unusual opportunity to communicate a feeling of identity rather than one of difference. In "Let 'Em Roll," the musical revue, an effort was made to maintain equal numbers of whites and Negroes in the dance choruses.[16]

Despite the Curtaineers' progressive social mandate and casting policy, however, very few plays confronted racial issues head-on. Company members rejected producing *Native Son* over "concern about doing any play in which violence and love interest between Negroes and whites were involved," and only Maxine Wood's *On Whitman Avenue* openly addressed racism in the form of discrimination in housing and employment. Even Gerson's progressive color-blind casting was subject to internal censorship when it came to sexual relationships. One company member acknowledged that Gerson recognized "the strong feelings in the community against miscegenation by casting families on a uniracial basis. Friends, colleagues, acquaintances, can be and usually have been presented interracially except where sexual intimacies have been suggested or implied."[17] This policy seems to have loosened by 1954, however, when a production of *Streetcar Named Desire* featured Walter Worthington as Mitch and a white actress as Blanche. (A publicity photo of the interracial couple appeared in both the *Pittsburgh Press* and the *Pittsburgh Post-Gazette*.)

The Curtaineers gradually developed a reputation for good acting and production values and attracted a regular stream of guest artists that included many white actors from the Playhouse company. (However, black actors appeared only occasionally at the Playhouse in these years.) Guest actors and short-term members came and went, interested primarily in the company's eclectic repertoire and a chance to perform in the Kaufmann auditorium. Still, the progressive social purpose of the group was a primary motivation for the company's full-time members. One African American actor told an interviewer that he would never have joined an all-black troupe that was only interested in putting on plays for fun.[18] Walter Worthington, for more than twenty years a leading figure in the African American theater community, used his increasing influence in local government and education to promote the IKS Curtaineers' work and social agenda.[19] The group made a significant contribution to the "cause of democratic understanding" by uniting black and white actors and entertaining integrated audiences in one of the city's most culturally diverse neighborhoods.

The Civic Light Opera

As with the Curtaineers, the origins of the Pittsburgh Civic Light Opera also reflected a passionate belief in the relationship between creative expression and social progress. When Abraham Lewis Wolk, a progressive Democrat and a leader in the city's first smoke-control efforts, was elected to the city council in 1938, he immediately began a campaign to support the indigenous arts community. His first (unsuccessful) effort was to argue for a city-funded municipal theater on Flagstaff Hill in Schenley Park to house the city's burgeoning little theater groups.[20] In 1939 Wolk secured a $5,000 municipal grant for a series of summer concerts performed on a temporary stage in Schenley Park. These initiatives seemed only to whet Wolk's interest in the arts as a force for urban development. In 1945 he convinced department store owner Edgar Kaufmann to give $50,000 to start an open-air light opera to be modeled on St. Louis's famous Municipal Opera Company. With Kaufmann's support, Wolk put together a board of directors rivaling in influence those of the Pittsburgh Symphony and the Carnegie Institute. They included Vira I. Heinz, Michael L. Benedum, Edgar Kaufmann, Oliver Kaufmann, the University of Pittsburgh chancellor (who agreed to let the company perform in Pitt Stadium), and corporate heads from Carnegie-Illinois Steel, the Union Trust Company, Westinghouse Electric, Weirton Steel, and National Steel. When the new organization was announced in 1945, the *Jewish Chronicle* exclaimed with delight: "At last there will be singing among the sooted hills of Pittsburgh."[21]

The concept of light opera in the summertime was not new to Pittsburgh. In 1896 Harry Davis had opened the Casino Comic Opera Company in the Schenley Park skating rink, claiming it was the "only theater in the United States erected for the sole purpose of presenting lovers of music with standard and comic operas during the hot summer months." In 1900 the Duquesne Garden Stock Opera Company launched twenty-five years of programming popular operettas such as *The Mikado, Olivette, The Geisha,* and *H.M.S. Pinafore* in its 8,000-seat assembly hall in Oakland. And in 1938 the Pittsburgh Savoyards, the city's first Gilbert and Sullivan troupe, began as a church choir raising money for a summer camp before spinning off into an independent company. What made Wolk's effort different was the new company's organizational structure. Neither an amateur endeavor, nor a business venture like the Casino and Duquesne Garden, the Civic Light Opera was a civic initiative funded entirely by wealthy citizens and the University of Pittsburgh. As Mayor David L. Lawrence stated in 1946, a "civic light opera is an indication of civic progressiveness."[22]

The CLO's first season "under the stars" at Pitt Stadium opened in June 1946 with Victor Herbert's *Naughty Marietta,* a crowd pleaser with local appeal, given Herbert's status as the Pittsburgh Symphony's first conductor from 1898 to 1904. That first season established the company's modus operandi: to produce well-known material, to import nationally known star players, to cast local performers (usually students) in the chorus and corps de ballet, and to present the shows in a casual setting at reasonable prices. According to a first-season ad: "Every production is starred with songs you have played and sung! Never have Pittsburgh and the Tri-State had such an opportunity for entertainment! All-star casts for every operetta. Renowned names of the professional stage, opera, concert. A great orchestra. Superlative staging under nationally famous directors. Low prices."[23] The new venture lost $50,000 in its first season, largely because of the weather, but Kaufmann was impressed by the total attendance figures (about 270,000) and the quality of the productions and agreed to support the next season.

In 1947 a new managing director was hired. William Wymetal was an opera director from Vienna by way of Hollywood, and soon the CLO was featuring stars like Jackie Gleason, Zero Mostel, Jack Cassidy, Elaine Stritch, John Raitt, Robert Alda, Nancy Walker, Jeanette McDonald, Imogene Coca, and ballerina Maria Tallchief. But Wymetal was also committed to using local talent, both amateur and professional. Corps de ballet positions were coveted by students at Carnegie Tech and the University of Pittsburgh and over the years helped to launch many New York careers (including those of Shirley Jones, Lenora Nemetz, Florence Lacey, and Kathleen and Rob Marshall). The orchestra, under the baton of Karl Kritz (later associate conductor of the PSO), attracted highly trained professionals, including many from the Pittsburgh Symphony.

Within a few years the CLO was pushed to respond to two key demands by patrons: to present the new breed of Broadway musicals, such as *Oklahoma!, Kiss Me, Kate,* and *Annie Get Your Gun,* and to get them out of the rain. In 1949 Edgar Kaufmann pledged $500,000 toward the construction of a seemingly fantastical modern indoor-outdoor amphitheater with a retractable roof. After a few false starts and several years of negotiations, the Kaufmann gift was increased to a million dollars and transferred to the city's Auditorium Authority for the purpose of building a new Civic Arena.[24] Meanwhile, the CLO moved from Pitt Stadium to a large tent erected next to the arena construction site (called the Melody Tent), where they performed for three seasons on a much smaller artistic scale but with considerably better financial success. In 1961 the Civic Arena finally opened. At a reported cost of $22 million, it featured a dome that was 415 feet in diameter and twelve stories high—reportedly the biggest such structure in the world. Yet despite an ideal location and numerous amenities, the Civic Arena was nearly the death of the CLO. By the end of the first season, the summer of 1962, audiences were complaining about the terrible acoustics in the enormous space, the bad visibility, the lack of intimacy, and the fact that the roof rarely opened because of a wind-tunnel effect that caused microphones to roar and scenery to blow around the stage. It was, after all the effort, a poor environment for theater or live performance of any kind. As Carl Apone of the *Pittsburgh Press* noted, "Watching a musical show there is like watching a flea perform on second base in Yankee Stadium" (Dec. 4, 1967, 21). Despite good reviews, a vibrant contemporary repertoire (*West Side Story, Little Me, My Fair Lady*) and a string of money-making nostalgic revues (*The Wayne Newton Show, Liberace, The Jack Benny*

Fig. 32. The Civic Light Opera performing at the Civic Arena with the re-
tractable roof open, ca. 1962. Source: Library and Archives Division, Historical
Society of Western Pennsylvania.

Show), the number of subscribers steadily declined after the CLO's move to the
Civic Arena.[25]

During the fifties two other companies attempted to follow the Civic Light
Opera's recipe for creating a new kind of semiprofessional theater. One was the
International Theater Pittsburgh, a drama and ballet company founded in 1955
by an influential board of directors that included members of the Heinz, Hunt,

and Benedum families. Modeled on London's Vic-Wells company, International Theater Pittsburgh was managed by Francis Mayville, a local impresario with operations in Pittsburgh and Miami. Over its three-year existence, the company staged an ambitious repertory: *Julius Caesar, Death of a Salesman, The Cretan Women, Medea, A View from the Bridge,* and *Anastasia*.[26] A similar venture, the Wagon Wheel Playhouse, opened in 1951 at the Fine Arts Club in Squirrel Hill. Using a combination of imported Equity actors and local people as bit players and apprentices, it managed to present one season of legitimate plays before disappearing altogether.[27]

Strawhat and University Theater

The postwar years saw a boom in amateur and semiprofessional summer stock companies, especially in suburban communities. These "strawhat" theaters included Bill Green's Arena Theater, which presented "summer stock under a tent" on Highway 51, the White Barn (1948), the Silver Fox Playhouse (1950), the William Penn Playhouse (later called the Apple Hill Playhouse, 1950), the Pine Playhouse (founded in 1951 by a group of Carnegie Tech alumni), the Red Barn (1960), and the Mountain Playhouse, which had been founded in 1938 as a little theater but by the 1950s was a fully professional company offering a twenty-week season of Broadway fare in a bucolic setting about sixty miles from Pittsburgh. Of these, perhaps Will Disney's Little Lake Theater, which opened in 1948 in a converted hay barn about fifteen miles south of Pittsburgh, had the largest impact on local theater. Disney, who spent twenty years as an actor, director, and teacher at the Pittsburgh Playhouse before launching Little Lake, mentored several generations of young actors (notably, Charles Grodin and Barbara Feldon) during his forty-four years at the Little Lake Theater.

University theater also experienced a postwar surge. Carnegie Tech's School of Drama continued to draw national attention for its innovative pedagogy, especially the work of Edith Skinner, author of *Speak with Distinction*—a primer that revolutionized speech and vocal training.[28] Audiences for the School of Drama's productions were drawn by the high quality of student acting, excellent productions, and the opportunity to see an eclectic range of classical texts. At Duquesne University the Red Masquers presented an annual four-play season, as

CAP and GOWN CLUB
UNIVERSITY OF PITTSBURGH
Thirty-first Annual
Production

PICKETS PLEASE!

by NICK SPANOS '38 *and* ROBERT SAFFRON '38

Staged by GENE KELLY
Dialogue by CARL CASS
NIXON THEATRE
ENTIRE WEEK - APRIL 4
NO MATINEES

A Bombshell of Fun and Music That Hits the Spot!

Fig. 33. Program for Cap and Gown Club show directed
by Pitt alumnus Gene Kelly, 1938. Source: Unknown (Curtis
Theatre Collection, University of Pittsburgh Library).

they had done for nearly half a century. At the University of Pittsburgh the all-
male Cap and Gown Club, founded in 1908, produced an original musical revue
each spring at the Nixon Theatre. In April 1938 former Pitt student Gene Kelly
choreographed and directed *Pickets Please* for the club just before moving to New
York City. Finally, the Pitt Players—successors to the original Academy Thespians
—produced a four-play season at the university's Stephen Foster Memorial Theatre, erected in the late 1930s through the efforts of the Tuesday Musical Club.[29]

The Heyday of the Pittsburgh Playhouse

Clearly, there was both depth and range in Pittsburgh's noncommercial theater offerings during the supposed cultural dark ages of the forties and fifties. Most prominent was the Pittsburgh Playhouse, by then the city's largest theater company and a leading cultural center for the city's white professional class, with many supporters coming from Squirrel Hill's Jewish elite, including the Weil, Rauh, Falk, Freehof, and Dreifus families.[30] By the early 1950s, the Playhouse was a substantial business enterprise with a $300,000 annual budget, 8,000 subscribers, a million-dollar building with three stages, a restaurant, a professional staff, a touring company, a children's drama school, and a professional-level conservatory. The organization had been thriving since the mid-forties, buoyed by increasing attendance and a growing national reputation. Herbert Gellendre's original Apprentice School, begun in 1937 as a conservatory-style training program for young adults, had evolved into two branches: a Saturday school offering classes in acting, dance, and technical theater for teenagers, and the Playhouse School, a state-accredited two-year conservatory course for young actors and technicians training for professional careers. In 1949 the Playhouse Junior was launched under William Leech, a former professor at Carnegie Tech. The venture was immediately successful, drawing hundreds of schoolchildren into the Playhouse on Saturday mornings to see original stage adaptations of well-known children's literature. The Playhouse Junior claims to be the oldest continuing children's theater company in the United States.

The small Hamlet Street building could not long support this level of activity. In 1948 the board of directors, led by Richard S. Rauh, and the Playhouse Guild launched a fund-raising campaign to erect a new building complex at 3401 Boulevard of the Allies.[31] But the project stalled because of a federal directive issued during the Korean conflict "prohibiting the building of theaters, amphitheaters and other structures whose general purpose was recreation and entertainment."[32] In 1951, with a $200,000 grant from the A. W. Mellon Educational and Charitable Trust, the board purchased the Tree of Life synagogue next door. The new 554-seat Craft Theater opened in 1952, increasing the building's seating capacity to about 900. By the mid-1950s the Playhouse complex featured two auditoriums, classrooms, meeting rooms, offices, technical shops, a cocktail lounge, and a popular members-only restaurant. The Playhouse on Craft Avenue became

Fig. 34. Architect's rendering for a new Pittsburgh Playhouse that was never built, 1949. Source: Unknown (Curtis Theatre Collection, University of Pittsburgh Library). Courtesy of Point Park University.

an island unto itself, offering its patrons the care and safety of an entire evening's entertainment in one building. It also served as the central nerve center for the local theater community.

The Playhouse's loyal and large audience was attracted by the opportunity to see recent Broadway hits, or as Frederick Burleigh often put it, "shows that people know about."[33] Burleigh generally gave his audience comfortable middle-brow fare, from boulevard comedy to serious dramas to new musicals. Each spring he produced an original revue created and performed by various Playhouse artists, including composer Charlie Gaynor and dancer-choreographer Gene Kelly (in 1938).[34] But he also experimented with new material, such as Marc Connolly's *The Green Pastures*, mentioned earlier, with an all-black cast—a courageous gesture in 1941 in a city with a clearly understood color line. In 1954, ten years before the civil rights movement began to have an impact on the repertoire at most of Pittsburgh's theaters, Burleigh produced Louis Peterson's *Take a Giant Step*, starring Walter Worthington and Althea Washington, about a black boy growing up in a white neighborhood. In addition, each season also included at least one work from other countries, such as Stanislaw Wyspianski's *The Wedding* (its first commercial production outside of Poland) and at least one new play.

Between 1938 and 1958, for example, the Playhouse staged twenty-five original scripts, several by local playwrights. Examples include Dorothy Rood Stewart's *This Is My Valley* (1949) and *Water Witch* (1951) and Joanna Roos's *Among Ourselves* (1957)—an ambitious piece about school segregation. Most of these plays did poorly at the box office because they lacked name recognition and ironically did not fit Burleigh's own standard of producing "plays that people know about." Still, toward the end of his career Burleigh listed his work with new plays as among his important accomplishments, asserting that modern regional theaters had to be willing to "gamble on that sort of thing."[35]

From its inception most of the Playhouse's actors were volunteers (except during the Gellendre years), though local players were paid a small stipend to cover expenses, and, on occasion, professionals from New York City were imported for particular roles. Volunteer status did not necessarily indicate a lack of training or prior professional experience, however. As Burleigh told an interviewer in 1959, "I have a great mixture of actors, some who have had professional experience in New York, some who have trained here locally at Carnegie Tech for the theater, and others whom I have developed myself over a period of twenty years."[36] Many had substantial professional credits. Helen Wayne Rauh trained at Carnegie Tech, worked with George Sharp's professional stock company and did commercial radio dramas at KDKA, a local station, before beginning her thirty-six-year tenure at the Playhouse. Lincoln Maazel, formerly with the Los Angeles Opera, joined the Playhouse in 1949 and continued until the late 1960s while also working as a nightclub singer and acting in films, on television, and as a narrator for symphony concerts. The Playhouse also gained a reputation as a training ground for stars such as Sada Thompson, Shirley Jones, Barbara Feldon, and George Peppard, all of whom had been students or actors there during the forties and fifties. By 1959 the Playhouse was recognized as a first-tier civic theater and labeled one of the nation's "great going concerns."[37]

Yet toward the end of the 1950s the organization began to falter both financially and artistically. Subscription sales did not keep pace with the growing costs of operating the large building complex, the schools, and the Playhouse Junior, which subsidized ticket costs for area children in order to promote greater accessibility and therefore did not earn significant revenue. As financial problems increased, the board of directors and the staff began to differ over the essential mission of the Playhouse and its future course. Was it a production company or a community center? Should it be amateur or professional, mainstream or avant-garde? A board-initiated effort to upgrade the acting company by importing a core group of New York professionals was quickly undermined by Burleigh, who insisted that he "found it impossible to get the type of actors who were versatile enough to fit [his] particular program."[38] The tension increased in 1957 when the Rockefeller Foundation offered to help transform the Playhouse into a progressive nonprofit regional theater similar to Houston's ten-year-old Alley Theatre. As Playhouse business manager Richard Hoover remembered it, "[The Rockefeller Foundation] offered money to us on the condition that Fred Burleigh be removed as full artistic director and that we demonstrate our interest in becoming more progressive rather than so tied to the strings of community, amateur theater. Since we didn't want to let Fred go, we opened the Theater Upstairs during the 1958 season to attract the attention of the Foundation."[39]

The Theater Upstairs, carved out of unused attic space, had a small proscenium stage and sixty-seven seats. Burleigh used the theater to program "experimental" work—a mixture of avant-garde and intimate popular dramas ranging from Beckett's *Waiting for Godot* (staged in 1959), *The American Dream* and *The Zoo Story* by Edward Albee (1962), *The Caretaker* by Harold Pinter (1963); Arthur Kopits's *Oh Dad, Poor Dad, Mama's Hung You in the Closet and I'm Feeling So Sad* (1964, 1965); *Tevya and His Daughters* by Arnold Perl (1960), and Synge's *Playboy of the Western World* (1962). On the whole, the Theater Upstairs succeeded in updating the Playhouse repertoire and broadening Pittsburgh's theatrical fare. Albee's plays were discomfiting and difficult (as they proved to be in cities all over the country), but Kopits's odd little play became the longest-running show in Playhouse history, playing to capacity audiences during two long runs in 1964 and 1965. Another key Playhouse initiative was the Vanguard Theatre Project, begun in 1962 to "bring performance of good theater into the high schools of Pittsburgh and surrounding areas." It was funded for three years by the Rockefeller Foundation. The project was developed by Miriam Cherin and Marcelle Felser as a mobile theater featuring three professional actors, all trained at Carnegie Tech. During its ten years of existence, Vanguard took suitcase productions of *Antigone, Waiting for Godot,* and *Rhinoceritis* (a combination of Ionesco's *Rhinoceros* and Brecht's *The Informer*) to local high schools and colleges.

Despite these efforts, however, claims that Burleigh and his supporters were out of touch with the changing times grew louder and were heard by board

Fig. 35. The Pittsburgh Playhouse in 1958, featuring three marquees for three theaters. Source: Unknown (Curtis Theatre Collection, University of Pittsburgh Library). Courtesy of Point Park University.

members concerned about the company's growing deficit and loss of clout within the cultural community. Some of Burleigh's efforts to regain the ever-dwindling subscription base were successful, notably a nostalgic burlesque-style revue called *Naughty Nifties* that featured vaudeville-era star Bert Carr and sold an unprecedented 18,596 tickets in the spring of 1964. But that kind of throwback programming merely further alienated board members interested in moving the company into the future. As Philip K. Herr, executive director of the board, saw it after the 1963–64 season, the problem was how to decide "what will sell tickets and enhance the Playhouse image."[40]

The American Conservatory Theatre

In 1965 Pittsburgh's postwar urban renewal project was being declared a resounding success. The air was cleaner than it had been in 150 years, the industrial litter had been cleared from the "golden triangle," and plans for new office towers, including the sixty-story U.S. Steel building, were reshaping both the skyline and the city's future as a major corporate headquarters. The term "renaissance"—first introduced in the late forties as a public relations tool to boost civic morale and leverage financial support—was now an accurate description of the city's metamorphosis. The Smoky City had truly been reborn.

The Pittsburgh Playhouse was also undergoing a renaissance of sorts in 1965. Or at least that was the hope of the beleaguered board of directors when they decided not to renew Fred Burleigh's contract for a twenty-fifth season. The decision to fire Burleigh was a long time in coming—introduced in 1957 when the Rockefeller Foundation made its first offer of support and again in 1963 when the foundation returned with a new proposal. Rockefeller money was to be used for a joint operation between the Playhouse and Carnegie Tech to "bridge the gap between the university theater and commercial theater . . . under the guidance of a distinguished man of the theater."[41] Although the boards of both institutions knew that Burleigh was not the "distinguished man of the theater" the foundation had in mind, it took them two years to agree on who was.

When Burleigh was finally fired, the executive committee asked managing director Richard Hoover to consult with William Ball about "implementing a repertory season for the coming year."[42] Ball, a leading off-Broadway figure known for his adventurous staging of Molière's *Tartuffe* in 1965, had trained at Carnegie Tech and even appeared at the Playhouse in a 1952 production of *Ah, Wilderness!* By 1965 he had a plan to create a new model for the American theater. In Ball's words, it would be "a non-profit, tax exempt educational institution resembling the European concept of Conservatory—adapted so that development and performances are integral and inseparable parts of the professional's creative life. Training and production shall be indigenous, as the one to the other, not working as separate programs with separate personnel. All participants in the conservatory—as in a ballet company—will always be in training."[43] The Rockefeller offer seemed tailor-made for Ball's ambitious agenda, and his American Conservatory Theatre and the newly constituted Carnegie Tech–Playhouse Company contracted to stage eleven plays between June and December 1965. The three producing organizations would maintain separate identities and separate boards of directors. Ball would control the artistic product, and the Playhouse's Richard Hoover would be the general business manager.

The innovative design of the American Conservatory Theatre at the Playhouse included a seventy-five-member company made up of Equity actors (mostly Ball's associates in New York), non-Equity actors (mostly Playhouse regulars), and an apprentice group (students from Carnegie Tech). The allotted budget for the six-month season was $400,000 and was based on grants from the Rockefeller Foundation, the A.W. Mellon Educational and Charitable Trust, the Sarah Mellon Scaife Foundation, Carnegie Tech, and the Pittsburgh Playhouse (including $35,000 donated by individual board members). Ball arrived in Pittsburgh flush with the promise of an unusually generous production budget and the freedom to pursue his own aesthetic agenda. He immediately initiated a national publicity campaign, commenting on his "brand new idea" in publications such as the *New York Times* and the *Saturday Review*. But he also had to charm the locals. His company toured the city, visiting various ethnic neighborhoods and even spending a day at a steel mill watching the production process and greeting laborers. In addition, Ball issued the following "Letter of Thanks" in his opening program:

> To our patrons—the citizens of Pittsburgh—who have shown such interest in our program and plans, we are proud to be among you for these months. To this whole city, which has been so friendly and so warm, we can only try to make ourselves worthy and appreciative. . . . Because Pittsburgh has extended so enthusiastic a welcome to us, you have made our fears of loneliness disappear into your blue, smogless sky.[44]

Following his European-derived design, Ball initiated a rotating repertoire staged between the Hamlet and Craft theaters. He opened by remounting his Lincoln Center success, *Tartuffe* (featuring Sada Thompson, a former Playhouse actor), and a new production of Edward Albee's *Tiny Alice*. The rest of the season reflected Ball's mission to stage both new plays and international classics and included *King Lear*, Pirandello's *Six Characters in Search of an Author*, Anouilh's *Antigone*, Giraudoux's *The Apollo of Bellac*, Williams's *The Rose Tattoo*, Goldoni's *The Servant of Two Masters*, Miller's *Death of a Salesman* (featuring Richard Dysart), a mounting of the popular British satirical revue *Beyond the Fringe*, featuring "Playhouse favorite" René Auberjonois, and the road production of Martin Duberman's *In White America*, starring Cicely Tyson. The ambitious six-month season was a qualified success. The local critics, including Harold Cohen of the

Fig. 36. American Conservatory Theatre Company in 1965 (Cicely Tyson is fourth from left). Source: Unknown (Curtis Theatre Collection, University of Pittsburgh Library). Courtesy of Point Park University.

Post-Gazette, Kaspar Monahan of the *Pittsburgh Press*, and George Anderson of the *New Kensington Daily Dispatch*, uniformly praised the high level of acting and the cultural sophistication of Ball's programming choices. And during the six-month season attendance was a respectable 68 percent of capacity, with over 75,000 tickets sold for 270 performances.[45]

But there were serious problems. By September Ball had already exceeded his $400,000 budget, with nearly four months left to go. A substantial portion of Ball's expenditures were reportedly "devoted to development and promotion of ACT's own corporation."[46] The administration began to realize that continued affiliation with the ACT agenda would signal the end of the Playhouse's autonomous activities, including the children's company, the school, the Vanguard troupe, and a newly launched resident ballet company. The board drafted a memo to Ball defining new terms for continuing their relationship. These included oversight of the budget by the Playhouse board and public recognition by ACT of the autonomy of Playhouse Junior, the Vanguard Theatre, the Play-house School, and other long-standing community commitments. Ball refused the terms and on December 12, 1965, resigned from any "further association with the Pittsburgh Playhouse." The American Conservatory Theatre maintained a partial affiliation with Carnegie Tech (a stipulation of the Rockefeller grant), but nevertheless left the city. By July 1966 the company had found a new home in San Francisco, hosted by the chamber of commerce, and soon launched its first season by restaging the Pittsburgh repertoire and using the sets and costumes financed and built by the Pittsburgh Playhouse.

Interestingly, though William Ball's residency lasted less than six months, it quickly engendered two resilient narratives about the Pittsburgh-ACT experiment, what one might call the local version and the national version. In the local telling, Ball is the villain, an irresponsible megalomaniac who used the city and its well-meaning, well-heeled theater patrons to fund a start-up venture that was never intended to remain in Pittsburgh. In the opinion of Lottie Falk, a Playhouse board member and initial supporter of William Ball, "Either you were Ball's mad slave and follower or his mortal enemy—there was no in-between."[47] In the national version of the tale, however, Pittsburgh is the villain. This was certainly the message of *A Theater Divided: The Postwar American Stage*, by Martin Gottfried, which used the Pittsburgh-ACT relationship as a case study amplifying the danger of providing serious theater to provincial (that is, conservative) audiences. "Pittsburgh is a strange theater town," writes Gottfried, "and the Pittsburgh Playhouse a peculiar operation. . . . Unable to understand serious theater and completely uninformed about new methods of administration, [the Playhouse board] watched ACT's audiences dwindle—and perhaps even gloated over it. The business executives who sat on the board gave negligible help."[48] Gottfried's information is clearly incorrect. A more measured assessment is that Ball and his company would probably not have stayed in Pittsburgh no matter how accommodating the Playhouse board of directors or local audiences might have been. This is the opinion expressed by Joseph Zeigler in *Regional Theater: The Revolutionary Stage* (1973). Zeigler concludes, "Their eyes were on larger vistas from the beginning; they were in Pittsburgh because the National Theater had to start somewhere."[49]

THEATER AS CIVIC IDENTITIES

1968 to 1979

Pittsburgh, March 21, 1975. Thirty-five people are crowded into the grubby, ramshackle building transformed into a theater by a maze of 200 white sheets hanging from the ceiling. Most of the spectators are sitting cross-legged on the floor, a few are standing, one or two are seated in folding chairs, but everyone is just a few feet from the actors. On the "stage" is a filthy white toilet. Two men sit tied to it by their feet. One of the men is moaning, occasionally begging for water. It's a typical Pittsburgh Laboratory Theatre evening; the obscure contemporary text (Arrabel's *The Labyrinth*) is provocative, and the in-your-face acting—exacerbated by the close quarters and the oppression of the set design—is hard to watch. But none of this is news to the Lab subscribers who sit in the center of the maze. They are, for the most part, a young crowd—college students and artists who share Royston's interest in experimental theater. But the Lab faithful include some older subscribers as well. Dr. Ford Curtis, for example, an eighty-something Pitt

English professor who knows more about local theater than just about anyone in town, has been a subscriber for several years now. (He's the one seated in the folding chair.)[1]

The Final Years of the Original Playhouse

The ACT experiment under William Ball left the Playhouse with a deficit of over $500,000, the largest in the organization's thirty-year history.[2] Unwilling to give up the idea of turning the Playhouse into a professional nonprofit venture, the board agreed to sponsor one "independent" season featuring an Equity company directed by Carnegie Tech professor Lawrence Carra. But budget problems continued to escalate, and by the fall of 1966 a "Campaign to Save the Playhouse" was necessary to keep the school open. Support came from the general public and local foundations (Howard Heinz, Thomas Mellon Evans Foundation, A. W. Mellon, Westinghouse), and the National Council on the Arts, which gave $25,000; the Playhouse was saved by what the *Post-Gazette* called "a last ditch fund raising campaign" (Dec. 14, 1966, 1).

Despite the crisis brought on by Ball's fiscal irresponsibility, a majority of the board remained keenly interested in converting the Playhouse into a professional resident theater company. Richard Hoover, who had stayed on as general manager through the ACT period, began negotiations with John Hancock, the twenty-seven-year-old director of the Actor's Workshop in San Francisco and, like Ball, a reported wunderkind. Having heard rumors about the Playhouse's "meddling" board of directors, Hancock agreed to come to Pittsburgh only on condition that no one would interfere with his choice of repertoire. "I am hoping to offer the kind of theater that the cultural revolution has been forging of late in other communities," he said after accepting the position, "which means we'll probably lose from 25–30 percent of the Old Guard audience that wants a diet of *Under the Yum Yum Tree* and other commercial light-weights. But I think we can replace the defectors from the ranks of students and blue collar workers who have an intellectual curiosity and who will find stimulation and excitement in Brecht, Shakespeare, Maeterlinck, Beckett, Osborne and even early Clifford Odets" (*Pittsburgh Post-Gazette*, July 21, 1966, 12). Hancock was given an exceptionally

Fig. 37. Pittsburgh Laboratory Theatre production of *Outcry* in 1979, featuring Bingo O'Malley. Source: Unknown (Curtis Theatre Collection, University of Pittsburgh Library). Courtesy of Pittsburgh Laboratory Theatre.

large first-year budget, about $715,000. He labeled his season "A Theater of Excitement" and produced an eclectic but hardly revolutionary repertoire that included Brecht's *A Man's a Man, A Midsummer Night's Dream, A Streetcar Named Desire, A View from the Bridge, Two for the Seesaw, Three Sisters,* and John Osborne's *The Entertainer.*

There was trouble right from the start. Hancock was arrogant and openly antagonistic to the Playhouse staff, which led to Hoover's resignation in the spring of 1967. More problematic was the occasionally controversial nature of Hancock's directorial concepts. The set for *A Man's a Man,* for example, included an onstage urinal, a fact that was widely reported (though not condemned) in the press and eventually polarized the audience into two camps fighting over the "rights" of the avant-garde stage versus the "rights" of polite entertainment. Attendance plunged to 38 percent capacity. Hancock responded by attacking the Pittsburgh audience: "It's a challenge. But the city's still so stodgy. People on the streets are tight, Germanic, little old ladies with clear plastic frames on their glasses. All the people between twenty and forty seem to have gone away. It's been a hard place to keep up company morale, but we're still intent on trying" (*Pittsburgh Press*, Nov. 21, 1966). While attendance improved over the second half of the season, Hancock's relations with the Playhouse staff and a majority of the board did not. He was fired in June 1967. A small but powerful coterie of board members resigned in protest, leaving the organization with a weakened administration and a fractured community presence.

This latest upheaval, both internal and external, put the Playhouse in an even more precarious financial and cultural situation; after two seasons of experimentation and infighting, the deficit continued to rise while public interest (and ticket sales) began a serious decline. In response, the Playhouse launched a campaign to "raise theater consciousness" among its subscribers and in the larger community, but the struggle to fill the organization's three theaters continued under a new general manager, Robert Novak. The next season featured a combination of popular musicals (*Once Upon a Mattress*) and canonical works like *Henry IV, Part I* and *Arms and the Man*, directed by Jon Jory. By the end of 1967 the Playhouse was carrying a deficit of $563,820, and by the next June the board announced the cessation of all Playhouse activities and a total staff layoff.[3] In August, Point Park College offered to take over the building's operations. The Pittsburgh Playhouse reopened in the fall of 1968 with its executive committee reporting to Point Park's board of directors, and over the next five years it attempted to return to its roots as a civic theater with a paid staff and volunteer actors. Helen Wayne Rauh rejoined the company for a role in *Dear Me, the Sky Is Falling*, capping a thirty-four-year relationship with the organization. Other long-time Playhouse actors returned as well, including Lincoln Maazel, who played Lenora Nemetz's father in the musical spoof *Cindy*. But while all three Playhouse stages were busy on a regular basis with plays (including the world premiere of Tom Thomas's *The Interview*, starring and directed by José Ferrer), a new film festival in the Craft Theater, and Nicholas Petrov's newly formed Pittsburgh Ballet Theatre, the organization was unable to recapture its audience or to recover financially. In 1973, after thirty-nine years, the executive committee voted to disband the Pittsburgh Playhouse as an independent, nonprofit incorporation and turned it over to Point Park College.

Heinz Hall for the Performing Arts

The Pittsburgh Playhouse was not alone in its struggle to remain relevant in the rapidly changing culture of the late sixties and early seventies. The city's few remaining commercial playhouses—the New Nixon, the Penn, and the Stanley—were also in financial trouble. For even though the advent of film and radio had been negatively affecting live theater since the 1920s, television utterly reinvented consumer patterns and permanently altered the entertainment landscape. When Pittsburgh's first television station, WDTV, went on the air in January 1949 with a program shot live from the stage of the Syria Mosque, only about 9 percent of American homes contained a television set. Five years later, that percentage had increased to 64.5.[4] By the 1960s, most Americans were more accustomed to finding their "theater"—stories told through dramatic narrative techniques—on both the big and small screens than in the theatrical playhouse.

The advent of television is certainly one explanation for the ill fate of the New Nixon, Penn, and Stanley theaters after World War II. But an equally compelling reason is the decline of the downtown Penn-Liberty corridor between 1955 and 1970, when the city lost 100,000 residents to the suburbs. The long time downtown retailers that lined Penn and Liberty soon followed, leaving commercial storefronts vacant or housing culturally marginal businesses. Liberty Avenue, once an elegant urban boulevard, became the center of Pittsburgh's sex trade, with novelty shops and adult theaters like the Art Cinema (where German "talkies" once played in the 1930s) stretching for several blocks. Pittsburgh's few remaining commercial theaters had no place in this changed landscape. In 1963 United Artists gave up its lease on Loew's Penn, removing the movie screen and projectors. Although the building soon reopened as a road house known as the Penn Theater Auditorium, over the next four years it was usually dark, opening sporadically to host blockbuster touring shows like *The Owl and the Pussycat* (starring Eartha Kitt) and *Hello, Dolly!* (starring Carol Channing). The New Nixon—plagued for years by the clutter of porn shops and related street traffic—stopped booking live touring shows altogether in the early 1970s.

The first effort to arrest the downward spiral of the Penn-Liberty corridor began in 1967, when the Howard Heinz Endowment abandoned plans to build a new symphony hall next to the Civic Arena and paid $850,000 for the dilapidated Penn Theater with the idea of making it a symphony hall. The Heinz Hall project was spearheaded by philanthropist and corporate head Jack Heinz, Symphony Society president Charles Denby, and Theodore Hazlett, former secretary of the Urban Redevelopment Authority during Renaissance I, and in 1967 president of the A. W. Mellon Educational and Charitable Trust.[5] Their immediate goal was to find a more suitable home for the symphony, which had been unhappily housed in the Syria Mosque for many years.

To test the feasibility of the space, in late 1969 and early 1970 the PSO staged two public performances in the Penn Theater. When the concerts proved successful with both the artists and the audience, the plan quickly moved forward.[6] The Pittsburgh Symphony Society, with underwriting from the Howard Heinz Endowments, hired the local architectural firm of Stotz, Hess, MacLachlan, and Fosner to transform the movie palace into a hall for the performing arts. The $10 million restoration also involved substantial construction work.[7] The back wall was removed to increase the size of the stage and backstage areas and to provide new dressing rooms and rehearsal space. On the advice of acoustical expert Heinrich Keilholz, a large plaster sound reflector was added to the proscenium arch. The number of seats, newly refurbished in crimson velvet, was reduced from 3,486 to 2,847 to provide more legroom. Finally, several businesses that had fronted Sixth Avenue, including the Mayflower, a popular coffee shop, were removed to expand the entrances so as to accommodate the arrival and departure of 2,000–3,000 visitors at one time.

Heinz Hall for the Performing Arts opened on September 10, 1971, with a gala concert featuring Mahler's *Resurrection* Symphony.[8] The program choice was meant as a clever nod to the role that Heinz Hall was expected to play in the rebirth of Pittsburgh's downtown cultural life. By that time, the scope of the project had expanded to envision housing for the Pittsburgh Opera, founded in 1940, the Pittsburgh Ballet Theatre, founded in 1969, and the Civic Light Opera.[9] Like the Kennedy Center for the Performing Arts in Washington, D.C., which had opened a few days earlier, Heinz Hall was envisioned by its supporters as "more than a handsome building. . . . It was built to satisfy the aspirations of many: those who envisioned a more magnificent hall for the city that is their home—those who will perform in it for the public's pleasure—those who will come to see and hear and have their lives enriched. It stands as a testimonial to the civic spirit that has supported Pittsburgh's cultural organizations over the years."[10]

Fig. 38. Heinz Hall (formerly Loew's Penn) under restoration, 1970. Source: Library and Archives Division, Historical Society of Western Pennsylvania.

Newspapers across the country covered the Heinz Hall opening. The *New York Times* called the rehabilitation of the Penn Theater "a dramatic example of the best kind of urban renewal" and an "example that other cities might well study while searching for solutions to some of their urban and arts problems" (Sept. 12, 1971, 82). The Heinz Hall opening celebrations continued throughout the fall of 1971, as the other resident organizations held their own galas. For the struggling Civic Light Opera, Heinz Hall represented more than a fancy new address. It was truly a rescue operation for the twenty-five-year-old institution, which had "temporarily" shut down at the close of the 1968 season, when the increasingly untenable conditions at the Civic Arena and an ever-dwindling audience left the organization with losses of about $250,000. In anticipation of its reopening in the summer of 1971 under the new general manager, William Thunhurst, the CLO's gala fund raiser on November 24 featured a national roster of musical theater stars that included Ethel Merman, Joel Grey, and former Pittsburghers Lenora Nemetz (then appearing on Broadway in *Cabaret*) and Florence Lacey. The evening's biggest applause, however, belonged to local performer Barbara Russell, who gestured toward the glittering palatial interior of the meticulously restored hall and asked, in her best Pittsburgh accent, "For this they had to tear down the Mayflower?"

Pittsburgh's Resident Theater Movement

Over the first half of the twentieth century, the various kinds of noncommercial theater in the United States were guided by two impulses: to promote art over profit and to decentralize American theater by drawing it away from New York City. After the Second World War a third impulse was added: to make independent theater a professional enterprise in both preparation and practice, as opposed to the avocational philosophy of the little theater movement. This new idea, dubbed the resident or regional theater movement, was spurred by the work of Margo Jones, artistic director of Theater '47 in Dallas; Nina Vance, founder of Houston's Alley Theatre; and Zelda Fichandler, who established Washington, D.C.'s Arena Stage in 1950. All three were visionary leaders of a new type of American public theater that emerged in the postwar years: fully professional, committed to producing new American plays as well as classics, rooted in the host community, and permanently nonprofit by virtue of a tax-exempt status.[11] During the 1950s and 1960s several dozen nonprofit regional theaters were founded on this model and were supported by generous funding from new art-centered private philanthropies and government agencies, notably the Ford Foundation and the National Endowment for the Arts, established in 1965.[12]

Pittsburgh entered the resident theater movement later than other cities, though not nearly as late as has often been reported.[13] Whereas Pittsburgh was said to have no "professional" theaters until 1975, in fact the city played host to more than twenty noncommercial theater companies that came of age in the late 1960s and early 1970s. They varied from experimental to political to community-oriented. But all were staffed by professionally trained directors, actors, playwrights, designers, and administrators committed to theater as a profession, not an avocation, and to being rooted in the community as financially independent nonprofit institutions. In that sense, all were professional, whether they paid salaries or not. A more useful way to classify the city's many resident theaters of the 1970s, then, is to refer to budget size and union affiliation rather than professional versus amateur status.

Black Horizon Theater

During the civil rights era Pittsburgh's racial tensions centered on high unemployment, poor housing, and lingering discrimination suffered by African Americans at all levels of community life. By then the decade-long diaspora out of the Lower Hill had not only destroyed the community's vibrancy but had also disenfranchised African Americans by breaking up their largest residential voting block. In response, many key black community institutions—the Urban League, the NAACP, the *Pittsburgh Courier,* and the newly formed Citizens Committee for Hill District Renewal—began a battle to save what was left of the Hill by opposing any further attempts to raze housing and businesses along Centre and Wylie avenues.[14] This rescue effort was led by Rep. K. Leroy Irvis, a former assistant district attorney who had represented the Hill District in the state assembly since 1958.[15] It was also supported by a new wave of cultural activism being fueled by poets, painters, actors, dancers, and musicians working out of neighborhood meeting places like the Hill Arts Society, the Halfway Art Gallery, and Hill House on Centre Avenue—formerly the Irene Kaufmann Settlement House, which had been given to the community when the Jewish Community Center established a new home in Squirrel Hill.

In 1965, in the midst of this charged sociopolitical climate, a group of young poets calling themselves the Centre Avenue Poets' Theater Workshop emerged. These included Nick Flournoy, Charlie P. Williams, Robert Lee Penny, and Frederick August Kittel, a twenty-one-year-old wandering scholar who shed his German father's name, took his African American mother's name, and, as August Wilson, went "down onto Centre Avenue to learn from the community how to be a man."[16] The poets were schooled in the legacy of the Harlem Renaissance and the performing style of Beat-era writers. As members of the black community, however, they were increasingly influenced by the emerging aesthetic politics of black nationalism—a concept introduced to the group by Gaston Neal, an older and more established Hill District poet and civil rights activist. (Neal left

Pittsburgh in 1966 to start the New School of African American Thought in Washington, D.C.)

In its first few years the Centre Avenue Poets' Theater Workshop operated primarily as a writers' workshop and peer support group, its members writing, listening to music, and talking about their work in restaurants, coffee shops, and a local hangout called Irv's Bar (*Pittsburgh Post-Gazette*, June 1, 1987, 2). Their loosely conceived definition of theater was confined mostly to impromptu (and often uninvited) recitations in art galleries and jazz clubs along Centre, Wylie, and Fullerton avenues. (Wilson admitted that he was poorly received when he "gave" his poetry to the crowd at the Halfway Art Gallery.)[17] Few members of the group had seen much theater while growing up on the Hill, probably because the neighborhood's once plentiful African American independent theater companies had largely disbanded. Wilson once reported that he was twenty years old when he saw his first play—the Vanguard Theatre Project's *Rhinoceritus* at the Fifth Avenue High School. As Wilson remembered it, "What the hell is this, I wondered—there was nothing to relate to in it. I wasn't impressed." Wilson was equally unimpressed by John Hancock's production of *A Man's a Man* at the Pittsburgh Playhouse: "I lasted about twenty minutes."[18] He was apparently also unaware of the work of the city's two integrated companies: the Curtaineers and the Freedom Readers, formed in 1965 as a collaborative of theater artists "dealing with integration, the leading challenge of our time" (*Pittsburgh Post-Gazette*, Dec. 4, 1965, 32). Thus when the Centre Avenue Poets' Theater Workshop began convening in the mid-sixties, the legacy of the city's African American theater activity of the 1930s and early 1940s seems to have disappeared from the collective cultural memory. "It never occurred to us there had been [black] people doing theater before us," Wilson remembered in 1999. "Every day we walked by Walter Worthington's record store, never knowing that twenty years before he'd had a theater."[19]

In spite of this estrangement from the contemporary white and integrated theater community—or perhaps as a result of it—in 1968 the Centre Avenue Poets' Theater Workshop underwent a metamorphosis and emerged as Black Horizon Theater of Pittsburgh.[20] The new company was clearly influenced by the Black Arts movement, the aesthetic and spiritual sister of the Black Power concept being articulated by Amiri Baraka (Leroi Jones), an Obie award–winning playwright and poet. In 1968 Baraka's two community-based black nationalist theater companies (Harlem's Black Arts Repertory Theater School and Spirit House of Newark, New Jersey) were spurring the development of black theater groups in cities around the country.[21] Rob Penny and August Wilson, founders of the Black Horizon Theater, intended to follow Baraka's model by merging political action with theatrical practice in their commitment to Black Nationalism and to politicizing the Hill District community. But it was Rob Penny's newfound interest in playwriting that moved the idea to action. In 1967 he wrote two one-act plays—*Dance of the Blues Dead* and *Deeds of Blackness*. Wilson decided to direct them and prepared himself by studying *The Fundamentals of Play Directing* by Carnegie Mellon's Lawrence Carra. Black Horizon's first productions took place in 1967 in a school auditorium in the Upper Hill.[22] In 1968, Wilson discovered a collection of contemporary black plays and poems published in the *Tulane Drama Review*, which was "the first time [he] had seen black plays in print."[23] Between 1968 and 1971 Black Horizon Theater produced works by Rob Penny, Amiri Baraka, Ed Bullins, Sonia Sanchez, and Douglas Turner Ward at numerous theaters and auditoriums in the city and out of state.[24] Wilson served as the group's principal director, with Penny as the resident playwright. Company members included Claude Purdy, Marsha Lillie, Maisha Baton, Ron Pitts, Mary Bradly, and Sala Udin, another political activist who later became a Pittsburgh city council member representing the Hill District.

In 1971 a few members from Black Horizon set out to create satellite theater companies in other African American neighborhoods in the Pittsburgh area, but the only group to emerge from the plan was a new theater located in a Hazelwood housing project where August Wilson's family was living. Called the Ujima Theater (the word *ujima* means "collective work and responsibility" in Swahili), the new company was organized by Penny, Wilson, Ron Pitts, and Mary Bradly. Ujima's first project was an adaptation of the popular movie *Superfly*—which Wilson reconfigured into an antidrug vehicle (*Pittsburgh Post-Gazette*, June 1, 1987, 2). The production, underwritten by the University of Pittsburgh, raised $10,000 for recreational activities in Hazelwood. Ujima went on to produce through the mid-seventies, at which time it seems to have splintered into a variety of individual pursuits as several members left the city.[25]

August Wilson stayed on the Hill, writing and occasionally publishing poetry while working at a series of minimum-wage jobs. In 1972 he wrote his first play, *Recycle*, an "avant-garde experiment" that mingled verse and prose dialogue and was reportedly about the end of his first marriage.[26] By the mid-seventies Wilson's interest in community-based theater was waning; he complained that his volunteer actors often failed to show up for evening rehearsals. He turned instead to writing poetry and the occasional one-act play, including *Homecoming,* about the blues singer and guitarist Blind Lemon Jefferson. Around this time Wilson collaborated with Maisha Baton and Claude Purdy on a musical satire called *Black Bart and the Sacred Hills,* which was later rewritten and staged in Minneapolis and Los Angeles.

Kuntu Repertory Theatre

Rob Penny also chose to stay in Pittsburgh after the dissolution of the Black Horizon and Ujima companies, living on Bedford Street in the Hill District and teaching courses in black consciousness and revolutionary theater at the University of Pittsburgh after joining the faculty in 1969. Though Penny was known primarily as a published poet, he also continued exploring his neighborhood in plays like *Little Willy Armstrong Jones,* the tragic story of a nightclub owner turned drug dealer. Vernell Lillie first noticed Penny's work in late 1973 when a student performed a monologue from *Little Willy* in her course in contemporary black theater. Lillie, a director and specialist in psychodrama, came to the University of Pittsburgh from Texas by way of graduate study in education at Carnegie Mellon. She was instantly impressed with the clearly stated social agenda of *Little Willy,* combined with Penny's evocative language, and suggested to her colleague that they stage a reading of the play. This led to a new community-based theater company devoted to producing plays, like Penny's, that examined "black life from a sociopolitical-historical perspective" and were dedicated to moving both "performers and audience to social action."[27]

The Kuntu Repertory Theatre made its official debut in 1975 with a production of *Little Willy Armstrong Jones* at Pitt's Stephen Foster Memorial Theatre.[28] Under Artistic Director Vernell Lillie it became the first black theater company in residence at a Pittsburgh-area university.[29] At first the company was made up primarily of faculty and students, but over time a growing roster of actors, designers, and technicians from the larger community joined the effort (including August Wilson, who served as an acting coach on several early productions).

Fig. 39. Ben Cain in Kuntu Repertory Theatre's 2005 revival of
Rob Penny's *Little Willy Armstrong Jones*. Source: Jason Blair, courtesy of CIDDE, University of Pittsburgh.

Kuntu's repertoire was focused on black life and social issues, with most plays
drawn from the contemporary Black Arts canon. In its first few years, Kuntu
staged works by Ed Bullins, Kathleen Collins, Alice Childress, and Lorraine
Hansberry. Lillie was also open to producing the work of emerging playwrights
connected to Kuntu. When August Wilson brought *Homecoming* to her attention,
she directed it herself in October 1976 as part of an evening of three one-act
plays. This was the first Wilson play to be produced by a resident theater company. (The earlier production of *Recycle* had been self-produced by Wilson.)

From its inception Kuntu's repertory was rich and varied, though its voice was most fully heard in the work of playwright-in-residence Rob Penny, who wrote prolifically for the company. Penny's dramaturgical style was influenced by his politics, particularly his growing belief in cultural nationalism, and an aesthetic built on his love of African-derived performance modes. His plays often used musical structure to meld highly poetic sequences (which Penny called "pulses") with traditional scenes (which he called "movements"). These early works were also unabashed morality tales that placed responsibility on his failed protagonists (like the drug-dealing Little Willy) but also targeted American racism and discriminatory practices in contemporary Pittsburgh. Some, in fact, were written in direct response to feedback from Kuntu's audience. When one audience member noted the lack of attention to black feminists, for example, Penny responded by writing *Good Black Don't Crack*, the story of the romantic journey of a middle-aged woman circa 1975. Some of Penny's Kuntu plays (notably *Good Black* and the highly regarded *Who Loves the Dancer?*) were produced elsewhere, including Woodie King's New Federal Theater in New York, the Billie Holiday Theater in Chicago, and the Ododo Theater in Tucson. But the Hill District native remained deeply rooted in Pittsburgh and the mission and daily work of Kuntu Rep until his sudden death in 2003.

In addition to its annual main stage series, Kuntu undertook educational and community-based initiatives ranging from a college touring production of scenes and monologues from the Black Arts canon (created by Lillie) to psychodrama classes (offered to schools, jails, and senior citizens' centers) to the Kuntu Writers' Workshop, a community-based writing program launched in 1976 and headed by Penny and Wilson with support from the University of Pittsburgh's Curtiss E. Porter. The Kuntu Writers' Workshop was designed to teach young writers how to take "the written word and oral tradition to the communities, in the way of the Griot, in the style of our ancestral heritage and for the reason of keeping those traditional and creative speeches alive and at work."[30] Penny led the playwriting section, Wilson led the poets, and Maisha Baton led a group interested in developing children's literature. After Wilson went to St. Paul in 1978 and Baton to New Mexico around 1979, Penny oversaw the playwriting workshop, today the second oldest black writers' workshop in the nation.

Activist Theaters

Theater played a role in Pittsburgh's changing political culture of the late 1960s, as it did elsewhere. In 1969, the city parks and recreation department and the Pittsburgh Council on the Arts sponsored an initiative called the Community Action Theater (CAT) intended to help residents of eight "poverty neighborhoods" develop their own activist theater organizations (*Pittsburgh Press*, Dec. 3, 1969, 9). Targeted areas included Homewood, the Hill District, East Liberty, the North Side, and South Oakland. Only the last group took hold, however. Headed by Louis Lippa, the South Oakland CAT presented a series of plays at the Paul Younger Center, including one written by Joe Yusko, a steel worker never before involved in theater.

Two other groups agitated within the black community in the 1970s: the short-lived Demundi Theater and Bob Johnson's Theater Urge. Demundi was a quirky self-labeled "proprietary operation" run by playwright-producer-teacher Frederick Louis Richardson and based at the Hill House on Centre Avenue. During its one season Richardson staged the first local production of Jean Genet's *The Blacks,* as well as two of his own scripts focusing on contemporary black life, *Me and Mrs. Jones* and *The Taking of JoAnn,* about Joann Little, a black woman who killed her jailer when he tried to rape her. A similar focus defined Bob Johnson's Theater Urge, founded in 1975 as a subsidiary of the Black Dance Theater Ensemble. Johnson, a dancer and actor from New York, came to the University of Pittsburgh in 1969, where he was a colleague of August Wilson, Rob Penny, and Vernell Lillie.[31] Theater Urge debuted in January 1976 in an East Liberty storefront with a provocative mock blackface minstrel show, *Black Butter: A Black Dirty Show.* Johnson's purpose was to "continue the Revolution and remind people —Lord Jesus—there was a time when this was accepted."[32] During the bicentennial celebrations in 1976, Theater Urge continued its activist agenda by staging an adaptation of Langston Hughes's poems entitled *Hues of Langston.*

In addition to his work with Theater Urge, Johnson also worked independently, notably as the director who mounted the first production of a full-length play by August Wilson. In 1982 he convinced Wilson, by then living in St. Paul, to let him stage *Jitney* at the Allegheny Repertory Theatre (ART) in Oakland. Johnson, with co-director Beryl Berry, chose his actors from the local black theater network: Sala Udin (Black Horizon), Ron Pitts (Ujima), Milt Thompson, Monte Russell (Kuntu Repertory), and Curtiss Porter (University of Pittsburgh).[33] The production was well received by the critics. Donald Miller praised the "strikingly human performances" without "self-consciousness or carelessness in the acting. . . . All of the players seem as though they have just stepped off the street" (*Pittsburgh Post-Gazette*, Nov. 5, 1982, 21). The weekly *Market Square* noted Wilson's "rich" sense of irony and enjoyed the realism of the play's Hill District setting (Nov. 3, 1982, 4).

Experimental Theaters

Two of the most innovative experimental companies to come of age in the early 1970s were the Lovelace Marionette Theatre and the Pittsburgh Laboratory Theatre. Margo Lovelace, an alumna of art classes at the IKS and Carnegie Tech, first studied theatrical puppetry with German puppeteer Erhard Reis and Sergei Obraztsov of Moscow's Central Puppet Theater. After several years of itinerant work under different names (including Lazarus Puppets and Margo's Moppets), Lovelace established her resident marionette company first in a studio in East Liberty in 1957 and later in a 100-seat theater in a converted garage on Ellsworth Avenue in 1964. In the 1970s the company moved to the Carnegie Institute, where they staged an ambitious repertoire that included Giraudoux's *The Apollo of Bellac*, performed in 1972, Molière's *Love's the Best Physician* (1973), and Jean Cocteau's *The Wedding on the Eiffel Tower* (1967, 1970, and 1977). The Lovelace company was perhaps the most honored theater in the city, winning the bronze medal at the International Festival of Marionette Theaters in France (1972). Lovelace also produced two award-winning films (including *Museum Piece*, which was nominated for an Academy Award), traveled to Russia to teach and perform, was in residence at the Smithsonian Institution, and collaborated with Mabou Mines, Lee Breuer's avant-garde troupe. In addition, Lovelace and company collaborated locally with the Iron Clad Agreement on a production of the agitprop play *Gov't Owned Apples*, and with the Pittsburgh Public Theater on Aleksei Arbuzov's *Balyasnikov*. Over the years Lovelace and her company members taught puppeteering technique to thousands of Pittsburgh-area schoolchildren. She also mentored young apprentices, including Peter Sellars, the renowned theater and

Fig. 40. Lovelace Marionette Theatre in 1967 (Margo Lovelace at far left). Source: Unknown (Curtis Theatre Collection, University of Pittsburgh Library).

opera director, who began apprenticing with Lovelace in 1967 when he was in the sixth grade. "I had the most wonderful training in Pittsburgh," Sellars told an interviewer. "At Lovelace we'd do one adult play a season, and I'd be exposed to those and to the worlds of James Joyce and Martin Buber, who became more normal to me than popular playwrights like Tennessee Williams and Edward Albee."[34]

Exposure to new worlds was also at the heart of the Pittsburgh Laboratory Theatre, an experimental company founded by Bill Royston in 1971. In the 1960s Royston had worked a stint at the Pittsburgh Playhouse and had participated in the New Theater Workshop, a group that began meeting in 1968 at the Place, a "theater coffee shop" in Market Square, to discuss experimental theory and theatrical practice. By 1971 he was teaching at the Youth Learning Center at St. Peter's Episcopal Church in Oakland, where he produced an environmental staging of Edward Albee's *Tiny Alice*.[35] Soon after, the Pittsburgh Laboratory Theatre began its twelve-year run as the era's most aggressively avant-garde theater company.

Royston was deeply influenced by the work of Jerzy Grotowski, founder of the Polish Laboratory Theatre and the leader of a stripped-down, no-frills "poor theater" movement intended to purify the "decadent" commercial theater process. Following Grotowski, the Pittsburgh Lab explored environmental staging by using what Royston referred to as "created and negotiated" spaces. In his definition, created spaces relied on a highly conceptualized environment, such as the giant maze made of white sheets used to stage Fernando Arrabal's *The Labyrinth,* or the series of descending scaffolded platforms used in a production of Ionesco's *Exit the King.* Negotiated spaces, on the other hand, left the space as it was found, as in a 1975 production of Harold Pinter's *The Homecoming* performed in an Edwardian-era sitting room located in the St. Peter's Annex. In both cases the audience and the actors shared the same space, often sitting within a few feet of each other. Royston was also keenly interested in new definitions of what constituted a theatrical text and frequently adapted existing plays by radically cutting and resituating the action until it evolved into a new work that he labeled "environmental transformations." In addition, Royston followed Grotowski's experimental approach to rehearsal. As he explained in 1976, "First we work together in a training situation to explore ourselves, our art. These sessions are private and closed; hence, the term 'laboratory.' Next, we decide on the nature of the work, and each member defines his role within the given piece. At this point, other actors and technicians not in our company are brought in to augment our resources. These newcomers are assimilated into the training program, adding their ideas and perspectives."[36]

Over its twelve years, the Lab invited some intrigue and controversy. Royston complained of the lack of press coverage for the city's alternative troupes, his disgust with theaters run like corporations (he derisively referred to Ben Shaktman of the Pittsburgh Public Theater as a "businessman"), and his disappointment that he could not get grants because of the Lab's small audience and lack of visibility. Other problems were rooted in the Lab's controversial repertoire and its ramshackle building. In 1974 the space was vandalized and robbed of its lighting and costume stock two weeks before an opening, only to be rescued (ironically, given Royston's open criticism of local foundations) by contributions from the Pittsburgh Foundation, the Alcoa Corporation, and a few private donors. In 1975 the space was shut down during the run of *The Labyrinth* as a result of a patron's complaint over unsafe conditions in the Annex. Royston refused to believe that the complaint had anything to do with building codes, however, and blamed the incident on a "vindictive individual bent on censorship and suppression of experimental theatrical modes" (*Pittsburgh Post-Gazette*, Mar. 29, 1975, 9).

Despite its troubles, the Pittsburgh Laboratory Theatre received its non-profit, tax-exempt status and, as local funders warmed up, reached an operating budget of $100,000 by the end of the 1970s. During these years many local actors were trained and developed at the Lab, notably Bingo O'Malley and Kate Nicholas. But perhaps Royston's most lasting contribution to Pittsburgh theater was his so-phisticated and adventurous knowledge of world literature; under his guidance Pittsburgh audiences were introduced to avant-garde playwrights such as Fernando Arrabal, Jean Genet, Peter Handke, Slawomir Mrozek, and Peter Barnes.[37]

Actors' Theaters

Like their forebears during the little theater revolution, many of the small non-commercial companies that came and went during the seventies were moti-vated by a desire to choose the repertoire without worrying about box office appeal or traditional entertainment values. They tended to produce contempo-rary plays that experimented with structure, tone, characterization, and narra-tive techniques. Often they were self-described "actors' theaters" that focused on the actor as an active agent in setting the theater's aesthetic and economic agenda.

Among Pittsburgh's resident companies that fit this model were the Open Stage Theater; the Atelier Theater, the Artichoke Theater, the Fine Line Theater Company, the Workshop, Soho Repertory Company, Pennsylvania Repertory Company, the Carnegie-Mellon Theater Company, the Mattress Factory Players, the Metropolitan Stage Company (Metro), and the Odd Chair Playhouse. All were known for staging contemporary plays of serious intent and uncertain commercial appeal. These included Dos Passos's *U.S.A.* and Anouilh's *The Re-hearsal* at CMU's Atelier Theater, *Dracula/Sabbat* by Leon Katz at the Artichoke Theater, a deconstructed Shakespeare called *Measure Still for Measure* at the Penn-sylvania Repertory Theater, and an original "jazz musical" called *Liberty Avenue* at the Soho Rep. Even the more commercial actor-centered companies had their edgier moments in the seventies. Tom Thomas's Odd Chair Playhouse was best known for its polished summer stock productions of musicals (*Cabaret, Hair,* and John Guare and Mel Shapiro's Tony-winning *Two Gentlemen of Verona*). Odd Chair sometimes stepped into the realm of social commentary and dramaturgical innovation, most notably with its 1975 production of *Lenny,* about the radical comedian Lenny Bruce, which included a very young Rob Marshall in the cast.

In marked contrast to the middle-aged, middle-class amateurs of the little theater, most of the companies in the 1970s were created and run by young artists. This could reflect the rapid growth of university theater programs and a change in attitude among its graduates. A journalist noted in 1979, "It used to be that the graduates held their diplomas in one hand and one-way tickets to New York in the other. But now, rather than seeking out-of-town thespian opportunities, they are creating their own in Pittsburgh. Six of the ten companies based here were founded by CMU alumni or faculty members, two are administered by Pitt people, and the oldest group is under the direction of a Point Park grad."[38] The Pittsburgh Poor Players, for instance, founded in 1970 by a group of Carnegie Mellon graduate students, featured contemporary social problem plays, including new plays by company members. They were the first local company to produce *Sticks and Bones* (1973), David Rabe's savage satirical attack on the nation's involvement in the Vietnam War. The production featured Michael Keaton (then known as Michael Douglas) "as the shallow, guitar-playing Rick" (*Pittsburgh Post-Gazette,* June 4, 1973, 23).

Another vital student-led company was the Iron Clad Agreement, a traveling repertory company founded in 1975 by Wilson Hutton and Julia Swoyer, a doctoral candidate at Carnegie Mellon. Iron Clad produced original pieces based on Pittsburgh history from a politically left perspective. (The group's name referred to a shady business arrangement among the founding partners of Carnegie Steel.)[39] With Pittsburgh's politically complicated industrial heritage as ripe material, the Iron Clad Agreement covered a range of topics and perspectives and mounted an acclaimed stage version of Thomas Bell's *Out of This Furnace* in 1977. Working without sets or props and with the house lights on to force a "sense of community," the actors performed in nontraditional spaces such as union halls and engaged the audience in a dialogue after each performance. During the 1980–81 season, its final year in Pittsburgh, the company stopped traveling and performed a resident season at Carlow College's Antonian Hall.[40]

The most visible and critically acclaimed of the student-initiated professional companies from the seventies was Theatre Express, founded in 1975 by eleven Carnegie Mellon students as a national touring company "dedicated to the creation of exciting new expressions in theater" that included vaudeville, expressionism, mime, circus, and farce.[41] After a year on the road, under directors William Turner and Caren Harder the group launched an ambitious first season at a community center in South Oakland that included *Cat's Cradle*, the first staging of a work by Kurt Vonnegut. Over the next four years Theatre Express produced at a variety of local spaces before finding a permanent home on Baum Boulevard. It became a member of the national Theatre Communications Group and began a "developmental" relationship with Actors Equity. The repertoire was both decidedly noncommercial and adventurous: Beckett's *Endgame;* Shepard's *Angel City;* and Fassbinder's *Preparadise, Sorry Now,* and two experimental operas by Turner: *The Unlit Corridor: A Vampire Vaudeville;* and *Made by Two,* an adaptation of a Gertrude Stein play. But despite its reputation for good acting and exciting production concepts, Theatre Express had trouble finding and keeping an audience. When Turner resigned in 1980, Jed Allen Harris, associate artistic director, took over the struggling company, but it disbanded within the year after a burst water pipe caused serious damage to the theater.

Special Events

Pittsburgh had been a commercial road town since the late eighteenth century, but in 1974 a decidedly new type of road show began appearing under the auspices of the 99 Cent Floating Theatre—a quirky presenting organization headed by University of Pittsburgh theater professor Dick Mennen. The 99 Cent Floating Theatre was originally conceived as part of the Guest Company plan, a collaborative organized by Pitt, Carnegie Mellon, and the Playhouse Theater Center (under Point Park College) to bring avant-garde theater companies to Pittsburgh for short runs. The Guest Company partnership quickly folded, but Mennen pursued his mission to bring the country's leading avant-garde theater troupes to Pittsburgh audiences for less than a dollar per seat by convincing local institutions and patrons to donate space (including auditoriums and housing for the visiting performers) and getting the artists to accept a

Fig. 41. Theatre Express in Leon Katz's *The Marquis de Sade's Justine*, 1978. Source: Unknown (Curtis Theatre Collection, University of Pittsburgh Library). Courtesy of Theatre Express.

percentage of the box office receipts and additional donations (usually from passing a hat).

During its eight-year existence, the 99 Cent Floating Theatre presented an eclectic range of alternative theater that included the Iowa Theater Lab, the Multigravitational Aerodance Group, the Chicago Body Politic, the New York

Theater Commotion, Milwaukee's Theater X, the Performance Group, Mabou Mines, SQUAT, Charles Ludlam's Ridiculous Theatre Company, and a one-man show by local performance artist Stephen Pellegrino called *A Legend (in his own mind)*. In keeping with its name, the 99 Cent Floating Theatre moved from space to space and neighborhood to neighborhood. It also reached a diverse audience, as a journalist reported: "Blacks from the Hill District, teenagers from rock shows, students form everywhere, Steeler fans, symphony subscribers, and even a County Commissioner attend—and pay less than a dollar to do so."[42] When Mennen left the city in 1977, leadership of the organization was passed to Leon Katz, a playwright on the faculty of the University of Pittsburgh.[43] Under Katz the mission of the renamed Floating Theatre Company remained the same: to foster alternative theater by resisting traditional industry demands. As Katz told an interviewer in 1979, "Authenticity is the major criterion—not audience appeal."[44]

Authenticity was ostensibly the major reason for the Living Theatre Company's choice of Pittsburgh as a site for the creation of a new portion of their *Legacy of Cain* cycle. Judith Malina and Julian Beck's labor of love was perhaps the most infamous experimental performance company in the world, having spent years mounting various versions of *Paradise Now* all over Europe and the United States, including one shown at Carnegie Mellon in 1968. When a reporter asked Beck "Why Pittsburgh?" he answered that they wanted to "create for people who aren't in the habit of going to the theater. . . . It's industrial here and we wanted to break the image hard hats aren't interested" (*Pittsburgh Press*, Mar. 16, 1975, G-2). Another reason for choosing Pittsburgh must surely have been the $22,500 grant received from the A.W. Mellon Educational and Charitable Trust.

In 1974 sixteen members of the Living Theatre spent the better part of nine months in Pittsburgh researching, rehearsing, and eventually performing *The Money Tower*, their homage to the 1892 Homestead steelworkers' rebellion and the 1935 strike, which had led to the formation of the Steelworkers Organizing Committee and the United Steelworkers of America. During the residency, members of the performing collective lived together in a house on the North Side (where they put in a community garden), rehearsed at the Stephen Foster Memorial Theatre, and offered various works of protest performance, including a ritualized bloodletting in front of a Mellon Bank branch office on the North Side intended to criticize the relationship between money, power, and violence in capitalist societies.[45] In September 1975 the Living Theatre presented a series of outdoor stagings of *The Money Tower* over a three-week period. The set was a forty-foot steel structure with five wooden platforms between which the actors moved and from which they scattered fake money. The tower could be assembled and knocked down in an hour. The company performed *The Money Tower* on the streets in Homestead, Hazelwood, Manchester, Braddock, the South Side, and the Hill District.

A year later, America's bicentennial prompted a variety of special theatrical productions, from Don Brockett's *Celebration '76*—an open-air musical revue staged outside the Gateway Center office towers—to community pageants created and performed in Mt. Lebanon, Turtle Creek, Allison Park, and the Hill District. The most significant of these events was *Steel/City*, an original full-length documentary play about the history of Pittsburgh's steel industry by Gillette Elvgren and Attilio Favorini of the University of Pittsburgh. Like Bartley Campbell's *The Lower Millions* of almost a century earlier, *Steel/City* sought to explore Pittsburgh's working-class psyche by looking closely at events in the city's industrial past. But whereas Campbell's melodramatic story line was largely invented, Favorini and Elvgren located their characters and dialogue in actual events taken from archival sources, autobiographies, steel company records, minutes of union meetings, letters, and interviews. The entire third act, for example, was taken verbatim from oral histories. *Steel/City* opened in March 1976 as part of Pitt Rep's annual season and was revived that summer with the original student cast. NBC's *Today Show* broadcast twelve minutes of the work on live television, and the full production was invited to be a part of the Smithsonian Institution's Festival of American Folklife in August. Other productions were staged in the summers of 1977, 1978, and 1992.[46]

City Players Company and the Pittsburgh Public Theater

In 1974 Louise Brown, city parks director, began work toward creating a municipally funded professional theater company to occupy the new Allegheny Community Theater, located in the former Carnegie Free Library and Music Hall (built in 1889) that had recently been renovated into a flexible 200-seat performance space.[47] With a grant from the Comprehensive Employment and Training Act

Fig. 42. The Allegheny Community Theater under construction, 1972. Source: Unknown (Curtis Theatre Collection, University of Pittsburgh Library).

(CETA), a federal initiative to support community-based arts programming in U.S. cities, Brown hired Marjorie Walker, an instructor at Carnegie Mellon, to assemble a troupe of trained actors, designers, technicians, and craftsmen. The City Players, Pittsburgh's first municipally sponsored professional theater company, was charged with performing and teaching in the community twelve months of the year.[48]

The City Players began by leading theater workshops for schoolchildren in recreation centers and classrooms, before offering its first season of free performances at the Allegheny Community Theater in the summer of 1975 with productions of *The Death and Life of Sneaky Fitch* by James Rosenberg and a stage version of Bram Stoker's *Dracula*. The press responded with enthusiasm. The *Post-Gazette's* Donald Miller commented on "the most unusual set seen here in memory" and described it as the best local staging he could recall (Aug. 19, 1975, 24). That fall the City Players toured high schools and senior citizen centers with a production of *A Christmas Carol,* then returned to the Allegheny Community Theater in January 1976 with *The Beggar's Opera*, directed by Gregory Lehane.

This pattern of alternating a touring season in schools and community centers with a resident season at the Allegheny Community Theater continued for the next three years under the direction of Mark Lione, who replaced Walker as artistic director in 1977. During these formative years the City Players built its reputation by producing a mixture of contemporary American plays, among them *Sexual Perversity in Chicago,* original works such as Carnegie Mellon professor Jewell Walker's *Tuesday* and *The Circus,* and classics like *Waiting for Lefty, The Misanthrope,* and *Bus Stop.*

While the City Players began with a rare showing of local government support, the Pittsburgh Public Theater was launched through the more common practice of private patronage. In 1973 Margaret Rieck and Joan Apt, who had long served the local arts community, began exploring the possibility of founding a new professional resident theater in town. Both were motivated by the city's bad reputation in the national theatrical press (particularly Martin Gottfried's scathing indictment of the Playhouse's audience) and rejected the notion that Pittsburgh could not support a professional noncommercial theater. As Rieck said in 1985: "I found myself thinking it's absurd theater can't succeed in Pittsburgh, which has so many universities and is the third largest corporate headquarters. It began to be a patriotism, a loyalty and a defensiveness about Pittsburgh."[49] Apt had close ties with local foundations and knew how to navigate the funding terrain. Rieck was in conversation with two of the city's leading cultural gatekeepers—Richard Cyert, president of Carnegie Mellon University, and Mellon Bank's Andrew Mathieson—both of whom encouraged her to pursue the idea. Together they enlisted Ben Shaktman, a young New York director, and in 1974 the three began formulating a blueprint for a resident professional theater company modeled on the criteria outlined by the League of Resident Theatres (LORT), including the use of union-affiliated actors and directors (which differentiated them from the non-Equity City Players). In 1974–75 the three made the rounds of local philanthropies, galvanizing interest in the project, obtaining promises of financial support, and assembling a board of directors.[50]

In 1975 Mayor Peter Flaherty agreed to donate the Allegheny Community Theater for four months of the year—an arrangement that would split the use of the city-owned playhouse between the City Players and the new Pittsburgh Public Theater. Led by a fourteen-member board of directors and a forty-member Advisory and Development Council, the Public became the first Pittsburgh theater to

Fig. 43. City Players Company performing *Androcles and the Lion* in a city park, 1975.
Source: Unknown (Curtis Theatre Collection, University of Pittsburgh Library).

join the League of Resident Theatres (founded in 1965 in order to represent the
interests of nonprofit regional theaters and to conduct special contract negotiations with Actors' Equity Association).[51] The company's first season featured
The Glass Menagerie, Twelfth Night, with Leonard Nimoy as Malvolio, and a highly
regarded production of *One Flew Over the Cuckoo's Nest* starring Tom Atkins, a
Pittsburgh actor with a growing national reputation.[52] They ended in the black—
the $444,000 operating budget was raised through box office receipts and grants
from local charitable foundations—having served 7,100 subscribers. The press
reviews were largely positive, especially for Atkins's portrayal of the tragicomic
McMurphy in *Cuckoo's Nest.* The following fall the PPT returned with productions of *Henry V* and a new translation of *Uncle Vanya,* both directed by Shaktman, as well as the first staging of Athol Fugard's *Sizwe Bansi Is Dead* outside
New York City, directed by the New Federal Theater's Woodie King Jr. (August
Wilson once told *Post-Gazette* theater critic Chris Rawson that this production of
Sizwe was the first complete piece of theater he ever sat through.) Again the
fledgling company ended the season in the black, playing to a total of 36,707 people, a group that included over 10,000 subscribers.

By the start of its third season at the Allegheny Community Theater, the Public had become the most visible and fiscally strongest theater company in the city. The local press routinely touted it as the "only professional" company in town, despite the ongoing work of the City Players, who continued to share the Allegheny Community Theater with the PPT. The Public was not without its critics, however. According to *Pittsburgh Magazine*,

> [Many locals] resent the PPT because its General Director, Ben Shaktman, is not a Pittsburgher, nor are most of the principals involved in his productions. Shaktman . . . appoints mostly New York directors, auditions and casts mostly New York actors, imports mostly technical people from New York. Since the PPT was established, more than three years ago, not one of its 11 plays have been directed by a Pittsburgher . . . Then why call it the Pittsburgh Public Theater, people ask? . . . The theater has nothing to do with Pittsburgh really.[53]

Shaktman countered this growing critique by making the point that a professional theater was required to hire from outside and noted that city residents did not expect the professional athletic teams to hire Pittsburghers. Despite the tension between the Public's staff and the local theater community, however, the company continued to grow steadily, adding a casting coordinator and a publicity director, expanding to a five-play season, and initiating special event programming funded through a grant from the National Endowment for the Arts.

By the late seventies the repertoire had settled into a seasonal recipe consistent with most of the nation's LORT companies: a mixture of international classics, American classics, recent hits from off Broadway, and occasionally a work from the avant-garde or political theater. Between 1977 and 1979, for example, the Public staged *The Importance of Being Earnest, The Seagull, Mr. Roberts, For Colored Girls Who Have Considered Suicide When the Rainbow Is Enuf,* and *Slow Dance on the Killing Ground,* all to extremely positive reviews. By the end of its fourth season, the company had 13,500 annual subscribers and was playing to over 97 percent capacity.[54] With an operating budget of $785,369, it had become the strongest and most prominent theater company in the city's history.[55]

By 1979, Pittsburgh was in the unusual position of having its two professional resident theater companies operating, rent free, out of the same space: the Allegheny Community Theater. When the Public Theater petitioned the city to

Fig. 44. Pittsburgh Public Theater performance at the Hazlett Theater, 1980. Source: The Darkroom, courtesy of the Pittsburgh Public Theater.

extend its lease to nine months a year, what had been a low-simmering tension between the two groups came to a boil. In April 1979 Mayor Richard Caliguiri agreed to grant the Public an extended lease for the following season (at the token price of one dollar per year). That decision rendered the City Players Company essentially homeless, since the company could not survive as a professional producer with only a three-month season. The resulting controversy played out in the local press and within the theater community. City Players Artistic Director Mark Lione resigned, because he could not "justify that the city would give three-fourths of its theater to an outside group when they have their own company" and complained that no one from Citiparks or the mayor's office ever explained the rationale behind the decision.[56] Whatever the reason, by 1979 the Pittsburgh Public Theater clearly had broader community support (including a powerful board of directors) and a larger audience, and was thus better positioned to be regarded as Pittsburgh's leading "professional theater company." The PPT launched its fifth anniversary season in the Allegheny Community Theater with five plays, including Sam Shepard's *Buried Child*, which had just won the Pulitzer Prize for drama. The City Players Company, with ongoing CETA funding, continued to conduct workshops in the schools. In 1979 the University of Pittsburgh offered the City Players a new home, including office space and the use of its Studio Theater in the Cathedral of Learning. A deal was struck, and by early 1980 the troupe was embarking on a new institutional identity.

9

THEATER AS CULTURAL CAPITAL

The 1980s

Pittsburgh, July 26, 1985. At 7:40 P.M. the afternoon downpour has given way to a hot and humid summer evening. Downtown along Penn Avenue, a middle-aged husband and wife are hurrying as fast as they can across Sixth Street, past a crowd of young children dressed in their Sunday best, and through the ornate bronze doors of Heinz Hall to see the Civic Light Opera's production of *The Man of La Mancha.* Four miles to the east, a more casually dressed crowd outside the Stephen Foster Memorial in Oakland stands on the stone steps listening to an Elizabethan-style troupe of strolling musicians before heading inside to see the Shakespeare Festival's dark, edgy version of *Measure for Measure.* A quarter mile up Forbes Avenue, another crowd presses into CMU's tiny Studio Theater for the Metro's production of *Agnes of God,* while a mile to the east, others stream into Chatham College's Eddy Theater to see the American Ibsen Theater's highly touted version of *The Dutch Courtesan.* In nearby Garfield, college-age patrons are climbing up the dark, dirty stairwell that leads into the New Group Theatre's open loft, where inside an assortment of fans are blowing in a vain attempt to cool off the space before the lights go up on Strindberg's *Creditors*. And a few more miles to the north, people in shorts and halter tops gather under a tent at Hartwood Acres to see the CMU Repertory Theater's staging of *Sweeney Todd*, despite the warning in today's *Post-Gazette* review: "CMU's 'Sweeney Todd' not summertime froth."[1]

∽⤫∾

The Cultural District and the Benedum Center for the Performing Arts

In the 1970s a small group of political and corporate leaders led by Jack Heinz began engineering another urban renewal effort for Pittsburgh's downtown triangle. Renaissance II was launched in 1981 with an overhaul of the aging Market Square area anchored by the magnificent Pittsburgh Plate Glass complex of six buildings designed by Philip Johnson and John Burgee. A wave of Gilded Age–like conspicuous construction quickly followed: Mellon Bank Centre, Oxford Centre, Fifth Avenue Place, and Two Chatham Center, confirming Pittsburgh's status as the third largest corporate headquarters in the United States and its *Rand-McNally Almanac* rating as "America's most livable city" in 1984. But there the analogy with the city's Gilded Age ends. The promised business expansions failed to materialize as anticipated; instead, the 1980s saw a devastating downturn in the region's industrial economy and a dramatic population decline, as a century of steel production came to a catastrophic end with the loss of more than 100,000 union jobs.[2]

A key feature of Renaissance II, the part that eventually came to fruition, was the drive to establish a performing arts district along the historic Penn-Liberty corridor—the same stretch that had once housed the dime museums, variety and burlesque theaters, amusement halls, and destination playhouses of the past. The Cultural District, an ambitious real estate initiative, emerged from a series of studies commissioned by the Allegheny Conference and the Heinz Endowments. Like the so-called Cultural Acropolis of Renaissance I, the Cultural District plan saw the arts as an economic engine capable of revitalizing the downtown and

Fig. 45. Three Rivers Shakespeare Festival's Good Companions performing on the steps of the Stephen Foster Memorial Theatre, 1980. Source: Gary Grant, courtesy of the University of Pittsburgh's Department of Theatre Arts.

stimulating the city's economy. But unlike the earlier scheme, which called for new construction and the near wholesale demolition of an established city neighborhood, the Cultural District initiative involved the rehabilitation and reuse of historic buildings.[3] In 1983 the Cultural District initiative was folded into the newly created Pittsburgh Trust for Cultural Resources, a not-for-profit organization managed by board chairman Robert Dickey III, then by Carol Brown, who became the organization's first president in 1986. Under Brown a public relations campaign re-envisioned the once dirty, seedy Penn-Liberty area as a place where "on any night of the year" Pittsburghers would be able to experience "performances by major cultural groups . . . experimental theater . . . the sound of rehearsals . . . a revamped Penn Liberty corridor, filled with pedestrians . . . proud 19th century architecture setting off exciting new buildings . . . tree-lined shopping streets and late-hour crowds in the restaurants . . . [and] concerts in the riverfront park."[4]

The Cultural Trust's first major project was to restore and renovate the Stanley Theatre at Seventh and Penn—a $43 million public-private effort launched in 1983 with the help of a $17 million Urban Development Action Grant and support from the Benedum Foundation.[5] It had become increasingly clear that Heinz Hall could not accommodate the demands of the Pittsburgh Symphony Orchestra, which owned the building, as well as the Pittsburgh Opera, the Pittsburgh Ballet Theatre, the Civic Light Opera, the Pittsburgh Dance Council, road shows, and other special bookings. The project's goal was to provide the city's major performing arts companies with a handsome, well-equipped auditorium and newly constructed rehearsal rooms, dressing rooms, and office space, while restoring the best features of the original 1928 movie palace.

The Benedum Center for the Performing Arts opened in September 1987. The inaugural gala, produced by the Civic Light Opera, featured local artists who performed works by Pittsburgh song writers ranging from Stephen Foster to Fred Rogers, the children's television innovator.[6] The press saw the event as a sign that the postwar vision of renewal through the arts was finally coming true for Pittsburgh. The Benedum marked the "second cornerstone" of the plan, the first being Heinz Hall, which had opened in 1971. Proceeds from ticket sales at the Benedum were projected to be $7.5 million per year. "You don't need to get out your calculator to figure out that that would enrich the city by $750,000 in amusement taxes."[7] The new Benedum Center was the first really significant sign of the Cultural Trust's potential as a cultural force. It also proved what arts funders and arts managers had been claiming since 1982, when an economic impact study conducted by the Pittsburgh–Allegheny County Cultural Alliance showed that local arts organizations generated significant income through salaries, wages for professional services, taxes, and locally purchased materials and supplies.[8] For many Pittsburghers, then, seeing the lights of the Benedum Center marquee go on for the first time indicated that in postindustrial Pittsburgh the arts were not only good for the city's heart and soul, but also good for its bottom line.

Seeding the Resident Theater Boom

In the 1980s, Pittsburgh's resident independent theaters became more influential, economically viable, and publicly visible than ever before, transforming what had essentially been an alternative, underground movement into a mainstream cultural commodity. This was largely the result of new fiscal strategies for funding arts organizations, owing to the nearly wholesale adoption of 501(c)3 nonprofit IRS status. Even small-budget theater companies could seek operating support from charitable foundations and individual donors willing to support the arts in exchange for a tax write-off. This in turn influenced the funding practices of the local foundations, with Ted Hazlett of the Mellon Foundation leading the charge. Reluctance to fund what had been labeled "community arts" gradually gave way to a generous flow of grants for local arts groups, including small theaters. Soon foundations were not only funding local theater companies, they were also recognizing the value of small arts groups to the larger cultural community. By the early 1980s, a new generation of program officers, notably William Lafe and Janet Sarbaugh of the Pittsburgh Foundation and the Heinz Endowments, considered advocacy for small arts organizations to be a critical component of their positions.

In 1979 fourteen theater companies united to form the Alliance of Theaters, a coalition of professional theatrical groups in the Pittsburgh area. The alliance indicated a new vitality in local theater. "You need a few strong groups to feel strong, and now we have them," noted Margo Lovelace. The goals of the alliance were similar to those of the Federation of Non-commercial Theaters and the Negro Drama League during the 1930s: to provide a network for sharing information, resources, and support and to bolster the role of theater in the local culture. One key difference was that most resident theaters of the seventies were nonprofit corporations, not all-volunteer civic clubs. As such, they had to compete in the arts marketplace—that is, they had to attract a real audience. As Leon Katz of the Floating Theatre observed in 1979: "Two things are primary. Visibility and money, and then we go forward together. No matter what, the theater groups are here and growing all the time. The only thing they will succumb to is inattention" (*Pittsburgh Press*, Oct. 14, 1979, E-2).

Indeed, inattention, particularly from the local press, must have contributed to the malaise that had settled on Pittsburgh's theater culture after World War II. In the 1950s and 1960s, the *Pittsburgh Press*, the *Sun-Telegraph*, and the *Post-Gazette*, the city's three remaining dailies, were no longer reviewing the work of independent theaters, even though these papers had devoted considerable space to the little theater movement of the 1930s. And even as the resident theater movement began to change the landscape in the 1970s, the daily papers continued to review only the "professional" theaters: the Pittsburgh Public Theater, the Civic Light Opera, and the touring commercial shows. "I'm puzzled by the lack of interest from the critics," the Metro's David Ball remarked in 1979. "If critics must exist, they should be part of the process of a city's theatrical development. My hope is that theater criticism grows with theater in Pittsburgh."[9] Given these conditions, the theater community turned to the city's small, alternative publications for coverage and support. But although Bruce Steele (of the *University Times*), Michele Pilecki (*Market Square*), Richard Mennen (*Pittsburgh New Sun*), and Alice Carter (*North Hills News Record*) were writing thoughtful and well-informed reviews, in the later 1970s and early 1980s these small-circulation weeklies simply could not affect mainstream consumer habits or influence potential funders.

That situation had changed by the mid-1980s, however, when both the *Post-Gazette* and the *Press* were using writers specifically hired to cover the work of the local companies. Previews and reviews by Christopher Rawson and Susan Harris Smith were serious, well informed, and inherently enthusiastic about the role of indigenous theater in Pittsburgh. And while Rawson and Smith were certainly not the first well-trained critics working for Pittsburgh dailies, they were the first to emphasize the role of the local, noncommercial theater industry over the commercial stage. Their reporting and critical writing had a significant influence on changing the standards for covering local theater.

New Resident Theaters of the 1980s

Twenty-six new theater companies were founded in Pittsburgh during the 1980s. Some lasted only a season or two; others lasted longer but did not survive the decade. Still others continued into the 1990s.[10] Most of these theater companies fit the actors' theater model of the 1970s; that is, the actors set their own aesthetic and economic agendas. Certainly that describes the New Group Theatre, which was founded in 1982 by a small collective of local actors interested in "the production of plays, old and new, that have a strong, relevant statement to make about the world around us . . . [and] new plays, particularly by local playwrights."[11] In 1983 the company rented space in an old building in Garfield where they produced low-budget, high-energy stagings of many neglected playwrights of the modernist canon, including Dario Fo, T. S. Eliot, Emanuel Fried, and Jean Cocteau. The New Group also staged new plays by several company members, notably Cheryl Young and Martin Giles, the latter developing a reputation as a witty, wordy, and cerebral playwright "intoxicated with language" and the power of theatrical metaphor.[12]

Glen Gress and Edward Kinchley Evans's Acting Company (originally called the Laurel Highlands Regional Theatre Company) also made its mark beginning in 1985 with a mission to "invite and encourage our audiences to join with us in our study of the human condition."[13] The Acting Company purchased an unused church in Lawrenceville, where they presented an expansive repertoire that included both familiar works (plenty of Tennessee Williams, for instance) and obscure work such as a stage adaptation of the expressionist film *The Cabinet of Dr. Caligari* and original pieces by Evans, the company's playwright-in-residence. Still another actor-managed company was the Upstairs Theater, founded in 1988 by E. Bruce Hill, Denise Pullen, Clare Ratway, and Tom McLaughlin. After a nomadic existence, including stints at a gallery, a church, and an Italian beneficial society, the Upstairs Theater eventually settled in an old industrial building on Penn Avenue, where they produced a wide range of contemporary American plays.

The actors' theater model was not the only game in town, however. The Allegheny Repertory Theatre emerged in 1980 as a producing agency designed to help "talented Pittsburghers gain the exposure and recognition they deserve."

The ART was a self-described "melting pot for Allegheny County's theatrical community," providing administrative, design, and technical support for several fledgling companies and for many highly regarded independent productions, including Bob Johnson's staging of August Wilson's *Jitney* in 1982.[14] During this period the ART also produced its own shows (*Look Back in Anger, Travesties, March of the Falsettos, Beyond Therapy*) at the Lion Walk Arts Center and the Famous Rider. Another group of the era, Pellekin Multi-Arts, Inc., stood out because of the idiosyncratic vision of the company's founder and artist-in-residence, Stephen Pellegrino, a self-described blue-collar artist. Pellegrino wrote, composed, choreographed, designed, and performed (sometimes alone, and sometimes with a changing cast of local actors, musicians, and dancers) under the Pellekin umbrella beginning in the late 1970s. In 1985 he launched his Drywall series—a kind of ongoing meditation on the "frenzied existence between the world of the blue collar worker and that of the artist" that served both as homage to and as a critique of Pittsburgh's industrial heritage and working-class ethos.[15] During the 1980s and beyond, Pellegrino/Pellekin's Drywall events took various forms, from dance concerts to museum installations to full-blown spectacle theatricals, and were performed in museums, playhouses, and various outdoor sites around the city.

In some ways, however, the most radical theater company of the 1980s was the American Ibsen Theater, "the people who made Scandinavian angst a mainstay of summer entertainment."[16] The AIT was founded in 1983 by Michael Zelenak and Rick Davis, Yale School of Drama graduates whose goal was to rescue Ibsen's plays from the dusty restraints of the realistic stage. "We make no pretense of reality," Davis noted in an interview. "We don't want to tie the theater down to trying to imitate real life. We ought to do more. We think the theater should be thrilling."[17] During its three summer seasons in residence at the Chatham College Eddy Theater, the American Ibsen Theater was both thrilling and unconventional, thanks to its vividly conceptual directors and the visceral work of resident set designer Christopher Barreca. The inaugural production of *A Doll House* turned Nora's famous parlor into an empty expanse framed by eighteen doors "arranged in a rigid line diagonally across the stage to capture the characters in a sort of domestic cage" (*Market Square*, June 29, 1983, 3). The company's emotionally charged production of *Ghosts* put the audience directly on the stage (seated amid several tons of trucked-in dirt) and looking out into an empty auditorium—a staging conceit that culminated in the "slow, painful closing of the curtain at the end . . . sealing audience and actors into the claustrophobia of Osvald's brain" (*Post-Gazette*, June 4, 1986, 21). The AIT's best-known production was the 1984 gender-bending version of *Hedda Gabler* directed by Carnegie-Mellon's Mel Shapiro, which featured Charles Ludlum, founder of the Ridiculous Theatre, in the title role. Shapiro warned in the theater's newsletter: "People will have to understand that when they walk into the theater, it's anything goes time. And I think that was the intention of Ibsen's writing, too; it was anything goes. He's writing about an outrageous woman who, unfortunately for herself, wasn't outrageous enough."[18] The American Ibsen Theater folded after its third season for the usual financial reasons, but not before establishing a loyal following and a national reputation based on its bold production concepts and the scholarly celebrity of its four dramaturgs, Rolf Fjelde, Brian Johnston, Leon Katz, and Royston Coppenger.

The Three Rivers Shakespeare Festival

In terms of audience numbers, the most successful new theater initiative of this era was the Three Rivers Shakespeare Festival, founded in 1980 by Attilio Favorini as a semiprofessional theater company in residence at the University of Pittsburgh. The city's first classical repertory theater began with a marketing campaign that deliberately alluded both to the city's working-class heritage and to the current success of its professional sports teams, which had won the World Series in 1979 and the Super Bowl in 1980. Favorini announced in interviews that his group would offer "vigorous, vital, unpretentious Shakespeare, because that's what the city is like" (*Pittsburgh New Sun*, June 26, 1980, 5). Despite such civic boosterism, however, Favorini's first program message acknowledged the considerable challenge of mounting a classical theater company in the Steel City. He noted, "The world knows us for our laboring strength, industrial might, ethnic richness, and invincible athletes—and well it should. But much of our burgeoning culture remains obscured, as if the darkness at noon which used to blight our city still hung over the streets. Our logo of 'Shakespeare rising' is partially an image of light shed on that part of the city still overshadowed."[19]

The Shakespeare Festival's inaugural season at the Stephen Foster Memorial

Theatre featured *The Taming of the Shrew* and *Romeo and Juliet*, performed by professionals from the City Theatre (at that time under contract with the university) and Pitt graduate students. The house directors were Gillette Elvgren, Stephen Coleman, and Kathleen George; the house designers were Henry Heymann, Tony Ferrieri, and Lorraine Venberg; and the composer-in-residence was Christine Frezza. The festival atmosphere was enhanced by picnic suppers on the lawn outside the theater accompanied by Good Companions, a group of Elizabethan-costumed players and singers, as well as by several free outdoor performances hosted by Pittsburgh Citiparks and staged nearby in Schenley Park. The first few seasons were extremely successful, garnering both large (near sellout) houses and excellent reviews. The buzz even caught the attention of a writer for the *Wall Street Journal*, who noted that "the free 'Romeo' drew 800 people, 200 more than could be seated."[20] And just as the Pittsburgh Public Theater had done in the mid-1970s, the Shakespeare Festival quickly established itself as a key cultural commodity among civic leaders. "It used to be that you had to go to one of the Stratfords—England, Ontario, or Connecticut—to see Shakespearean drama at its best. No longer," noted the *Pittsburgh Post-Gazette*: "Shakespeare is alive and well in Pittsburgh" (July 16, 1982, 8).

By 1984 Pittsburgh was the home of the fifth largest Shakespeare Festival in the United States, according to the Shakespeare Association of America, and was using Equity actors under guest artist contracts. The festival company had expanded its programming to include appearances at schools and special fundraisers by internationally recognized classical actors like Claire Bloom and Derek Jacobi. The group continued to expand as a "professional classical theater in residence at the University of Pittsburgh" and added a parallel two-play season by the Young Company, a graduate student troupe that staged low-budget postmodern interpretations of works by Shakespeare and related contemporary playwrights, including the area's first production of Ann-Marie MacDonald's *Good Night Desdemona, Good Morning Juliet*. In the late 1980s, the Shakespeare Festival embarked upon an era of more intellectually adventurous staging. Of note were Coleman's *Julius Caesar*, described as "a soaring symphonic tribute to Shakespeare's austere Roman tragedy," Elvgren's insightful *Merchant of Venice*, with a "rich vein of farcical humor and genuine compassion for the misused Shylock," and guest director Yosef Yzraely's wrenching *Measure for Measure*, with a memorable dance of death at the end featuring "a small globe spinning in a pool of

Fig. 46. Three Rivers Shakespeare Festival's "Superbard" brochure, 1989. Source: Tim Hartman, courtesy of the University of Pittsburgh's Department of Theatre Arts.

light."[21] By the end of its tenth season in August 1989, the nationally recognized Three Rivers Shakespeare Festival had played to over 250,000 patrons.

Commercial Theater

The renovations of Heinz Hall and the Benedum Center significantly expanded the city's capacity to host large-scale commercial touring shows, thus launching a new era for Pittsburgh as a "road town." By the late 1980s the Pittsburgh Symphony's Broadway series and the PACE Theatrical Group were regularly importing "bus and truck companies" which, like the combination companies of the late nineteenth century, produced recent Broadway hits featuring nationally known performers—though usually not the stars of the Broadway stage, who preferred to make their big money in television and film. But these big-ticket imports were not the only commercial theater in town during the decade: locally based producers, including On Cue Productions, Unicorn Productions, J. Pohl Associates, and Patina Productions, also mounted commercial shows in dinner theaters and cabaret clubs in and around the city.

One of the most noteworthy of the local commercial producers was Don Brockett, a writer, actor, director, teacher, and producer who began his theatrical career as the musical director at the Wagon Wheel Playhouse in 1949. In 1960 Brockett wrote a satirical musical revue for public television station WQED called *Who Needs a Show Train?* Its success led to a series of stage revues produced in various venues in and around Pittsburgh, as well as several engagements elsewhere, most notably in Phoenix with comedienne Phyllis Diller in 1964 and several bookings in New York City that culminated in an off-Broadway run of *Sweet Feet* in 1972. *Who Needs a Show Train?* also marked the beginning of Brockett's thirty-five-year partnership with comedienne and actress Barbara Russell.

By the early 1980s Brockett Productions was a wide-ranging commercial enterprise that included everything from successful tours of Brockett's *Big Bad Burlesque,* performed at New York's Orpheum Theater, to hundreds of industrial shows featuring local performers in song and dance numbers designed to sell products. (Trade fairs and sales meetings have provided a rigorous training ground for several generations of local performers who went on to national careers.) But it was the Brockett and Barbara revues, with their unflinching spoofs on Pittsburgh life (*Sunday Afternoon at the Airport, Babushka Power, Last Polka in Pittsburgh, Yinz Air,* a local-dialect reference to USAir), that set his work apart. The *Post-Gazette* reviewer praised them for "their irrepressible high spirits and their determined resistance to anything hinting of civic niceness. . . . Brockett's slashing remarks about our political figures have never been more cutting and more hilarious" (Feb. 15, 1977, 11). In a similar vein, Brockett began producing *Forbidden Pittsburgh,* modeled on the long-running *Forbidden Broadway* musical spoofs, in 1985. By putting new lyrics to familiar show tunes, Brockett's annual summer installments satirized local culture with songs about everything from the mayor's pronounced Pittsburgh accent to a streetwalker bemoaning the rapidly disappearing sex trade along the Penn-Liberty corridor ("Give Me Liberty or Give Me Penn"). Brockett's satirical voice and unflinching perspective were called "downright ruthless" and "slashing,"[22] yet his *Forbidden Pittsburgh* lyrics could also be unabashedly sentimental, as in this version of "One" from *A Chorus Line*: "One, Thank you, Rand

McNally, We always knew what you have found. One, Pardon while we rally, We're ten feet off the ground. One final moment as all of us point with pride. We frankly love the great city where we reside."[23] Brockett's loyalty to his hometown clearly informed all his work.

The University Theaters

Among the city's three degree-granting theater programs, the most significant growth occurred at Point Park College, where the presence of the professional Playhouse Theater Center helped to push the undergraduate training to new levels of intensity and rigor during the 1980s. Under director James Prescott and a faculty that included Ken Gargaro, Don Wadsworth, Kate Young, Raymond Laine, and William Duncan, the college's ambitious bachelor of fine arts conservatory programs began producing well-trained musical theater performers who went on to professional careers in New York and Los Angeles.[24] Carnegie Mellon University continued to produce highly polished actors, directors, and designers, as it had done for seventy years. And at the University of Pittsburgh new master of fine arts programs in acting and directing and a doctoral program in theater studies increased the number of talented and (near) professional-level artists living and working in the city.

In terms of enriching local theater, however, the two most significant byproducts of these academic training programs were the professional activities of the faculty and the intellectual enrichment provided by the university repertoire. At Carnegie Mellon University, Mel Shapiro and Donald Marinelli started the Carnegie-Mellon Repertory Theater in a tent at Hartwood Acres, a county park north of the city, in the summer of 1984. Playwriting professor Arthur Giron developed a working relationship with the Public Theater, where his *Becoming Memories* and *Edith Stein* were produced in 1985 and 1987. And Barbara and Cletus Anderson, senior faculty of CMU's prestigious design program, worked prolifically as costume and set designers at several area professional theaters as well as for locally produced television and films, including several directed by George Romero.[25]

University of Pittsburgh faculty artists worked regularly with the Three Rivers Shakespeare Festival and City Theatre, where the institutional relationship allowed for regular cross-pollination between the academic and professional sectors. Pitt Repertory Theatre continued to connect to the larger community through programming that emphasized the relationship between theater and civic life. In 1983, the university worked with local Jewish organizations to co-sponsor a Jewish Play Festival and Jewish Playwriting Conference. Featured were productions of *The Windows of Heaven*, a postwar piece about the Jewish ghetto in Lodz, and C. P. Taylor's *Good*, a controversial new play about the metamorphosis of an average citizen into one of Hitler's "exterminators."

Above all, Pittsburgh's wealth of university and college theaters—Duquesne, Chatham, Carlow, and Robert Morris—influenced the local arts ecology by giving theater patrons opportunities to see rarely produced plays. In 1984 Carnegie Mellon staged *The Greeks*, a massive stage spectacle from the Royal Shakespeare Company that combined plays by Aeschylus, Sophocles, and Euripides with sections of *The Iliad* and *The Odyssey*. The nine-hour performance, which featured a student cast, could be seen in one day if one chose. Another challenging production for this era was Peter Harrigan's controversial staging of *Spring Awakening* at the University of Pittsburgh in 1987, in which Frank Wedekind's story of the "vigorous intelligence, nervous energy and mercurial temper of youth" included a pantomimed masturbation sequence and a homosexual kiss (*Pittsburgh Press*, Oct. 29, 1987, D-4).

A Decade of Stabilization and Institutionalization

In the early 1980s several of Pittsburgh's established theater companies—the Lab, the Express, the Floating Theatre—went under, while others reached new levels of maturity. One actor-centered company that thrived for a time was the Metro. In the words of Carnegie-Mellon professor David Ball, it was a theater "like Shakespeare's and Molière's. Each actor has a share in the company—its policies, its work, or its profits."[26] The original group was made up of ten actors pulled from professional companies all over the United States (including the La Mama Experimental Theater Company in New York, the Guthrie in Minneapolis, and the American Conservatory Theatre in San Francisco), but by the 1980s the Metro had evolved into a summer Equity house performing in Carnegie Mellon's Studio Theater. Although the Metro garnered consistently good reviews

Fig. 47. The Metro's production of *A Midsummer Night's Dream*,
1981. Source: Unknown (Curtis Theatre Collection, University of
Pittsburgh Library).

and had a loyal subscription audience (cultivated over the years by Ball through
a series of charmingly eccentric "dear subscriber" letters), the company could
not survive the loss of its CMU space in the fall of 1985 and disbanded shortly
thereafter.

A number of organizations continued to flourish during the 1980s. Under
Vernell Lillie's leadership, Kuntu Repertory Theatre produced at least one Rob

Penny play each season, in addition to works from the evolving Black Arts canon, notably a 1984 production of *A Raisin in the Sun* that featured television star Esther Rolle, and the critically esteemed Pittsburgh premiere of August Wilson's *Ma Rainey's Black Bottom* in 1987. During this period Kuntu also toured its theme-driven multimedia collages (*Profiles in Black, Lift Every Voice and Sing, Still I Rise*) to colleges and performance festivals as far-flung as the New Orleans Jazz Heritage Festival and the Edinburgh Fringe Festival in Scotland. The Civic Light Opera, which had essentially been reborn in 1971 when it became a resident of Heinz Hall under the guidance of the charismatic W. L. Thunhurst, entered the 1980s fully revitalized. Charles Gray, a stage director whose career had often brought him to Pittsburgh and the CLO, became executive director and general manager in 1983. Gray raised the visibility of the company, which moved to the Benedum Center in 1987, and helped to found the National Alliance for Musical Theater, a consortium of light opera companies from Connecticut to California that shared costs by mounting joint productions. During the eighties the CLO continued to cast local professional talent in featured roles and to use locally trained singers and dancers in the chorus, among them future Tony Award winners Rob Marshall, Kathleen Marshall, and Rob Ashford. The Playhouse Theater Center also underwent a rebirth when it affiliated with Point Park College. In 1984 the old Craft Street stage was refurbished and christened the Rockwell Theater with a production of *A Little Night Music*, launching an era of producing large-scale musicals featuring Equity leads and choruses cast with talented students from Point Park College's conservatory training programs in dance and musical theater.

The City Players and the Pittsburgh Public Theater grew substantially during the 1980s, becoming the region's dominant year-round companies. The City Players had the roughest journey, beginning with the loss of the Allegheny Community Theater on the North Side in 1979. The company was offered a new home at the University of Pittsburgh, where it was renamed the City Theatre under the direction of Pitt faculty member Stephen Wyman.[27] When Marc Masterson became artistic director in January 1981, he was immediately confronted with a more serious problem: under Ronald Reagan the federal government ended its sponsorship of the CETA program, which had been paying his and the actors' salaries. Operating funds now had to come from other sources, including in-kind support from the University of Pittsburgh and a new contract with the presenting organization Gateway to Music to produce children's theater in the schools. Over the next few years, core members of City Theatre (Masterson, Larry John Meyers, Holly Thuma, Michael Cook, David Kuhns, and John Hall) toured local schools by day and in the evening rehearsed and performed at the New City Theater, a 115-seat facility on Bouquet Street owned by the university. With its own performance space and administrative support provided by Pitt's theater arts department, the City Theatre had a clear advantage over other small resident companies. As Masterson recalls, "We could put every dollar we had into artists. I didn't pay much, but it was more than the other theaters, and it got me some very good actors."[28]

During this growth period, City Theatre's core group of actors gradually moved on, mostly to other cities, and an ad hoc casting system was installed. A contract with Actors' Equity allowed Masterson to hire a certain number of union actors per show—which led to an ongoing relationship with established local professionals like Helena Ruoti, Bingo O'Malley, Lenora Nemetz, Don Marshall, and David Butler. Over time, Masterson and Associate Artistic Director Jed Allen Harris built a reputation for producing and directing experimental American plays.[29] City Theatre regularly featured the work of challenging con-temporary playwrights such as Sam Shepard, David Mamet, Irene Fornes, and George C. Wolfe and lesser known works by emerging regional playwrights, in-cluding John Olive and Stephen Dietz. City Theatre's productions also developed a signature look based on the style of the two house designers, Tony Ferrieri and Lorraine Venberg.

By the mid-1980s, with an annual operating budget of about $300,000 and several thousand subscribers, the company had outgrown both its tiny per-formance space and its dependence on the University of Pittsburgh. In 1988 Masterson's influential board of advisors decided to establish the company as an independent fiscal entity. Other changes included the addition of a two-play sum-mer season at Hartwood Acres and a play reading series called Tuesday Night Theater, run by literary manager Dennis Kennedy. The company launched a capital campaign and was able to purchase and refurbish the Bingham Street Methodist Church and parish house on the city's South Side.[30] In November 1991 the seventeen-year-old City Theatre finally opened its own doors with a produc-tion of *Bricklayers,* a story about generational tensions among a Pittsburgh work-ing-class family by a local playwright, Elvira DiPaolo.

Fig. 48. City Theatre's production of *Indians*, featuring Larry John Meyers, 1982.
Source: Unknown (Curtis Theatre Collection, University of Pittsburgh Library). Courtesy
of The University of Pittsburgh Department of Theatre Arts.

On the city's North Side, the Pittsburgh Public Theater entered the 1980s in sole possession of the city of Pittsburgh's newly rechristened Hazlett Theater and clearly in an institutional league of its own. By 1980 the operating budget topped $2 million and the company's thirty-member staff included marketing and fund-raising professionals, in-house designers, a large production crew, a literary manager and casting director, a community programs coordinator, and a new executive director reporting directly to Ben Shaktman, who took the title of artistic director. The PPT's main stage season was increased to six shows, and a new Plus Six workshop series was added, promising a second season of new works that, according to Shaktman, would "stretch the form of the art to its stress points." But after a dismal box office return and some controversy over the content of the new plays, the Public's board of directors refused to continue to sponsor the new works initiative. Disappointed by the board's interference, Shaktman resigned at the end of the 1981–82 season. Larry Arrick was named the new artistic director, but accusations of a nepotistic casting system, coupled with steadily increasing debt, led to a call for Arrick's resignation in 1984. Arrick was replaced by William Gardner, who as producing director became the company's first leader not specifically hired to perform double duty as a stage director.

Gardner immediately oversaw a half-million-dollar renovation of the Hazlett Theater that expanded the seating capacity to 457 and added a new bar and lounge area—both attempts to increase revenue and control the deficit. And though he maintained the Public's policy, consistent with that of other League of Resident Theaters, of hiring New York City professionals, he also hired many local actors and designers, notably Tom Atkins, Helena Ruoti, Larry John Meyers, Cletus Anderson, Barbara Anderson, and Henry Heymann. Just as significant, Gardner engineered a campaign to secure the company's place within the Pittsburgh community. In 1987 the Public became the first theater in the nation to host an annual benefit performance for a local AIDS task force, for example, and under outreach department directors Mary Guaraldi (1983–87) and Rob Zellers (hired in 1987), the PPT sponsored more ambitious arts enrichment programs than any other company in the city. These included preshow site visits to local schools ("an important element in preparing the new young audience for their first experience with live, professional theater"); lecture-demonstrations by staff members and guest artists; technical assistance for theater productions at secondary schools; backstage tours of the Hazlett; career day seminars; public forums on issues in the plays; a theatrical training program for inner-city youth with little or no practical experience; and a program called Open Stage offering city residents free tickets to matinee performances.[31]

But Gardner's biggest civically inspired undertaking was his determined pursuit of August Wilson, who was then emerging as one of America's leading playwrights after winning a series of prestigious awards. Though it took several years, the Public finally got the rights to the Pulitzer Prize–winning *Fences* at the end of the 1988–89 season, staging the first fully professional, big budget production of a Wilson play in the playwright's hometown. Wilson's long-time colleague Claude Purdy directed a cast that featured Monte Russell, a Homestead native and former Kuntu actor, in the role of Cory. The show became the best-attended production in the Public's fourteen-year history—selling out all but two performances in an extended run that garnered extraordinarily strong reviews. The *Pittsburgh Press* claimed that the production was "far more effective than the New York version with Billy Dee Williams. Purdy's wholly convincing, substantive and tempered production engages from the start. Authentic delivery replaces artificial, precise stage diction and low-key acting avoid grandstand staginess" (June 1, 1989, C-3). The *Pittsburgh Courier* pointed to the "moans, groans, cheers and standing ovations" from the sellout audiences (June 17, 1989). *In Pittsburgh* cited the elegance of the play's "inherent rhythms and pace" (June 7–13, 1989, 11). But it was George Anderson in the *Post-Gazette* who most fully captured the effect of Wilson's long-overdue homecoming:

> There was an extraordinary scene at the Pittsburgh Public Theater on Sunday at the final performance of August Wilson's "Fences." The capacity audience gave the cast a standing ovation that was timed at seven minutes long, an eternity in the theater. There was cheering and an outpouring of emotion that had the cast nonplussed. Actors hugged and shook hands with spectators in the first rows as the ovation built and sustained itself beyond what anybody at the theater had ever experienced. It was a dramatic conclusion to the most successful show the Public Theater has ever done. (July 13, 1989, 16).

Following on the heels of the *Fences* triumph, the Pittsburgh Public Theater ended the 1980s with the largest subscriber base in its history—topping 16,000—and an operating budget of almost $4 million. Gardner and the board of directors began looking for a larger space that would accommodate the theater's

Fig. 49. Pittsburgh Public Theater's production of *Fences*, 1989. Source: Ric Evans, courtesy of The Pittsburgh Public Theater.

growth as well as its ambitions. That effort ended a decade later when the Pittsburgh Public Theater became the resident company of the O'Reilly Theater in the Cultural District, the first stand-alone playhouse erected in the downtown since 1928. The inaugural production in the elegant new playhouse was the world premiere of *King Hedley II*, the latest installment of August Wilson's Pittsburgh cycle.[32]

Theatrical Activity in the Western Country

Pittsburgh's rising theatrical prominence during the 1980s was based on several key factors: the institutional maturation of a handful of the city's established resident theaters; a boom in the number of nonprofit companies—a few of whom were gaining national reputations; and a reinvigorated commercial industry based substantially on the Cultural Trust's efforts to resurrect the Penn-Liberty corridor. During the 1980s twenty-six new resident theaters were founded in the city, joining another fourteen or so established companies, to create the largest number of noncommercial troupes the city had seen since the 1930s. In addition, Pittsburgh and its environs were humming with other types of theater—touring road shows at the Benedum Center and Heinz Hall, strawhat suburban troupes, university-based companies, commercial dinner theaters, and a hundred or so amateur companies that continued to flourish in the region's diverse neighborhoods. (The resiliency of amateur activity suggests that an essential relationship between community identity and the opportunity to create theater remained an integral part of civic life in the 1980s, just as when the first settlers arrived in the western country more than two hundred years earlier.) When added together, this range of activity accounts for a richer and more varied theatrical menu than at any other time of the city's history.

We return to the audience, where this history of Pittsburgh theater began. By the 1980s the city's theater audiences were more diverse than ever before—no longer "iron-fisted burgers" and elite Presbyterians, but a cross section of citizens gravitating toward widely different styles of theater. Yet at the end of the 1980s the citizens of Pittsburgh still had one thing in common with the first generations of settlers. Whether they were gathering in an ornate concert hall in the new Cultural District or in a dirty second-floor warehouse in Garfield, whether they were telling their own stories or witnessing the lives of distant others, and whether they were watching highly trained professionals or their own neighbors, in 1990 as in 1790, Pittsburghers continued to enter the "theater" seeking meaning, illumination, joy, catharsis, redemption, and, above all, simple pleasure.

10

CONCLUSION

Pittsburgh in Stages

It is a rule of thumb that historians need to put at least a decade between themselves and the history they narrate. Ten years' distance allows patterns to emerge that invariably tie generations together and demonstrate the validity of an oft-quoted Harry Trumanism that the only thing new in the world "is the history that you don't know." This is the primary explanation for why this volume ends in 1989—exactly ten years before I began active research on this project. An equally compelling reason is that the 1980s saw the decisive end of Pittsburgh's industrial-era prowess and thus seems an appropriate point of closure for a narrative that has traced the city through stages of economic and cultural development—from frontier outpost to the world's largest steel producer to a midsized postindustrial city struggling to reinvent itself. Here I will conclude with some observations on the contemporary Pittsburgh theater, a sort of interim report on a few key developments.

Smoky City Redux

There is no single reliable portrait of postindustrial Pittsburgh. Following the city's fall from preeminence as an industrial behemoth, Pittsburgh has become one of the world's great medical research centers, a vibrant university town, a leader in the environmental protection movement, and one of the safest, cleanest, and most affordable places to live in the United States. At the same time, detractors hold that Pittsburgh is a rust belt town stuck in an old-economy death grip, a flyover city disabled by a massive brain drain, and a conservative, working-class enclave with a dull and aging population.

Opinions about Pittsburgh's cultural profile are similarly contradictory. A magazine survey in 2006 rated Pittsburgh as the nation's third best midsized city in light of its diverse and vibrant indigenous arts community, including the area's many small-budget organizations and individual artists who live and work in the city.[1] And in recent years the downtown Cultural District has become a national model for arts-based urban renewal. Since 1990, the real estate development arm of the Pittsburgh Cultural Trust has refurbished two historic theaters, the Byham (the former Gayety Theater) and the Harris (the former Art Cinema) and built the O'Reilly Theater and the Theater Square complex, which houses the Cultural Trust's box office, a 790-space parking garage, the Cabaret at Theater Square, Café Zao, and the downtown studio of radio station WQED-FM.[2] And under Executive Director Kevin McMahon, who replaced Carol Brown when she retired in 2001, the Cultural Trust's producing arm has expanded from co-presenting the Broadway Series to managing the Dance Council's annual season at the Benedum Center and sponsoring a wide range of special events.

Yet from a national perspective twenty-first-century Pittsburgh is still known as a "working-class town with working-class tastes." Because of this resilient myth, outsiders continue to view Pittsburgh's cultural products through the imagined haze of smokestacks that have long since disappeared. Out-of-town journalists arriving to research stories on the arts in Pittsburgh still routinely start off their copy with some reference to the Smoky City, echoing James Parton's "hell with the lid taken off" line from 1868.[3] They also insist on evoking the notion of a monolithic "Pittsburgh audience" made up of conservative-minded theater patrons with Presbyterian sensibilities—much as Noah Ludlow characterized the "iron-fisted burgers" who refused to supply his traveling acting troupe with supernumerary stage virgins in 1815. Surely the potency of this myth lies behind what happened when the first national touring company of Mel Brooks's *The Producers* began its three-week run at the Benedum Center in 2002. The touring show was marketed as a virtual replica of the Broadway production, with dialogue and songs "nearly line by line unaltered."[4] However, before the show opened in Pittsburgh the word *fuck* was excised from the script, a detail instantly noted by the local press: "One change for the tour is surprising: In his very first song, Max uses many of the seven words you can't say on television, but his climactic yell (on Broadway and CD), 'who do you have to [bleep] to get a break in this town,' has been changed to spare our middle-American sensitivities" (*Pittsburgh Post-Gazette*, Sept. 19, 2002, C-3). Though no explanation was given for the change, the rumor was that the decision came from the top: Mel Brooks knew Pittsburgh from his own show days and feared that Pittsburgh audiences would not tolerate that vulgarity in one of their theaters.

A City of Theaters

Of course, there is no monolithic Pittsburgh audience, conservative or otherwise. The city is multicultural and can support a diverse range of theatrical fare. At least that is how it looks from the vantage point of 2007, in the midst of another significant theater boom marked by the proliferation of new or refurbished dedicated playhouses, a rise in commercial bookings, and the continued growth of the resident, noncommercial theater movement.

Not since the building booms of the nineteenth century has the city seen so many new and significantly refurbished dedicated playhouses. In the downtown, the palaces built by the Cultural Trust (the O'Reilly, the Byham, and the Cabaret at Theater Square) are just a few blocks from the Pittsburgh Playwrights' Theater, a rustic space carved out of a parking garage on Penn Avenue. Soon to be constructed is a 500-seat theater inside the August Wilson Center for African American Culture on Liberty Avenue. Expanding the Penn-Liberty corridor toward the east is the Open Stage Theater in the Strip District; in addition, workshop performance spaces may be found at Modern Formations, the Garfield Artworks, and the Dance Alloy's Neighborhood Dance Center. On the South Side, the City Theatre operates a 270-seat main stage theater and the 100-seat Lester Hamburg Studio. In Oakland, the University of Pittsburgh produces in and also rents the 478-seat Charity Randall Theatre (the former Stephen Foster Memorial Theatre) and the 153-seat Henry Heymann Theatre, while Carnegie Mellon mounts its drama school productions in the Purnell Center for the Arts, a $36.2 million complex containing the 500-seat Chosky Theater and the smaller Helen Wayne Rauh Studio Theater. In East Liberty, the Kelly-Strayhorn Theater (the former Regent movie house) serves a variety of local and touring theater and dance troupes. On the North Side, the newly renovated New Hazlett Theater, still owned and operated by the city, is home to several local organizations. This accounting does not include temporary, adapted-use theater spaces that are put up for site-specific productions—a practice that has been relatively common in Pittsburgh since the Population Company opened the New Theatre over the Allegheny in 1795.

But the increase in the number of dedicated and improvised playhouses is not the most significant statistic here. Far more compelling is the fact that in 2007 there are more noncommercial, resident theater companies than this bounty of new playhouses can accommodate. Since 1990 over thirty-five new artist-centered theater companies have been formed in the city proper. Many did not survive the decade, but others continue to produce, and a few have become major players, most prominently Quantum Theatre, the Pittsburgh Irish and Classical Theatre, and the Pittsburgh Musical Theater.[5] Quantum, founded in 1990 by Karla Boos, is an itinerant, ad hoc company that produces an iconoclastic repertoire in a wide range of found environments—from a rose garden to an abandoned warehouse to the cemetery where Stephen Foster is buried. Boos's vision is rooted in a kind of willful uncertainty (thus the company's name) that informs her theatrical process; each new space introduces new technical problems and discoveries, and each new company of actors—a mix of imported and local professionals—takes on the risks inherent in performing in unconventional, even uncomfortable spaces. Since 1990 Quantum has grown steadily, garnering national press attention and an invited appearance at the Festival de Otono in Madrid in 2005. Like Bill Royston's Laboratory Theatre, founded in 1971,

Fig. 50. Penn Avenue theaters in 2006: Heinz Hall, O'Reilly Theater, Cabaret at Theater Square, and the Benedum Center (the former Stanley Theatre) in the distance. Source: Ellen Kelson.

Quantum is steadfast in its commitment to an exploratory production process and to the economically risky idea of introducing Pittsburgh audiences to sometimes obscure works from the international stage. And also like the old Pittsburgh Lab, Quantum has a devoted audience. Still, Boos has pushed the 1970s-era definition of "environmental theater" into the postmodern age by matching plays and sites in decidedly ironic and often subversive ways. Her 2001 production of Abby Morgan's *Splendour*, a contemporary play about the fall of a fascist regime in Eastern Europe, for example, was staged in the Homestead Pump House, the site of the fatal battle of Homestead in which steelworkers and their families fought off a hired militia during the infamous steel strike of 1892.

Like Quantum, the Pittsburgh Irish and Classical Theatre (PICT) is also a fast-growing company with a loyal audience and an international reputation for its high production values.[6] Founded in 1996 by Andrew Paul and Stephanie Riso, PICT is committed to a repertoire that includes plays from the larger canon but emphasizes works by Irish-born playwrights, past and present (such as Sheridan, Beckett, Brian Friel, Marina Carr, Thomas Kilroy, and Martin McDonough). Over its ten-year history PICT has had a measurable impact on local theater. In keeping with its stated mission to "improve employment opportunities for local talent," director Andrew Paul routinely hires a large percentage of Pittsburgh-based artists—actors, directors, technicians, and designers. In recent years the company has also made its home in the University of Pittsburgh's Charity Randall and Heymann Theatres.

The Pittsburgh Musical Theater (PMT) is a significantly different kind of resident theater. More populist in orientation, PMT reaches a far bigger and more geographically diverse audience (by its own accounting, roughly 85,000 people attend each season from a ten-county area) with its repertoire of standard American musicals. Under Ken Gargaro, the founding director, PMT also houses the Richard E. Rauh Conservatory and the Young Performers' Institute, a training academy for career-minded high school students in the mold of the original Pittsburgh Playhouse School (1934–69).[7]

Other, smaller-budget theater companies abound. Ruth Willis's Open Stage Theater produces accessible productions of modern and contemporary plays. The Unseam'd Shakespeare Company, begun in 1993 by a group of doctoral students at the University of Pittsburgh and managed since 1997 by Laura Smiley, continues to deconstruct classical texts for a university audience. Both the New

Fig. 51. Quantum Theatre's production of *Richard II* in a nineteenth-century iron foundry, 2004. Source: Mary Mervis, courtesy of Quantum Theatre.

Horizon Theater (named after the original Black Horizon Theater) and the Pittsburgh Playwrights' Theatre produce plays from the Black Arts canon. The latter company, directed by steelworker-turned-playwright and producer Mark Clayton Southers, insists on the importance of programming economic and racial diversity in the midst of the Cultural District. And finally, Attack Theatre, a dance-based theater troupe headed by Michelle de la Reza and Peter Kope, and Squonk Opera, a contemporary musical ensemble buoyed by the scenic wizardry of founding member Steve O'Hearn, produce stage hybrids that reflect the constantly changing definition of what constitutes theater.

The Post–Ford Foundation Arts Ecosystem

In Pittsburgh, as elsewhere, the not-for-profit resident theater model continues to be the guiding structure for building a professional theater; currently all of the city's resident companies operate either as independent 501(c)3 charitable institutions or under the fiscal umbrella of other nonprofit cultural organizations.[8] Even so, the nature of the nonprofit arts sector has changed significantly since the Ford Foundation established the model for subsidizing the arts in the late 1950s and thus fueled the regional theater boom of the sixties and seventies. As early as the mid-1980s, cultural economists began warning that changing marketplace conditions and reduced government, corporate, and foundation support for the arts would soon force American nonprofits to change how they did business. This warning became reality in the 1990s, when many theater companies around the country either folded or were drastically downsized. Pittsburgh, with its long-established and generous foundation-based support for the arts, has fared considerably better than many other cities of its size.[9]

Nevertheless, in recent years a new arts economy has begun to emerge—defined in part by a reconsideration of the definition of profit and nonprofit that encourages organizations to become less dependent on foundation support and more entrepreneurial in increasing income beyond ticket sales. They have also entered into what some analysts refer to as the post–Ford Foundation era, in which the old model of relying on support from large donors so as to leverage other funding (from the government and the private sector) is no longer sustainable.[10] In response, over the last decade or so Pittsburgh's large resident theaters have become increasingly entrepreneurial.

This is the case with the city's largest company, the Pittsburgh CLO, formerly the Civic Light Opera. When Van Kaplan took over from Charles Gray in 1997, he initiated the CLO's participation in the Independent Presenters Network (IPN), a national producing partnership devoted to the creation of new musicals. Under Kaplan the company has been the lead producer on several new works (*Barry Manilow's Copacabana, Casper—The Musical,* and *Doctor Dolittle*) and has invested, through IPN, in a number of Broadway shows. The income from these investments helps sustain the CLO's nearly $10 million annual budget, as does its new relationship with the Cultural Trust's Cabaret at Theater Square, the 253-seat house on Penn Avenue that features musical revues produced by Kaplan.

A different kind of investment strategy was launched in December 1999 when the Pittsburgh Public Theater gave up its city-funded home at the Hazlett Theater on the North Side to become the resident tenant of the Cultural Trust's $25 million O'Reilly Theater. The O'Reilly stands almost squarely on the spot where Felix Brunot's Mercantile Library Hall (later called the Bijou and the

Lyceum) opened 129 years earlier. This is a noteworthy coincidence, given that Mercantile Library Hall was financed and built in the flush post–Civil War era by a group of wealthy businessmen to advance the "honor and prosperity of the community through information and culture," and the mission of the publicly and privately funded nonprofit Cultural Trust is "to stimulate the economic and cultural development of Pittsburgh through the development and promotion of a downtown arts and entertainment district."[11] Shortly after moving downtown, the board of directors at the Public Theater named Ted Pappas to replace Edward Gilbert as artistic director. Pappas, a director and choreographer based in New York, had a versatile track record directing new plays, musicals, and American classics in Pittsburgh (*Wings, Sweeney Todd, Who's Afraid of Virginia Woolf?*). And as the head of the Society of Stage Directors and Choreographers union, he also had the kind of business acumen and negotiating skills required to lead a large nonprofit organization in the post–Ford Foundation era. In keeping with the Public's role as a lynchpin Cultural District organization, Pappas has overseen an expansion of the company's community responsibilities, including a marked increase in the production of new plays (which serves both the local and national theater community) and new educational initiatives such as Mondays with the Public—a free lecture-workshop series echoing the Jeffersonian ideal of popular enlightenment that so inspired Felix Brunot back in 1870. And Pappas has also continued the Public's commitment, begun under William Gardner, to stage works from August Wilson's canon and to honor Pittsburgh's native son with first-rate productions featuring the nation's leading African American directors and actors.

Changes in the arts ecosystem have also affected the growth strategy at City Theatre in recent years. Since its move to the South Side in 1991, the company's budget has more than doubled, and under Artistic Director Tracy Brigden, who replaced Marc Masterson in 2001, the company has acquired additional property near its two theaters. Brigden's goal of providing an artistic home for local and national theater artists is in keeping with City Theatre's roots as a company inspired by the local professional acting pool and by the excitement of producing new American plays for an adventurous, serious-minded audience. Since 2001 the addition of a fund-raising initiative dedicated to commissioning new plays from nationally regarded playwrights as well as an annual weekend celebration, called Momentum, of new play readings and workshops has helped City Theatre to extend its reputation. Brigden has also made a commitment to the community—her efforts to turn the six-building City Theatre campus into a "town hall for the community" include launching a number of innovative audience enrichment programs that promote the civic role of theater.[12]

Putting Culture on Stage

There are numerous by-products from this level of theatrical activity. Because of increased employment opportunities, a critical mass of polished actors now use Pittsburgh as their base.[13] The increased activity among the resident theaters and the commercial houses has also been good for freelancers, including stage technicians and the many accomplished designers, directors, and musicians on the faculties at Carnegie Mellon, Point Park, and Pitt.[14] The result is a rich resident professional acting, directing, and design pool—perhaps the strongest since the heyday of the many stock companies in residence at the destination playhouses of a century ago.

Increased interest in the larger culture of making theater also seems to have led to a renaissance in the production of new plays since 1990. This is a significant development for Pittsburgh because, as this volume illustrates, the city has not been particularly successful in encouraging the creation of new plays, despite repeated efforts that began in the early twentieth century. William Moore Patch's Pitt Theater in 1913, for instance, or the Little Theater Lane project in 1930, or Black Horizon Theater in 1968, or Theater Express during the William Turner years in the late 1970s—all of these efforts to produce new plays by Pittsburgh playwrights were well intentioned. But all were short-lived and financially troubled, largely because audiences resisted new works by unknown authors. That fear still affects the repertoire, of course, and not just in Pittsburgh—it is a prevalent stumbling block for new play production in most cities and increasingly on Broadway. Still, since 2000 both City Theatre and the Pittsburgh Public Theater have increased their commitment to presenting premieres and have joined Carnegie Mellon University's summer Showcase of New Plays in producing their own high-profile new play workshops—the annual Momentum event and the Public Exposures series.[15] And under Artistic Producing Director Ron Allan-

Lindblom, the Pittsburgh Playhouse has consistently mounted full productions of new plays, many of them by Pittsburgh-based writers.

In recent years the national profile of many of the city's resident playwrights has improved as well. Since 1989, Pittsburgh has been home to three O'Neill National Playwrights' Conference winners—Frank Gagliano (1989), Elvira DiPaolo (1990), and Ted Hoover (1992)—and several finalists, including Tammy Ryan, Dennis Kennedy, and Amy Hartman. Of this group, Ryan and Gagliano are arguably the best known and most frequently produced resident playwrights. Ryan, who holds a master of fine arts in playwriting from Carnegie Mellon and is the winner of several prestigious national awards, has had a dozen productions in Pittsburgh and another dozen at various regional theaters around the country, including an acclaimed staging of *The Music Lesson* at Florida Stage in 2000. Gagliano, who taught playwriting at CMU and headed the Carnegie Mellon Showcase of New Plays from 1986 to 1998 before taking a position at West Virginia University, has had a score of productions in Pittsburgh, New York, and other cities.[16]

Perhaps the most significant evidence of change in contemporary Pittsburgh's attitude toward new plays, however, is the recent vitality of activity designed to nurture local playwrights. Since 1990 more than a dozen companies, festivals, and reading series have emerged devoted to producing new plays by Pittsburgh-based playwrights. Some of them, like the Pittsburgh New Works Festival and the Festival in Black and White, have become institutions.[17] The relationship between a theater community's support for developing new plays and its national reputation is best demonstrated by Seattle and Minneapolis: both established strong new play development programs in the 1980s, and both are now considered theater meccas. For Pittsburgh, then, the current level of activity can be understood as a hopeful indicator for the future, since the theater's lifeline has always been grounded in a playwright's ability to speak clearly to his or her own time in language that has the potential to be understood throughout time. Or, as Pittsburgh's de facto poet laureate August Wilson once explained, a playwright's job is to "take culture and put it onstage. . . . My plays are about love, honor, duty, betrayal—things humans have written about since the beginning of time."[18]

NOTES

Preface

1. See Bruce McConachie, "Narrative Possibilities in U.S. Theater History."

2. A large number of theater histories ignore Pittsburgh as an important setting for American drama, while others make only a passing mention, often pejorative. Kenneth MacGowan, *Footlights Across America: Towards a National Theater* (1929); Sheldon Cheney, *The Art Theater* (1917); Louise Burleigh, *The Community Theater Movement* (1917); Constance D'Arcy Mackay, *The Little Theater in the United States* (1917), mention only Carnegie Tech. One notable exception is Robert E. Gard and Gertrude S. Burley, *Community Theater: Idea and Achievement* (1959), which devotes a section to the Pittsburgh Playhouse.

3. Reducing a city or region to one characteristic on the basis of geography is commonplace. Pittsburgh has long been profiled by reductive and simplistic cultural labels.

Chapter 1: *The Theater as Community Life*

1. Source material for historical snapshot comes from *Pittsburgh Gazette,* January 14, 1817, 3; November 13, 1818, 1; December 8, 1818, 3; Parke, "Reminiscences of the Old Third Street Theatre," 104; Buck and Buck, *The Planting of Civilization in Western Pennsylvania;* Fleming, *History of Pittsburgh and Environs;* "Pittsburgh in 1816."

2. I am concerned with European-derived theater in Pittsburgh, though of course there were indigenous performance traditions. See Buck and Buck, *The Planting of Civilization in Western Pennsylvania;* Ward, *Breaking the Backcountry;* Downes, *Council Fires on the Upper Ohio.*

3. See Buck and Buck, *The Planting of Civilization in Western Pennsylvania;* Bishop, "In the Shadow of the Dream"; Glasco, *WPA History;* Rishel, *Founding Families of Pittsburgh;* Martin, *Killing Time;* Fleming, *History of Pittsburgh and Environs.*

4. Martin, *Killing Time,* 5.

5. *Pittsburgh Gazette,* November 13, 1818, 1. The *Gazette* was founded in 1786 by John Skull, a Federalist who supported the Washington-Hamilton regime. The anti-Federalist paper, *Tree of Liberty,* was sponsored by Hugh Henry Brackenridge in 1799. Skull retired from the *Gazette* in August 1816, and the newspaper was taken over by Morgan Neville,

John I. Skull, and later by Isaac Craig. See Andrews, *Pittsburgh's Post-Gazette;* Thomas, *Front Page Pittsburgh.*

6. Boucher, *A Century and a Half,* 383, 393; see also Ward, *Breaking the Backcountry;* Buck and Buck, *The Planting of Civilization in Western Pennsylvania;* Fleming, *History of Pittsburgh and Environs.*

7. Boucher, *A Century and a Half,* 393.

8. See Nathans, *Early American Theatre;* Brown, *The Theatre in America During the Revolution;* O'Dell, "Amateurs of the Regiment."

9. Martin, *Killing Time,* 35.

10. Fleming, *History of Pittsburgh and Environs,* 50; Brackenridge, "Pittsburgh in the Olden Time," 12; *Pittsburgh Gazette,* October 14, 1802, 13; January 5, 1808, 3; December 29, 1806, 3.

11. *Pittsburgh Gazette,* April 17, 1790, 1. The location of the Theatre in the Garrison is unclear, although it was located "in all probability in the redoubt [the Block House], which is still standing, as it likely contained the most suitable apartment of the purpose" (Chapman, "Amusements in Early Pittsburgh").

12. The Pennsylvania Population Company was a land speculation firm incorporated in 1792 by "eastern capitalists." See Hale, "The Pennsylvania Population Company," 122.

13. This theater may have stood in the less populated northern side of the village, since the article refers to buying tickets at a shop in "Cheapside"; more expensive homes and shops were on the southern side near the Monongahela River.

14. Lorant, *Pittsburgh,* 460.

15. Cuming, *Sketches,* 67.

16. The reference to "Indian dances" comes from the anti-Federalist newspaper *Commonwealth* (February 5, 1806), Theater and Drama Files, Carnegie Library of Pittsburgh, Pennsylvania Room.

17. Baynham, "A History of Pittsburgh Music," 12–13.

18. Buck and Buck, *The Planting of Civilization in Western Pennsylvania,* 350, 375.

19. Brackenridge, *Recollections of Persons and Places in the West,* 105; see Anderson, "The Intellectual Life," 226.

20. Cuming, *Sketches,* 67. Casting female roles with young men, a practice dating to ancient theater, was still common in amateur clubs of the era.

21. See E. Wilson, *History of Pittsburg,* 879; Boucher, *A Century and a Half,* 393–94.

22. Starrett, *Through One Hundred and Fifty Years,* 530. The relationship between the Academy Thespian Society and other groups is unclear; the Academy Thespian Society and the Thespian Society may have merged.

23. Parke, "Reminiscences of the Old Third Street Theatre," 104–6.

24. The start of the War of 1812 brought 2,000 additional residents in the form of military troops, thus artificially increasing the city's population.

25. The Bromly and Arnold company's appearance in 1803 was not the "first theatri-

cal production in the city" (Lorant, *Pittsburgh*, 460), nor was it the first traveling company to make it to Pittsburgh.

26. It was common from colonial times for traveling players to enhance or even invent their associations with famous European institutions.

27. Others were the result of a sense of common need for the common good, such as the organization of a series of fire companies beginning in the early 1790s. See Buck and Buck, *The Planting of Civilization in Western Pennsylvania*, 351.

28. Parke, "Reminiscences of the Old Third Street Theatre," 104.

29. Ibid.

30. Hill, *The Theatre in Early Kentucky*, 99–100.

31. Londré and Watermeier, *The History of North American Theater*, 86; Hill, *The Theatre in Early Kentucky*, 51–52.

32. Ludlow, *Dramatic Life*, 55.

33. Ibid., 65.

34. Turner's liberty with the play's title was a common practice during the period.

35. Londré and Watermeier, *The History of North American Theater*, 87, asserts that Drake and his followers supplanted the Turner company in both Cincinnati and Kentucky, perhaps explaining why they did not return to Pittsburgh.

36. Alger, *Life of Edwin Forrest*, 99–100.

37. Ludlow, *Dramatic Life*, 368.

38. Parke, "Reminiscences of the Old Third Street Theatre," 105.

39. Buck and Buck, *The Planting of Civilization in Western Pennsylvania*, 353.

40. Quoted in Nathans, *Early American Theatre*, 14.

41. Cramer, *The Navigator*, 66–67.

42. Buck and Buck, *The Planting of Civilization in Western Pennsylvania*, 153.

43. McClure, *Diary of David McClure*, 46, 53, 107.

44. McKinney, *Early Pittsburgh Presbyterianism*, 132–33.

45. *Mrs. Royall's Pennsylvania*, reports erroneously that there was no theater in Pittsburgh in 1828, Mrs. Anne Royall, *Mrs. Royall's Pennsylvania, or Travels Continued in the United States* (Washington, DC: printed for the author, 1829), Carnegie Library of Pittsburgh, http://www.carnegielibrary.org/locations/pennsylvania/history/royall.html (accessed December 21, 2006).

46. Ludlow, *Dramatic Life*, 55, 65.

Chapter 2: *Theater as Community Investment*

1. Source material for this historical snapshot comes from the *Daily Pittsburgh Gazette* (July–September 1833), the *Pittsburgh Messenger* (July–September 1833). See also Fleming, *History of Pittsburgh and Environs*.

2. There were a few other public rooms, or assembly halls, during this period, including Philo Hall (on Third Street over the post office) and Wilkins Hall on Fourth Avenue. Several Masonic halls were constructed in Pittsburgh in the nineteenth and early twentieth centuries, culminating in the massive Masonic Temple in Oakland.

3. Poggi, *Theater in America,* 348–49.

4. Boucher, *A Century and a Half,* 395; see also E. Wilson, *History of Pittsburg,* 879, 880.

5. See Wemyss, *A Chronology of the American Stage* and *Theatrical Biography.* These accounts are filled with factual errors, including Wemyss's assertion that the "Drama had no regular home in Pittsburgh until 1832" (*Chronology,* 13).

6. See Alger, *Life of Edwin Forrest;* McConachie, *Melodramatic Formations.*

7. Baldwin, *Pittsburgh,* 264.

8. Baynham, "A History of Pittsburgh Music," 350.

9. This did not keep Wemyss from experiencing financial problems right from the start, as evidenced by a series of increasingly threatening ads placed in local newspapers over the fall of 1833: "The Board of Directors have passed a Resolution, 'That the treasurer be authorized, to bring suit against all stockholders, who have not paid the 4th installment due upon their subscription'" (*Daily Pittsburgh Gazette,* October 10, 1933, 3). The ads are reminiscent of similar notices after the Theatre on Third Street opened in 1813 and indicate that, like their forebears, these elite investors believed in the need for a privately subsidized theater and, also like them, didn't pay up.

10. Pennsylvania enacted gradual abolition in 1780, providing "thereafter no child born in Pennsylvania should be a slave." But during the era of Jacksonian democracy racial tensions rose, leading to the loss of voting rights for black freemen in 1838. See Bishop, "In the Shadow of the Dream"; Epstein, *The Negro Migrant in Pittsburgh;* Glasco, *WPA History.*

11. An ad from 1861 lists two "colored" areas: the gallery (tickets twenty-five cents) and special boxes (fifty cents). Interestingly, the cheapest seats in the house were in the white gallery (fifteen cents).

12. Unattributed clipping, "In the Days of Old Drury," Theater and Drama Clipping Files, Carnegie Library of Pittsburgh, Pennsylvania Room.

13. See Johnson, "That Guilty Third Tier."

14. Unattributed clipping, Theater and Drama Clipping Files, Carnegie Library of Pittsburgh, Pennsylvania Room.

15. Martin, *Killing Time,* 117; Baldwin, *Pittsburgh,* 264–65.

16. Baldwin, *Pittsburgh,* 265.

17. Undated clipping, Theater and Drama Clipping Files, Carnegie Library of Pittsburgh, Pennsylvania Room.

18. This clipping had no page number. All citations from newspapers lacking page numbers were found in clipping files.

19. Andrews, *Pittsburgh's Post-Gazette,* 113.

20. Baldwin, *Pittsburgh*, 263.

21. The term *legitimate* dates to England's Licensing Act of 1737, which gave a few patent theater companies the right to perform selected dramas. The term *variety* derives from short entertainments, including the French *variétés-amusantes* and British music hall shows. It now means a collection of individual acts without a narrative relationship.

22. Fleming, *History of Pittsburgh and Environs*, 80. This was certainly the attitude of Neville Craig, who besides editing the *Gazette* from 1829 to 1841 was also a lawyer and city council member. In his own history of Pittsburgh published in 1851, he promoted the city's assets: natural resources, especially coal, the rivers, and railroads.

23. Walther and Kruger, "A Brief History of the Cultural District," 6–9.

24. See the *Pittsburgh Gazette*, September 5–12, 1833. It seems unlikely that Rice was a nationally known performer by the fall of 1833, as many histories of minstrelsy claim, since Wemyss's account book shows that Rice received twelve dollars a week for his stint at the Pittsburgh Theatre, about half the amount paid to the company's leading players (Witham, *Theatre in the Colonies*, 84).

25. Pittsburgh's claim to be the place of origin of Jump Jim Crow is found in several contemporary accounts, including Wemyss, *Twenty-Six Years*, and Nevin, "Stephen Foster and Negro Minstrelsy." Other accounts place the inspiration for the character in Louisville and Cincinnati. Rice may have continued to develop the character in all three cities before reaching New York. See Bean et al., *Inside the Minstrel Mask*; Mahar, *Behind the Burnt Cork Mask*.

26. Baynham, "A History of Pittsburgh Music," 31.

27. E. Wilson, *History of Pittsburg*, 881.

28. Emerson, *Doo-Dah!*, 124–27.

29. Boucher, *A Century and a Half*, 396.

30. Emerson, *Doo-Dah!*, 200. Foster also composed for a branch of comic opera called the "fairy spectacle." He collaborated with Charles P. Shiras, a poet and a boyhood friend, on an operatic adaptation of J. R. Planche's *The Invisible Prince*. It opened at the Pittsburgh Theatre in November 1853, for a six-night run (ibid., 205).

31. Information from the *Pittsburgh Dispatch*, the *Pittsburgh Daily Gazette and Advertiser*, the *Pittsburgh Morning Post*, the *Pittsburgh Gazette*, and the *Daily Pittsburgh Post*.

32. Krich, "The Amiable Lady," 262. Although many of her contemporaries debated whether Menken, billed as a "daughter of Israel," was Jewish or Spanish, as she claimed (ibid., 259), she was actually African American. See Barca, "Adah Isaacs Menken."

33. Little is known about the Sefton Opera House beyond its innovative removal of divisions between the second and third tiers of the gallery, creating an open space that could seat 1,000 people. See "In the Days of Old Drury."

34. A page from Wemyss's account book shows the payroll figures for 1833. An average weekly salary was about twenty-two dollars (Witham, *Theatre in the Colonies*, 84).

35. This heavy reliance on the prompter was common. Palmer's recollections are

taken from an unpublished letter (dated 1865) in the Library and Archives of the Historical Society of Western Pennsylvania and the Curtis Theatre Collection, University of Pittsburgh Library.

36. Gillespie, "Old Time Actor."

37. Alger, *Life of Edwin Forrest*, 168–69.

38. Glasco, *WPA History*, 296–97.

39. Emerson, *Doo-Dah!*, 68.

40. Emerson states that the version of *Uncle Tom's Cabin* performed in Pittsburgh was based on George Aiken's stage adaptation of Stowe's novel (ibid.).

41. Unattributed clipping, Theater and Drama Clipping Files, Carnegie Library of Pittsburgh, Pennsylvania Room.

42. Ibid.

43. It is worth adding a note of skepticism here, since many of the theater "notices" ostensibly written by the editors were really puff items placed by press agents and paid for by the theaters. See Conner, *Spreading the Gospel of the Modern Dance*.

44. Fleming, *History of Pittsburgh and Environs*, 99–100.

45. Krich, "The Amiable Lady," 264.

46. Campbell's first New York hit was *My Partner* (1879). His greatest success, in terms of production numbers and royalties, was *The White Slave*—a line from which is quoted on his gravestone in St. Mary's Cemetery in Lawrenceville: "Rags are royal raiment, when worn for virtue's sake; and rather a hoe in my hands than self-contempt in my heart."

47. In 1871 the founding of the AF of L (a federation of organized trades and labor unions of the United States and Canada) in Pittsburgh was still ten years away, and the Homestead Steel Strike of 1892, which crushed the nascent Amalgamated Association of Iron and Steel Workers, was also in the future. So perhaps Bartley Campbell thought that setting his labor strife melodrama in a steel mill was a safer option.

48. Plot synopsis from the *Pittsburgh Commercial Gazette*, quoted in Claeren, "Bartley Campbell," 213.

49. Merriman Scrapbooks, Curtis Theatre Collection, University of Pittsburgh Library.

50. In James Parton's famous travel essay of 1868, he visits an unnamed local variety theater and writes: "Not a woman present. The place was packed with brawny men and noisy boys, all washed, all well-disposed, though half mad with joyous excitement" ("Pittsburgh," 34–35).

Chapter 3: *Theater as Destination*

1. Source material for this historical snapshot is taken from James Parton's 1868 travel essay on Pittsburgh and a series of annual reports by the Young Men's Library As-

sociation and the Library Hall Company published in the *Daily Pittsburgh Gazette* (January 9, 1854; January 14, 1856; January 10, 1859; January 13, 1860; January 9, 1866.)

2. Bode, *The American Lyceum,* 69; see also Hoffsinger, *Correspondence Schools, Lyceums, Chautauquas.*

3. The first circulating library opened in 1812 on Fourth Street and was followed by a series of fee-based institutions, the most prominent being the Mercantile Library Association. The first free library was Colonel James Anderson's Library Institute of Allegheny City, where Andrew Carnegie studied as a recent immigrant in the 1850s.

4. Amateur thespian activity among the Victorian elite, unlike their forebears earlier in the century, was usually for private amusement. The Shakespeare Club (ca. 1878), a reading and study group organized by members of the Thaw family, and the Crusaders, another amateur club, staged private performances in members' homes. The Curtis Theatre Collection contains an elegantly printed card that reads: "The Shakespeare Club will meet at the residence of Henry Holdship, No. 79 Lincoln Avenue, Allegheny city, Friday Evening, April 1st, 1881."

5. The paper began in November 1873 as the *Printers' Labor Tribune,* was renamed the *Weekly Labor Tribune,* then the *National Labor Tribune* in 1874.

6. This "philosophy" was informed in part by Mathew Arnold's definition of culture (as opposed to anarchy), which pointed to the need to aspire toward "the best that has been thought and known in the world . . . the study and pursuit of perfection." Levine notes that this "sacralization" of the arts was propagated by value-laden terms like "high," "low," "pure," "rude," etc. (*High Brow/Low Brow,* 223–24); see also Grimsted, *Melodrama Unveiled,* 22–23.

7. In 1907 the sculptor John Massey Rhind was hired to literalize this reference by creating four bronze sculptures depicting Galileo, Michelangelo, Bach, and Shakespeare to represent those disciplines. They are located near the carriage entrance on Forbes Avenue.

8. Quoted in a letter to the board of directors of the Carnegie Institute, 1897. Carnegie first attempted to initiate this cultural center ten years earlier. In 1881 he offered Pittsburgh $250,000 to build a library if the city would allocate $15,000 annually for maintenance. The city did not accept because under Pennsylvania law municipal property tax assessments could not be used to maintain a free library. Around 1890 the state laws were amended and Pittsburgh officials asked for a renewal of the offer. Carnegie offered to build the million-dollar institute. The board of trustees included Henry Clay Frick, Andrew Mellon, public works director Edward Bigelow, and the artist Joseph Woodwell. The architectural firm was Longfellow, Alden, and Harlow.

9. Resident companies did not disappear entirely, however, as is often claimed. Londré and Watermeier state that by 1900 "the resident company had virtually ceased to exist" (*The History of North American Theater,* 184), while Brockett and Hildy describe a steady decline (*History of the Theatre,* 343–44). Both are clearly exaggerations. Pittsburgh alone maintained five resident professional companies in 1900 (see chapter 4).

10. Since the definition of middle class varies widely, I use the terms "laboring" and "professional" to differentiate between classes of working people. See Kleinberg, *The Shadow of the Mills;* Hinshaw, *Steel and Steelworkers;* Gottlieb, *Making Their Own Way;* Rishel, *Founding Families of Pittsburgh;* and Couvares, *The Remaking of Pittsburgh.*

11. "In the Days of Old Drury," Theater and Drama Clipping Files, Carnegie Library of Pittsburgh, Pennsylvania Room.

12. See the diary of Mary Thaw Thompson in the Thaw Family Papers, Library and Archives, Historical Society of Western Pennsylvania. Nine years after the Monday Group began, it was incorporated as the Twentieth Century Club, which still operates.

13. Lambdin's Museum, Pittsburgh's first public exhibition space, opened in 1828. Over the century the city had a variety of mostly short-lived commercial museums exhibiting both natural history objects and visual arts. The first fine arts museum organization was probably the Art Society of Pittsburgh, founded in 1873 (and incorporated in 1891) for the "mutual consideration of art subjects" (Fleming, *History of Pittsburgh and Environs,* 627).

14. The term "museum" was eventually appropriated by the popular stage, and "Dime Museums" began combining lobby exhibitions of curiosities (freak shows) with variety-style bills of fare. See Peiss, *Cheap Amusements;* Bank, *Archiving Culture;* Frick, *Theatre, Culture and Temperance Reform.*

15. *The Librarian,* September 25, 1876, Curtis Theatre Collection, University of Pittsburgh Library.

16. Ellsler was the brother of John A. Ellsler, a theatrical entrepreneur who dominated the industry in Ohio in the later nineteenth century. Londré and Watermeier, *The History of North American Theater,* 116.

17. *The Librarian,* November 1, 1876, 1. The juxtaposition of the story of Henry VIII's struggle with the Church of Rome and the outcome of the 1876 election is worth noting. Disputed election returns caused a deadlock until Democratic leaders accepted Rutherford B. Hayes's election in exchange for Republican promises to make compromises that provided the legal grounding for Jim Crow segregation and the disenfranchisement of black men.

18. Avenue Theater playbill, June 1900, Curtis Theatre Collection, University of Pittsburgh Library.

19. Korol, "When Electricity Came to Pittsburgh."

20. Various editions of the *Librarian,* Curtis Theatre Collection, University of Pittsburgh Library.

21. *Librarian,* November 1, 1876, 1, in ibid.

22. Bijou program, September 5, 1887, in ibid. In 1881 Library Hall was taken over by F. A. Parke, who ran it for five seasons. In 1886 Parke sold the unexpired lease to R. M. Gulick, a New York City–based theater owner who owned and ran the chain of Bijou theaters. (William Chalet is sometimes listed as the manager and might have been

the local point person.) Under Gulick, the Hall was remodeled and renamed the Chalet-Bijou. The new management tore out the back wall and enlarged the stage and raised the proscenium from 56 feet to 70 feet. They also added boxes and a new gallery and created a new entrance accessible from Sixth Street. (The seating capacity was then 2,600 with a full standing room capacity of 3,600.) When co-manager William Chalet left in 1887, R. M. Gulick again renamed the theater, calling it simply the Bijou. According to one account from 1902, the Bijou was at that time the largest "in point of seating capacity" auditorium for theatrical purposes in the United States. In the late 1880s H. M. Bennett, owner of the Bijou chain, bought up a majority of stock in the Library Hall Company. This led to a civil suit, which was carried to the state supreme court in 1891. When the Library Association lost, the hall was remodeled and the library was torn out.

23. Erle Mitchell, letter published in the *Billboard* (n.d.), Merriman Papers, Curtis Theatre Collection, University of Pittsburgh Library.

24. His funeral was held onstage at the Alvin and drew 15,000 people to Sixth Street. He is buried in Homewood Cemetery.

25. "Crash Recalls Great History of Old Alvin."

26. Boucher, *A Century and a Half,* 403.

27. Unattributed clipping, Theater and Drama Clipping Files, Carnegie Library of Pittsburgh, Pennsylvania Room.

28. Ibid.

29. Casino program, June 1896, Merriman Scrapbooks, Curtis Theatre Collection, University of Pittsburgh Library.

30. East End programs, 1895 to 1900, Merriman Scrapbooks, in ibid.

31. See Demarest, *The River Ran Red.* Sources vary as to the number killed during the battle.

Chapter 4: *Theater as Big Business*

1. Source material for this historical snapshot from September 15, 1905, comes from the *Bulletin,* September–October 1905; Theater and Drama Clipping Files, Carnegie Library of Pittsburgh, Pennsylvania Room.

2. The *Bulletin* was founded in 1876 by John W. Black and merged with the *Index* in 1930. As the city's leading society paper, it was filled with specialty columns devoted to the leisure interests of gilded Pittsburghers (and their imitators from the professional class). Columns like "Club News," "College News" (reporting primarily on activities at Princeton and Yale, where 18 percent of elite Pittsburgh men were educated), "Church and Charities," "Fashion," "The Arts," and "Music" shared the pages with photographs depicting the city's upper-class neighborhoods and other illustrations.

3. Robinson, *Willa,* 80.

4. Samuel F. (Nordlinger) Nixon and his partner, J. Fred Zimmerman (former treasurer of the National Theater in Washington, D.C.), began leasing and managing theaters in Philadelphia in the 1880s. When they joined Klaw, Erlanger, and Frohman in 1896 to form the Syndicate, they had considerable holdings, including several playhouses in the Philadelphia area.

5. Alvin Playbill, 1896, Library and Archives, Historical Society of Western Pennsylvania.

6. Boucher, *A Century and a Half,* 401.

7. Sesqui-Centennial and Historical Souvenir of Greater Pittsburgh, 1908, Library and Archives, Historical Society of Western Pennsylvania.

8. See Connelly, "The Life Story of Harry Davis," "The First Motion Picture Theatre"; Stepanian, "Harry Davis."

9. The first private moving picture showing in Pittsburgh occurred a few days earlier, when Gulick, the owner of the Bijou Theater on Penn Avenue, hosted a private showing of Edison's vitascope. Haller, "Film Arrives in Pittsburgh in 1896," 2.

10. Connelly, "The First Motion Picture Theatre," 23.

11. While the Nickelodeon was probably not the first movie house in the United States, it was the first to catch national attention and quickly became known as the "Pittsburgh idea" (Musser, *The Emergence of Cinema,* 421). Davis and Harris each made a good profit from the venture and quickly opened their own movie house chains. Davis's Bijou Dreams movie theaters were located in Pittsburgh, Rochester, Buffalo, Cleveland, and Toledo. For a brief time after 1906, Davis also ran Pittsburgh's first motion picture studio for the production of "photoplays" in the Alsop Building on Fifth Avenue. Davis brought in an Edison film maker, Gilbert M. Anderson, to run the studio. In the first year in Pittsburgh, Anderson shot a "chase film" in Hazelwood and captured the consecration of St. Paul's Cathedral in 1906. But Davis fired Anderson soon after, and the studio was abandoned (Connelly, "The First Motion Picture Theatre," 9). John P. Harris's independent Harris Amusement Company owned many movie theaters in Pittsburgh and its suburbs through the 1960s.

12. Curiously, Harry Davis, who clearly was the leading original partner in the Nickelodeon venture, has been marginalized or completely written out of the history in most studies of the film industry.

13. Daily attendance figures range from 6,000 to 10,000 (see Connelly, "The Life Story of Harry Davis" and "The First Motion Picture Theatre"); Cohen, "Plays at Fort Pitt." The larger number seems unlikely, given the number of chairs, the length of the program, and the hours of operation.

14. *Bulletin,* September 2, 1916, 11.

15. Grand Opera House program, Curtis Theatre Collection, University of Pittsburgh Library.

16. Nance O'Neill was also well known as the friend and purported lover of Lizzie Borden, the infamous Falls River ax murderer. They met after Borden was acquitted for

the murders of her father and stepmother in 1892. O'Neill made many Hollywood films in the 1920s and 1930s.

17. By the late teens, the Schenley had been converted to a full-time moving picture theater.

18. Witham, *Theatre in the Colonies*, 146.

19. Davis's stock players attained special status with serious theatergoers and drama reporters. One local writer noted during the summer of 1911, for example, that "people seem to forget, I fear, that stock actors must get up in their parts on very short notice and that they are expected to be as letter perfect at the first performance as they may be after long service in a single role with a traveling company. . . . If the playgoing people had an adequate idea of the tremendous transitions . . . [that] must be made within a week—indeed, must be made simultaneously—it seems to me there would be a higher regard for the mental attainments of stock actors."

20. Walther and Kruger, "A Brief History of the Cultural District," 18.

21. Cheney, *The Art Theater*, 15.

22. Theater and Drama Clipping Files, Carnegie Library of Pittsburgh, Pennsylvania Room.

23. Unattributed clipping, Anna Pearl McMunn Scrapbooks, Curtis Theatre Collection, University of Pittsburgh Library.

24. *Bulletin*, October 11, 1913, 10. Siebel was perhaps the best known of a group of working Pittsburgh playwrights and poets, among them the historian and playwright Samuel Church, whose *The Brayton Episode* was produced at the Alvin before it moved to Manhattan's Fifth Avenue Theater in 1905. The group also included the novelist Mary Roberts Rinehart, who had seven plays produced on local commercial stages in the first decade of the 1900s, and Jackson D. Haag, whose *Bachelors and Benedicts* was first staged in Pittsburgh before going on to Boston's Castle Square Theater in 1916. See "Boston Theater Playbills," Hypertextcatalog, www.hypertextcatalog.com/playbill/index.htm (accessed December 21, 2006).

25. A short life span seems to have been the fate of another art theater of the era—the Pittsburgh Theater Association, founded in 1916 under the direction of Thomas H. Dickinson. See Burleigh, *The Community Theatre*, 179.

26. *Pittsburgh Press*, June 7, 1959. The league's official records go back only to 1914. Curtis Theatre Collection, University of Pittsburgh Library.

27. The Drama League of America published a quarterly journal called *The Drama* containing new plays in addition to essays by theater critics.

28. Drama League of Pittsburgh Papers, Curtis Theatre Collection, University of Pittsburgh Library.

29. The School of Applied Design was renamed the College of Fine Arts in 1921.

30. See Fleming, *History of Pittsburgh and Environs*, 370; Kimberly, "A History of the Drama Department of Carnegie Mellon University," 5.

31. It is worth noting that Duquesne University created the area's first drama de-

partment in 1913, though it did not grant a degree. See Rishel, *The Sprit That Gives Life*, 20.

32. The first class of nine women and nine men studied Elementary Technic [*sic*], Rehearsal; Direction and Makeup, History of the Theater, Dramatic Literature, Dramatic Composition, Scene Painting, Costume Making, and History of Costume. Kimberly, "A History of the Drama Department of Carnegie Mellon University," 5.

33. See Payne, *A Life in a Wooden O*.

34. Ibid., 120.

35. Merriman Scrapbook, Curtis Theatre Collection, University of Pittsburgh Library.

36. Among Poel's legacies was a costume collection that was used by the School of Drama for many years. After eight years at the Shakespeare Memorial Theater at Stratford-upon-Avon, Payne became a professor of drama at the University of Texas at Austin in 1946 and founded the Shakespeare Festival at the Old Globe Theater in San Diego in 1949.

37. An early example of payola is the work of "Dramaticus," who wrote for the *Pittsburgh Gazette* in 1817. Dramaticus always managed to lavish praise on Mrs. Entwisle, the leading actress at the Theatre on Third Street. Her husband, John Entwisle, the theater manager and a playwright of some accomplishment, was no doubt capable of penning a convincing piece of "criticism" (Conner, *Spreading the Gospel of the Modern Dance*, 10).

38. Fleming names seven daily English language papers, a dozen foreign-language dailies, and twenty weekly suburban and/or specialty journals that were published in Pittsburgh in 1920 (*History of Pittsburgh and Environs*, 347).

39. Robinson, *Willa*, 98.

40. Conner, *Spreading the Gospel of the Modern Dance*, 10–12.

41. Andrews, *Pittsburgh's Post-Gazette*, 285.

42. The Shubert brothers began expanding their Philadelphia-based booking and leasing business into the New York region in 1901. At first the Shuberts cooperated with the Syndicate, but by 1904 the two organizations were actively at war. Then in 1905 the Shuberts made a deal with New York producer, playwright, and theater owner David Belasco, and together began building a circuit monopoly to rival the Syndicate chain. Sam Shubert was killed in May 1905 on a train en route to Pittsburgh "to wrest a Syndicate theater away from K & E" (Tenney, "In the Trenches," 5). In 1908 the Shuberts and the Syndicate attempted a reconciliation by forming the National Association of Theatrical Producing Managers to "arbitrate disputes and blacklist actors who jumped their contracts" (ibid., 7). The merger fell apart in 1909.

43. Belasco playbill, February 5, 1906, Curtis Theatre Collection, University of Pittsburgh Library.

44. All three organizations came to blows in Pittsburgh in 1907 when the Syndicate (specifically Klaw and Erlanger) decided to take a piece of the rapidly expanding vaudeville industry. "In 1907 came the historic battle between the Keith interests and the 'White Rats,' which made the Grand and Nixon deadly rivals," noted Harold Cohen in

the *Post-Gazette.* "The 'White Rats' were chiefly of the legitimate stage—George M. Cohan and Ethel Barrymore among them—who, through the reigning Shuberts and the firm of Klaw and Erlanger, had declared war on the Keith outfit and began to produce what they called 'Advanced Vaudeville.' The Nixon fired the opening gun, presenting Victor Herbert in person with his Forty Songbirds. The Grand answered with a string of celebrated vaudeville names and following this up with bills running as high as 20 acts" (September 26, 1936, 11).

45. Locations: American (North Side), Carnegie Music Hall (Oakland), Syria Temple (later called Syria Mosque, Oakland), Sheridan Square (Lower Hill), Simon (Lower Hill), Triangle (East Liberty), Hippodrome (in Machinery at the Point), and Empire (formerly called the East End, East Liberty).

46. "Pittsburgh First," *Pittsburgh Press,* December 1, 1923, 3. In this article the term *theater* refers to both live venues and some stand-alone movie houses.

47. Many Pittsburghers could not afford to buy tickets even at popular prices. Still, the democratization in theater pricing policies profoundly affected the Pittsburgh market.

48. Nixon programs, 1906–7, Curtis Theatre Collection, University of Pittsburgh Library.

49. These women were a considerable economic force by 1900, making up about 28 percent of the female working population in Pittsburgh (Kleinberg, *The Shadow of the Mills,* 149).

50. Merriman Collection, Curtis Theatre Collection, University of Pittsburgh Library.

51. George S. Kaufman was born in 1898 and grew up in various neighborhoods in Pittsburgh and New Castle. He graduated from Fifth Avenue High School and attended the University of Pittsburgh Law School for one semester while living in a boarding house at 6102 Walnut Street in Shadyside. He left Pittsburgh for New Jersey in 1910. See Goldstein, *George S. Kaufman;* and Teichman, *George S. Kaufman.*

52. The Liberty was a short-lived vaudeville house on Liberty Avenue near Wood Street. Liberty Theater program, April 1913, Barth Scrapbooks, Curtis Theatre Collection, University of Pittsburgh Library.

Chapter 5: *Theater as Distraction*

1. Source material for this historical snapshot from October 31, 1931, comes from programs, newspaper clippings, and promotional materials in the John Radovic Collection, Curtis Theatre Collection, University of Pittsburgh Library.

2. Fleming, *History of Pittsburgh and Environs,* 698.

3. Ibid., 699.

4. Hirschl, "Lillian Russell," 11.

5. Fleming, *History of Pittsburgh and Environs*, 699.

6. Shubert-Alvin program, Curtis Theatre Collection, University of Pittsburgh Library.

7. *Seven Day's Leave* was written by Walter Howard and became an international success during the war years. It was remade as a film in 1942 during World War II.

8. Duquesne Theatre program, March 3, 1919, in Pittsburgh Theater Programs, Library and Archives, Historical Society of Western Pennsylvania.

9. Unattributed clipping in the Theater and Drama Clipping Files, Carnegie Library of Pittsburgh, Pennsylvania Room.

10. Humphrey, *Pittsburgh and the Pittsburgh Spirit*, 360.

11. Lorant, *Pittsburgh*, 333, 335.

12. See McLean, *American Vaudeville as Ritual*; Stein, *American Vaudeville*; Trachtenberg, *The Incorporation of America*.

13. It is difficult to find official written evidence of restricted or racially segregated theaters after 1833. However, many sources note that the downtown playhouses had "colored" seating areas and many were "unfriendly" toward African Americans. A remark from 1936 indicates that the downtown theaters and concert halls were racially segregated and/or restricted: "Economic handicaps and the existence of the color line in theater and concert hall have few restrictions. Unwritten rules in musical, literary, art, and historical societies, and unexpressed but understood disfavor among their memberships have kept doors closed to Negroes in some of the most highly developed of the white community" (Glasco, *WPA History*, 293).

14. To address inequities shown to black performers working the white circuits, Sherman H. Dudley, a black vaudeville circuit comedian, began leasing and booking theaters in Washington, D.C., in 1912. He joined with producers Martin Klein, E. L. Cummings, and Milton Starr to form the Theater Owners' Booking Association (TOBA) in 1910 in the South and the Midwest. Its acronym was known as Tough On Black Asses among the African American performers forced to work under the harsh conditions imposed by the managers. George-Graves, *The Royalty of Negro Vaudeville*, 104–6.

15. Advertisements in the *Pittsburgh Courier*, 1914–30.

16. The PSO gave its first concert in 1896 under the direction of Frederic Archer. Victor Herbert was the chief conductor from 1898 to 1904. He was succeeded by Emil Paur from 1904 to 1910, the year the orchestra was disbanded.

17. Stage and Play Society program, Theater and Drama Clipping Files, Carnegie Library of Pittsburgh, Pennsylvania Room.

18. Wallace was the co-head of Carnegie Tech's School of Drama, with Ben Iden Payne, from 1924 to 1928, where he taught playwriting. Between 1928 and 1931 he ran his own professional company, the Chester Wallace Players, in addition to working with the Stage and Play Society. Chester Wallace Players Collection, Fine Arts Archives, Carnegie Mellon University.

19. Unattributed, undated newspaper clippings and programs, Theater and Drama Clipping Files, Carnegie Library of Pittsburgh, Pennsylvania Room.

20. The letter is in ibid.

21. Burleigh, *The Community Theatre*, xxxiii.

22. On the relationship between race and class in the little theater movement, see Chansky, *Composing Ourselves*, 3–7.

23. Between 1920 and 1930 the number of English-language daily newspapers in Pittsburgh declined from seven to three (*Post-Gazette; Sun-Telegraph; Press*). These changes reflected several mergers and acquisitions involving the Scripps Howard, Block, and Hearst newspaper syndicates. See Thomas, *Front Page Pittsburgh*, 145–58.

24. The founding officers were Earle John Cox, president; Lewis H. Able, vice president, Miss Rose Bell, secretary, and Fred T. Loeffler, treasurer (*Pittsburgh Mirror,* October 26, 1929).

25. December 1, 1923, 3. In the same article, the *Pittsburgh Sun* reported that Pittsburgh was the "fourth heaviest user of motion picture films in the country" and had become an important film exchange center with several storage and exchange businesses located on Forbes Street, including the Seltzer Film Exchange building.

26. Kann, *Show Places,* 71.

27. Million Dollar Grand programs, 1918, Curtis Theatre Collection, University of Pittsburgh Library.

28. Harry Davis Enterprises merged with the Clark and Stanley movie theater chain in 1927, forming the Stanley Corporation of America. In 1928 Warner Brothers bought it out and took possession of the Stanley on Seventh Street and the Million Dollar Grand on Fifth Avenue. The Warner marquee still marks the 1918 building.

29. *Bulletin,* December 1, 1923, 17; Aldine playbills, 1926–27, Curtis Theatre Collection, University of Pittsburgh Library. The Aldine was renamed the Senator in 1940 when the Harris Amusement Company took over its management and ran it as a movie theater. In 1950 it became the New Nixon after the original Nixon Theatre was torn down to make way for the Alcoa Building.

30. The opening was delayed two days because of the unexpected death of Marcus Loew. Walther and Kruger, "A Brief History of the Cultural District," 19.

31. In 1929 Loew's reported a box office gross of $1,750,000, and the corporation earned $240,000. Because of the stock market crash, around 1931 the Loew's chain began defaulting on dividends. About 1936, the Pittsburgh stockholders took control of the theater building, though the bookings and operations remained a part of the Loew's chain.

32. Loew's Penn program, Curtis Theatre Collection, University of Pittsburgh Library.

33. The Stanley Theatre was part of a $10 million development project that included the Clark Building next door. Walther, "A Brief History of the Cultural District," 20.

34. Stanley Theatre program, Merriman Scrapbooks, Curtis Theatre Collection, University of Pittsburgh Library.

35. Lorant, *Pittsburgh*, 481.

36. Kann, *Show Places*, 67.

37. Undated clipping, Theater and Drama Clipping Files, Carnegie Library of Pittsburgh, Pennsylvania Room.

38. Undated clipping, John Radovic Collection, Curtis Theatre Collection, University of Pittsburgh Library.

39. Ibid.

40. Ibid.

41. Programs, John Radovic Collection, Curtis Theatre Collection, University of Pittsburgh Library.

42. Harding immediately began work as a contract player for the Pathé company (later RKO). She played major roles in dozens of movies over the next three decades, culminating in *The Man in the Gray Flannel Suit* in 1956. Bannister's career was less successful, though he worked in both film and television as well as on the New York stage.

43. At the time of his death in 1951, Sharp was reportedly managing the Shubert Theater in Philadelphia (*Pittsburgh Press*, August 3, 1951, 10).

44. Londré and Watermeier, *The History of North American Theater*, 273.

45. Nixon programs, 1928, Curtis Theatre Collection, University of Pittsburgh Library.

46. Rheinhart, *The Life of Eleonora Duse*, 285–86.

Chapter 6: *Theater as Social Change*

1. Source material for this historical snapshot from April 9, 1937, comes from the *Pittsburgh Press*, March 29, 1937, 17; *Bulletin-Index*, April 15, 1937, 18; *Drama Review*, April 1937, 1; and Glasco, *WPA History*, 306.

2. How the other half of the Iron City lived was researched and chronicled in 1907 by a team of field sociologists employed by the Pittsburgh Survey, a project of the journal *Charities and the Commons* of the Russell Sage Foundation. Some fifty researchers lived and worked in several struggling communities (including the Hill District and Homestead) to study the social institutions and labor conditions of the city's wage earners and to document how a leading industrialized city was coping with rapid expansion.

3. See *Bulletin*, September 15, 1932, 18. The largest photographic documentation of Shantytown is at the Photo Antiquities Museum of Photographic History on East Ohio Street in Pittsburgh's North Side.

4. See the *Bulletin-Index*, November 24–27, 1930; Lorant, *Pittsburgh*, 482–87.

5. As many as 57,000 new members joined the American Communist Party between 1930 and 1934 (Klehr, *The Heyday of American Communism*, 153).

6. *New Theater*, February 1935, 4. On U.S. workers' theater movements, see Samuel et al., *Theatres of the Left*.

7. The oldest continuing union in Pittsburgh is Typographical Union No. 7, founded in 1836. Many trade unions (from marble setters to musicians to iron workers) were organized during the second half of the century. In 1881 the U.S. Federation of Organized Trades and Labor Unions was formed in Pittsburgh. The Pittsburgh Central Labor Union was chartered on October 20, 1901. See Archives Service Center of the University Library System, "Pittsburgh and Western Pennsylvania Labor Legacy Pilot Project: 1882–1935," University of Pittsburgh, http://www.library.pitt.edu/labor_legacy/18821935.htm.

8. This does not necessarily imply overt sympathy for socialist ideology among all of Pittsburgh's workers' theater groups. A study of Pittsburgh's United Electrical Workers notes: "One of the great paradoxes of the American labor movement is that it is and has primarily been, especially since the 1920s, a working-class movement outside of the broad stream of socialist thought. Most references to unions as the institutional expression of class struggle existed mainly in the early rhetoric of the movement, but rarely in its operating principles" (Filippeli and McColloch, *Cold War in the Working Class*, 3).

9. *Pittsburgh Press*, May 24, 1936, 7; *Bulletin Index*, May 27, 1937, 28.

10. William G. Beal, in *Time*, July 1, 1936, described the success of the New Theater's production of *Waiting for Lefty* as the "Pittsburgh phenomenon" and noted that he had "no explanation" for it. The "Pittsburgh phenomenon" that Beal (who identified himself as an employee of the National Broadcasting Company) refers to was surely the phenomenon of *Waiting for Lefty* itself—a play that captured the attention of both regular theater patrons and special-interest patrons brought into theaters all over the country on the strength of the play's prounion message.

11. In May 1935 the Federation of Non-Commercial Theaters was officially organized and was headquartered at the new home of the Pittsburgh Playhouse in Oakland. The federation set up a script-lending library and facilitated pooling scenery, props, and costumes owned by member companies. These included the IKS Players, Braddock Community Players, Hilltop Community Playhouse, Masquers, Kilbuck Players, New Theater, Crafton Players, and Drama League Players.

12. Most little theaters around the country were racially segregated, as Dorothy Chansky notes: "The self-selected Little Theater audience, regardless of class, geographical, or even internal differences, was very uniform in one sense: it was almost always racially segregated" (15).

13. Glasco, *WPA History*, 293.

14. The abandoned manuscript was housed in the Pennsylvania State Library. In 1970 it was rediscovered, microfilmed, and disseminated in manuscript form by Rollo Turner, professor of black history at the University of Pittsburgh. In 2004 Larry Glasco edited and published it under the title *The WPA History of the Negro in Pittsburgh*. Wright hired largely African American researchers and writers, including E. Marie Coleman—a theater colleague and a long-standing contributor to the black theater community in Pittsburgh.

15. See Glasco, *The WPA History of the Negro in Pittsburgh;* Bishop, "In the Shadow

of the Dream"; Historical Society of Western Pennsylvania, "Beyond Adversity"; Gottlieb, *Making Their Own Way;* Hoover, "The Place to Be."

16. Glasco, *WPA History,* 298–99.

17. Among them were the Carron Street Players (of the Carron Street Baptist Church) and the St. Benedict's Players (of the St. Benedict's Roman Catholic Church—the city's first black Catholic congregation). Ibid., 298.

18. Ibid., 299.

19. Ibid., 306.

20. A copy of this mission statement and the manuscript of *Independent Hamilton* are housed in the Walter Worthington Papers, Library and Archives, Historical Society of Western Pennsylvania.

21. Glasco, *WPA History,* 300.

22. Ibid., 300; Birchard, "The Curtaineers," 21.

23. Glasco, *WPA History,* 301, 303.

24. Birchard, "The Curtaineers," 21.

25. See Glasco, *WPA History,* 306.

26. The Columbia Council School was founded in response to the principles of social reform through education adopted by the National Council of Jewish Women at the Columbia Exposition of 1893.

27. The IKS Players were modeled on Chicago's Hull House Players, the nation's first Settlement House theater troupe, founded by the pioneering social worker Jane Addams for the production of "good plays" that would have a "salutary influence on the community" (Addams, *Twenty Years at Hull House,* 220).

28. Program and theater columns in the *IKS News,* Irene Kaufmann Settlement House Papers, Library and Archives, Historical Society of Western Pennsylvania.

29. See Kugemann, "In Between Cultural Heritage, Identity and the Integration Process."

30. Ibid. For more on German cultural life in mid-nineteenth-century Pittsburgh, see Faires, "Ethnicity in Evolution."

31. Clipping files, Curtis Theatre Collection, University of Pittsburgh Library.

32. The play was revised by Father Herman Kollig. During the 1980s the Veronica's Veil Players became a secular company producing standard comedies such as *Send Me No Flowers, Blithe Spirit, Abie's Irish Rose,* and *Arsenic and Old Lace.*

33. See "Newman Theater," Theater and Drama Clipping Files, Carnegie Library of Pittsburgh, Pennsylvania Room.

34. Mary E. Clancy Papers, Library and Archives, Historical Society of Western Pennsylvania.

35. Baird continued to head the University's Cap and Gown theater club even after he left Pitt to take a job as a senior research analyst for the Department of City Planning in 1917.

36. Merriman Collection, Curtis Theatre Collection, University of Pittsburgh Library.

37. Kelly, *Allegheny County*, 288. The South Park Playhouse was funded through tax dollars as a free service.

38. Merriman Collection, Curtis Theatre Collection, University of Pittsburgh Library.

39. Richard S. Rauh was the third generation of his family to be heavily involved in Pittsburgh's civic life. His grandfather was a musician with the original PSO. His father, Enoch Rauh, was a city councilman. His mother was the first woman to hold a cabinet post in Pittsburgh (and the first in any large city in Pennsylvania) when she became the head of the Department of Charities under Mayor Magee. In 1935 Richard married Helen Wayne (nee Sisenwain), the leading lady of the Pittsburgh Playhouse.

40. Proceedings of the Pittsburgh Playhouse, October 7, 1934, quoted in Moore, "The History of the Pittsburgh Playhouse," 6.

41. Program essay by Harvey Gaul, Pittsburgh Playhouse Collection, Curtis Theatre Collection, University of Pittsburgh Library.

42. Moore, "The History of the Pittsburgh Playhouse," 16.

43. Ibid., 17.

44. Kann, *Show Places*, 70. See also Butsch, *The Making of American Audiences*; Levine, *High Brow/Low Brow*.

45. Unattributed clipping, Theater and Drama Clipping Files, Carnegie Library of Pittsburgh, Pennsylvania Room.

46. Kann, *Show Places*, 73.

47. Unattributed clipping, Theater and Drama Clipping Files, Carnegie Library of Pittsburgh, Pennsylvania Room.

48. Lewis, "Pittsburgh's a Poor Road Town."

Chapter 7: *Theater as Regional Renaissance*

1. Source material for this historical snapshot from January 8, 1965, comes from the *Pittsburgh Post-Gazette* and the Pittsburgh Playhouse Collection, Curtis Theatre Collection, University of Pittsburgh Library.

2. Theater and Drama Clipping Files, Carnegie Library of Pittsburgh, Pennsylvania Room.

3. See the "Guide to the Four Evans Family Papers," Curtis Theatre Collection, University of Pittsburgh Library. The Four Evans made up the only complete American family in a war zone during World War II. After the war they continued their act, appearing in every major U.S. city and on television through 1960.

4. The city's remaining destination playhouses—all movie houses by then—were

also in various states of disrepair and declining prosperity. In November 1940, the entire roof and ceiling of the old Alvin Theatre (then called the Harris-Alvin) fell in during a film. No one was injured; still, the disaster signaled the beginning of the end.

5. Unattributed article, Theater and Drama Clipping Files, Carnegie Library of Pittsburgh, Pennsylvania Room.

6. Memorandum to the officers of the Allegheny Conference, in Mallett, "Redevelopment and Response," 180.

7. Ibid.

8. Edgar Kaufmann had originally given a million-dollar grant to the Pittsburgh Civic Light Opera, but agreed to Mayor Lawrence's request to use the money to launch the $7 million arena project if the Civic Light Opera could perform in the arena.

9. Concerns about the razing of this historic neighborhood were also raised by some city officials. In November 1956, Theodore L. Hazlett, executive director of the Urban Redevelopment Authority, publicly warned that the Hill demolition would cause a critical shortage of housing for African Americans. See Lorant, *Pittsburgh,* 504; Mallett, "Redevelopment and Response," 186.

10. Anonymous city official, quoted in Mallett, "Redevelopment and Response," 184; see also Glasco, "Double Burden."

11. The Negro Opera Company was founded by Mary Cardwell Dawson in 1941 and operated out of the Dawson School of Music in Larimer before evolving into the National Negro Opera Company with branches in several cities, including Pittsburgh. The Pittsburgh Opera Society, founded in 1939, was by the 1940s a semiprofessional organization with a sharing contract with the Pittsburgh Symphony. The Pittsburgh Civic Ballet, founded in 1927, was a semiprofessional community company in residence at the Arts and Crafts Center. Dancers with the Pittsburgh Ballet Theatre—a professional training studio begun in 1941—appeared with the Pittsburgh Opera, the Bach Choir, and the Tuesday Musical Club. The Pittsburgh Ballet Association, with a school on Reynolds Street in Point Breeze, trained students for professional careers and boasted four alumni dancing with Alicia Alonso's legendary Cuban Ballet in the early 1950s. The Bakaleinikoff Sinfonietta and the Fine Arts Society were founded by Vladimir Bakaleinikoff, assistant conductor of the Pittsburgh Symphony, to promote chamber music in all forms, with concerts held at the Historical Society in Oakland. The Bach Choir and the Mendelssohn Choir (dating from 1908) led a large field of concert singing groups in the city. The International Society for Contemporary Music presented new music ensembles from around the world in the Kresge Theater at Carnegie Tech. See *Cultural Activities in Pittsburgh and Allegheny County,* 10–43.

12. Birchard, "The Curtaineers," 22.

13. Undated clipping from "Called to the Colors," Theater and Drama Clipping Files, Carnegie Library of Pittsburgh, Pennsylvania Room.

14. Birchard, "The Curtaineers," 16–17.

15. Ibid., 31.

16. Ibid., 64.

17. Ibid., 67.

18. Ibid.

19. Worthington served for twenty-two years as a member of the Democratic Committee, and as executive director of the Western Pennsylvania Research and Historical Society led the way toward creating the African Heritage classroom at the University of Pittsburgh. See Walter Worthington Papers, Library and Archives, Historical Society of Western Pennsylvania.

20. See "Post-war Planning," *Bulletin-Index*, n.d. Theater and Drama Clipping Files, Carnegie Library of Pittsburgh, Pennsylvania Room.

21. Brignano, *Pittsburgh Civic Light Opera*, 11–15.

22. Ibid., 11.

23. Ibid., 14.

24. The first projected site for the company's new playhouse was a wooded area in Highland Park, but the plan was dropped because of neighborhood opposition before the City Council. The second site was an area in Schenley Park, but that too was protested by the estate of Mary Schenley. See Mallett, "Redevelopment and Response," 183.

25. Brignano, *Pittsburgh Civic Light Opera*, 80–82.

26. Barth Scrapbook, Curtis Theatre Collection, University of Pittsburgh Library.

27. Wagon Wheel file, Pittsburgh Theater Collection, Curtis Theatre Collection, University of Pittsburgh Library.

28. Edith Skinner Papers, Curtis Theatre Collection, University of Pittsburgh Library; see also Elizabeth "Bes" Kimberly Collection, Fine Arts Archives, Carnegie Mellon University.

29. The Foster Memorial was funded by pharmaceutical manufacturer Josiah K. Lily, an avid Foster collector. The Tuesday Musical Club was founded in 1889 as an "outlet for women musicians whose social status prevented them from doing anything professionally." It continues to operate as a performance club. See tuesmc.smartforaliving.com.

30. Nassif, "A History of the Pittsburgh Playhouse School," 23.

31. The architect's rendering for the never-built structure is in the Pittsburgh Playhouse Collection, Curtis Theatre Collection, University of Pittsburgh Library.

32. Nassif, "A History of the Pittsburgh Playhouse School," 179.

33. Gard and Burley, *Community Theatre*, 41.

34. *Bulletin-Index*, July 16, 1942, 17. One of the company's original revues, *Lend an Ear* (1940), had a successful New York run at the National Theater in 1948.

35. Gard and Burley, *Community Theatre*, 39.

36. Ibid.

37. Ibid., 35.

38. Ibid., 36.

39. Nassif, "A History of the Pittsburgh Playhouse School," 238.

40. Ibid., 325.

41. Ibid., 311.

42. Ibid., 336.

43. William Ball, in program for *Tiny Alice,* Pittsburgh Playhouse Collection, Curtis Theatre Collection, University of Pittsburgh Library.

44. Ibid.

45. Nassif, "A History of the Pittsburgh Playhouse School," 340–65.

46. Ibid., 365.

47. Ibid., 373.

48. Gottfried, *A Theater Divided,* 108.

49. Zeigler, *Regional Theatre,* 137.

Chapter 8: *Theater as Civic Identities*

1. Source material for this historical snapshot from March 21, 1975 is taken from the Pittsburgh Laboratory Theatre papers, Curtis Theatre Collection, University of Pittsburgh Library; *Pittsburgh Post-Gazette,* March 24, 1975; *Pittsburgh New Sun,* March 11, 1976; Gangaware, "An Interview with Three Directors."

2. Nassif, "A History of the Pittsburgh Playhouse School," 397.

3. Ibid., 429.

4. Butsch, *The Making of American Audiences,* 235.

5. Hazlett was a leading force in the cultural life of Pittsburgh from the 1950s through the 1970s. In his capacity as the president of the A.W. Mellon Educational and Charitable Trust and chairman of the Pennsylvania Council on the Arts, he championed the arts as an important factor in the economic health of the region and promoted both traditional arts institutions and experimental companies, especially during the critical years of the early 1970s.

6. Schneider, "Heinz Hall for the Performing Arts," 25.

7. While the final cost of the project is a matter of dispute, the Pittsburgh Symphony Web site lists it at $10 million.

8. Also on the gala program was a new work by Samuel Barber ("Fadograph of a Western Scene") commissioned by the Alcoa Foundation.

9. The other arts organization at Heinz Hall was the Pittsburgh Youth Symphony Orchestra, founded in 1946 by Marie Maazel and philanthropist Vira Heinz. The Pittsburgh Dance Council, founded in 1969, was added to the Heinz Hall roster in the early seventies.

10. See the Heinz Hall file, Pittsburgh Theater Collection, Curtis Theatre Collection, University of Pittsburgh Library.

11. The Internal Revenue Service's 501(c)3 code allowing for tax deductions for contributions to charitable and educational organizations was instituted in 1917. See Baumol and Bowen, *The Performing Arts;* Benedict, *Public Money and the Muse;* Lowry, *The Arts and Public Policy;* and Arian, *The Unfulfilled Promise.*

12. Between 1957 and 1976 the Ford Foundation distributed more than $400 million to U.S. cultural organizations. And in 1965 President Lyndon B. Johnson signed into law the National Endowment for the Arts to "develop and promote a broadly conceived national policy" in support of the arts. The NEA is headed by a president-appointed chairman reporting to the National Council on the Arts, an advisory panel of fourteen citizens with recognized knowledge in the field. In addition, since 1997 the council is required to appoint six members of Congress to serve in an ex officio, nonvoting capacity. See Conner, "National Endowments for the Arts."

13. See, for example, Gottfried, *A Theater Divided;* Novick, *Beyond Broadway.*

14. See Mallett, "Redevelopment and Response," 187–88.

15. Irvis was appointed assistant district attorney in Pittsburgh in 1957 and elected to the Pennsylvania House of Representatives in 1958. Over the next thirty years he served as the Democratic caucus chairman, minority whip, majority leader, and Speaker. See K. Leroy Irvis Papers, Archive Service Center, University of Pittsburgh.

16. Rawson, "Pittsburgh Playwright," A-5.

17. Snodgrass, *August Wilson,* 9.

18. Rawson, "Wilson Again Proves Home Is Where the Art Is," G-5.

19. Ibid., G-3.

20. The name of the company appears in print in several forms: Black Horizon and Black Horizons on the Hill; Black Horizon and Black Horizons Theater Company; and simply Black Horizons. I have chosen to use the name as it is written on Robert Penny's resume from 1974: Black Horizon Theater of Pittsburgh (Penny's resume is held privately by the Kuntu Repertory Theatre Company).

21. Baraka coined the term Black Arts in 1965, and poet Larry Neal published a widely disseminated essay called "The Black Arts Movement" in 1968. See Williams and Shannon, *August Wilson;* Elam, *The Past as Present;* Sanders, *The Development of Black Theater;* and Silver, *A History of the Karamu Theatre.*

22. "Rob Penny: Curriculum Vita."

23. Rawson, "Wilson Again Proves Home Is Where the Art Is," G-15.

24. In this period the Black Horizon Theater performed at the A. Leo Weil Elementary School, University of Pittsburgh Studio Theater, Soldiers and Sailors Memorial, Fifth Avenue High School Auditorium, Bidwell Training and Cultural Center on the North Side, and at Black Arts festivals in the Hill District and Homewood. The company also traveled, performing at Oberlin College in Ohio (1968), Tougaloo College in Mississippi (1970), Spirit House in New Jersey (1970), and Lee Cultural Center in Philadelphia (1970) ("Rob Penny: Curriculum Vita").

25. Claude Purdy moved to Saint Paul, Minnesota, where he worked with the Penumbra Theater. Ron Pitts left Pittsburgh and eventually reestablished Ujima in Columbus, Ohio, where it is still in operation.

26. Snodgrass, *August Wilson,* 11. The title of the play also appears in memoirs from the period as *Recycling.* See Baton, "August Wilson and Me."

27. Interview with Vernell Lillie, 2004; programs, brochures, and press releases, Kuntu Repertory Theatre archives, Department of Africana Studies, University of Pittsburgh.

28. Interview with Vernell Lillie, 2004. *Kuntu* means *way* or *mode* in Bantu, a term borrowed from a book that Lillie was using in her course in contemporary black drama.

29. It is wonderfully ironic that many of Kuntu's productions were mounted in a building honoring the work of Stephen Foster—the "father" of minstrel music. Fletcher Hodges, curator of the Foster collection, let the fledgling company use the stage and storage areas in these early years.

30. "Teacher's Study Guide for *Little Willy Armstrong Jones,*" 6.

31. Johnson attended the New York Metropolitan High School of the Performing Arts and studied at the Alvin Ailey Studio, Katherine Dunham School, and Lafayette Theater Workshop. He was an original cast member in the New York Shakespeare Festival's production of *Hair* and appeared in the premiere of Ed Bullins's *Goin' a Buffalo* at the American Place Theater.

32. Heimbuecher, "Pittsburgh's Black Theater Is Involved," 6.

33. Johnson had ART's administrative help and the use of its space at the Fine Line Cultural Center, the former Lab Theatre space at Fifth and Craig. The cast also included James R. Darby, Herman Mosley, and Gwendolyn Perry. Though ART supported the production in important ways, Bob Johnson (and the vestiges of Theater Urge) "produced" *Jitney* in the sense that Johnson had the artistic vision and the cultural connections—through his relationship with Wilson and his community of actors—to mount the production.

34. *Pittsburgh Press,* December 23, 1934, F-2. In the late seventies Lovelace encouraged the creation of the Marionette Theater Arts Council, an umbrella administrative structure run by a board of directors that included Carnegie Mellon's Earle Gister, Joan Apt, Marjorie Walker, and David Visser. That group oversaw a few more productions at the Museum of Art Theater, including Jorge Guerra's *The Days of the Great Buffalo,* but in 1983 the Lovelace Marionettes ended operations. Many of Lovelace's puppets were donated to the Pittsburgh Children's Museum.

35. The church's annex space was known as the Pittsburgh Laboratory Theatre from 1971 to 1979, the Soho Repertory Theater between 1979 and 1980, and the Famous Rider Cultural Center after 1980.

36. Swoyer, "Two Experimental Theaters," 84–85.

37. Royston disbanded the company in 1983 when he took a position in Philadelphia.

38. Unattributed article, August 1979, Theater and Drama Clipping Files, Carnegie Library of Pittsburgh, Pennsylvania Room.

39. In 1887 an agreement was reached whereby stockholders in the Carnegie Steel Company could buy at cost the shares of a deceased stockholder. It also stated that, at any time, three-quarters of the interest in the company and three-quarters of the associates in the company could request that an associate be obliged to assign, transfer, and sell his interest back to the company at book value. This stratagem designed by Phipps (with Carnegie the unseen author) allowed them to force out partners who threatened their interests.

40. After touring the East Coast and Great Britain, the company moved to New York City in 1981 and disbanded in 1985. Ironclad Agreement file, Pittsburgh Theaters Collection, Curtis Theatre Collection, University of Pittsburgh Library.

41. Press release, Theatre Express file, in ibid.

42. Swoyer, "Two Experimental Theaters," 83.

43. Leon Katz came to Pittsburgh in 1968 as the Andrew Mellon Professor of Drama at Carnegie Mellon. In 1978 he took a position at the University of Pittsburgh, where he stayed until moving to Yale University in 1981. During this period his plays were produced by the Artichoke Theater, the Experimental Theater, Theatre Express, and the Pittsburgh Laboratory Theatre.

44. Unattributed article, August 1979, Theater and Drama Clipping Files, Carnegie Library of Pittsburgh, Pennsylvania Room.

45. The irony of accepting grant money from the Mellon Foundation to stage theater critiques of its parent corporation was noted by the local press.

46. See Elvgren and Favorini, *Steel/City;* Favorini and Elvgren, "I Sing of Cities."

47. The renovation was initiated in the early 1970s by Steven George, director of the City Parks and Recreation Department, and Ted Hazlett of the A.W. Mellon Educational and Charitable Trust, which provided a million-dollar grant. The original tenant, the Vanguard Theatre, left shortly after the space opened in 1973 when the city decided to rent it to a variety of community groups ("Seven Theater Spaces in Pittsburgh," 69).

48. In 1970 Pittsburgh's Department of Parks and Recreation (Citiparks) began sponsoring the Park Players, an amateur summer theater company led by Carnegie Mellon professor Lynn George and staffed by CMU student actors, including at one time or another Cherry Jones, Holly Hunter, John Wells, and Marc Masterson. The Park Players continued until 1980.

49. Unattributed clipping, Theater and Drama Clipping Files, Carnegie Library of Pittsburgh, Pennsylvania Room.

50. See Mennen, "Theater"; G. Anderson, "PPT's Shaktman"; Uricchio, "Setting Stage for Success"; and Rawson, "Triumphant Triumvirate."

51. By the early 1970s there were scores of LORT theaters in cities all over the country, and with them an informal roster of professionally trained actors, directors, and designers who worked the circuit on a single-show contract basis. In many ways the LORT culture was the logical continuation of the combination touring company of the 1870s and 1880s, since it allowed professional theater artists to pursue careers outside New York City.

52. Tom Atkins grew up in the Pittsburgh area and graduated from Duquesne University in 1965. His national credits include many television and film roles, work in the leading regional theaters (Actors' Theater of Louisville; Goodman Theater; American Conservatory Theatre; Long Wharf; Harford Stage), and the New York Drama Desk Award for his performance in the Broadway production of David Storey's *The Changing Room*. Since the late 1990s Atkins has worked steadily on Pittsburgh stages, most notably as Art Rooney in Rob Zeller and Gene Collier's *The Chief*.

53. Gutkind, "Pittsburgh Public Theater," 41.

54. According to Alice Carter, under the Shaktman-Reick-Apt management team the subscription strategy included selling blocks of tickets to corporations and firms, which increased the number of subscriptions sold in the Public's first five years and accounts for the high capacity rates reported by the theater. However, since many subscribers did not use their tickets, actual attendance was sometimes much lower.

55. Budget figures are from "Pittsburgh Public Theater Financial Summary, 1974–1985," records held by the PPT. Attendance figures are from an unpublished research report by Lynne Conner, 1986 (author's collection).

56. Unattributed clipping, August 1979, Theater and Drama clipping files, Carnegie Library of Pittsburgh, Pennsylvania Room.

Chapter 9: *Theater as Cultural Capital*

1. Source material for this historical snapshot from July 26, 1985, is taken from advertisements and reviews published in *In Pittsburgh,* the *Pittsburgh Press,* and the *Pittsburgh Post-Gazette* for July 1985; programs, brochures, and clippings, Curtis Theatre Collection, University of Pittsburgh Library.

2. Between 1950 and 1990 Pittsburgh's population dropped from 676,806 to 369,879, and Allegheny County's population dropped from about 2,000,000 to less than 1,500,000. See Hoerr, *And the Wolf Finally Came;* McCollester, "Less Than Miraculous."

3. The original plan called for the rehabilitation of the Stanley Theatre (now the Benedum Center for the Performing Arts), a central plaza housing an office building, parking garage, and a new playhouse for the Pittsburgh Public Theater (now the O'Reilly Theater) and Theater Square, a park at the corner of Seventh and Penn avenues (Katz Plaza), the rehabilitation of the Art Cinema (now the Harris Theatre), and new sidewalks and decorative banners for Penn and Liberty avenues. Later arts-based real estate ventures included the purchase and rehabilitation of the Gayety/Fulton Theater (now the Byham Theater) and the renovation of a flatiron building at Wood and Liberty (now the Wood Street Galleries).

4. Unpublished slide-show presentation script, December 18, 1985; Cultural Trust file, Curtis Theatre Collection, University of Pittsburgh Library.

5. As the project moved forward, additional grants came from the Howard Heinz

Endowment, the Vira I. Heinz Endowment, the Pittsburgh Foundation, and the Eden Hall Foundation.

6. Performers included Don Brockett, Lynn Beckstrom, Joe Franze, Joe Negri, Karen Prunczik, Dakota Staton, Maggie Stewart, the Mendelssohn Choir, the CLO ensemble Mini-stars children's troupe.

7. *Pittsburgh Post-Gazette,* September 29, 1987, B-12; *In Pittsburgh,* September 9–15, 1987. Pittsburgh's 10 percent amusement tax, charged to both commercial and nonprofit arts organizations in the city, had been a source of controversy since the 1960s.

8. The PACCA study was the first of its kind in Pittsburgh and heralded a new era of arts management in which corporate-style strategies for long-term planning were first initiated. See *In Pittsburgh,* September 17–23, 1986, 1, 6.

9. Unattributed clipping, August 1979, Theater and Drama Clipping Files, Carnegie Library, Pennsylvania Room.

10. These theaters lasted only a season or two: American Place Theater, the Winter Company, Word of Mouth Theater, Homewood-Brushton Renaissance Players, School-Time Theater, Iron City Theater, American Experimental Theater, First Step, Perfect Circle Theater, African American Renaissance Theater, the Women's Theater, Pittsburgh Renaissance Theater, Veronica's Veil Players, and A Renaissance Player. These lasted longer but did not survive the decade: Famous Rider Theater Company, American Ibsen Theater, Allegheny Repertory Theatre, Carnegie Mellon Repertory Theater, and Pittsburgh Deaf Theater. These continued into the 1990s: Saltworks, Pittsburgh Mime Theater, Pelliken Multi-Arts, New Group Theatre, Wilkinsburg Arts Theater, Upstairs Theater, Laurel Highlands Regional Theatre/The Acting Company, and the Three Rivers Shakespeare Festival.

11. Press release, September 18, 1982, New Group Theatre papers, Curtis Theatre Collection, University of Pittsburgh Library.

12. *Pittsburgh Post-Gazette,* July 16, 1985.

13. Garth Emory Schafer, "The Acting Company of the Laurel Highlands Regional Theatre," http://www.geswho.net/The_Acting_Company/index.html; mission statement at http://www.geswho.net/The_Acting_Company/mission.html.

14. Program notes for *The Misanthrope,* October 1983, Curtis Theatre Collection, University of Pittsburgh Library.

15. Program notes for *Legend (in his own mind),* November 1980, author's collection.

16. Michele Pilecki, review in *Market Square,* July 24, 1985, 4.

17. Undated article, *In Pittsburgh,* author's collection.

18. *AIT: The Repertory Reader* 1 (Spring 1983): 4, Curtis Theatre Collection, University of Pittsburgh Library.

19. Complete brochures and programs are in the Three Rivers Shakespeare Festival Archive, Curtis Theatre Collection, University of Pittsburgh Library.

20. Undated clipping, Three Rivers Shakespeare Festival Papers, Curtis Theatre Collection, University of Pittsburgh Library.

21. Undated clippings from the *Pittsburgh Press* and *Pittsburgh Post-Gazette,* in ibid.

22. *Pittsburgh Post-Gazette,* April 15, 1988, 12; *Pittsburgh Press,* April 27, 1989.

23. Don Brockett Papers, Curtis Theatre Collection, University of Pittsburgh Library. Brockett also acted in local television (he played Chef Brockett on *Mister Rogers' Neighborhood)* and in the films *Flashdance* and *The Silence of the Lambs.* See Alice Carter's biographical essay, Don Brockett Papers, Curtis Theatre Collection, University of Pittsburgh Library.

24. Point Park alumni from this era include Rob Ashford, Tome Cousins, Melina Kanakaredes, and Billy Hartung.

25. The Andersons joined the CMU School of Drama in 1968 as faculty costume and set designers. Their book, *Costume Design* (1984), is a standard text in the field.

26. Program notes, *The Maids* (1978), Metropolitan Stage Company Papers, Pittsburgh Theater Collection, Curtis Theatre Collection, University of Pittsburgh Library. The Metropolitan Stage Company originally consisted of two performing groups, the Metro and the Workshop (headed by James Rosenberg and devoted to developing new scripts).

27. City Theatre Records, Curtis Theatre Collection, University of Pittsburgh Library.

28. Interview with Marc Masterson, January 20, 2006.

29. Ibid.

30. City Theatre's earlier attempt to purchase the former Duquesne Brewery building on the South Side failed when the owner could not provide a clear title for the property. See Rawson and Abels, "The Company That Dares to Be Different," G-4.

31. "Outreach Department" notes, Pittsburgh Public Theater season programs, author's collection.

32. "An August Heritage: The Pittsburgh Cycle—August Wilson 4/27/45–10/2/05," *Pittsburgh Post-Gazette,* http://www.post-gazette.com/pg/03001/497623.stm (accessed December 20, 2006); on Wilson's national impact, see Elam, *The Past as Present.*

Chapter 10: *Conclusion*

1. See Kloostra, "Top 25 Arts Cities."

2. Other Cultural Trust sites include several small galleries along the Penn-Liberty corridor, a projected riverfront park and a green-certified condominium style housing project to be built along the southern bank of the Allegheny River.

3. See, for example, Apple, "Where Steel Was King"; Neil, "Arms of Steel."

4. Ann Miner, *"The Producers." Talkin' Broadway: Pittsburgh,* 2002. http://www.talkinbroadway.com/regional/pitt/p41.html (accessed December 20, 2006).

5. Other new companies that have produced for at least one season since 1990 include: Promoters of Art, Pyramid Productions, Flying Pig Theater, Pittsburgh Queer

Theater, Genderbridge Theater, Irish Repertory Theater Pittsburgh, Artists Raising Consciousness of Humanity Inc., Axiom Theater, Pittsburgh Theater Laboratories, Perspective Theater, Pittsburgh New Voices, Pittsburgh New Works Festival, Pinnacle Players, South Park Theater, East End Productions, Proudly Presents Productions, We Quit Our Day Jobs, Acorn Theater Company, New Teeth Productions, Barebones Productions, Gemini Theater, Dog and Pony Show, Bricolage, Saints and Poets Theater, Pittsburgh Playwright's Theatre, Pittsburgh Playback Theater, Open Stage, New Horizon Theater, Jewish Theater of Pittsburgh, Primestage, No Name Productions, Theater of the Night, Timespace, Thoreau NM, Grex and Totally Bard.

6. In 2003 PICT toured with its production of Brian Friel's *The Faith Healer* to thirteen venues in Ireland, and in 2004 the company's production of *Major Barbara* appeared at the Galway Arts Festival and at the Pavilion Theater in Dublin.

7. The PMT school was endowed by actor and critic Richard E. Rauh, son of Pittsburgh Playhouse founders Richard S. Rauh and Helen Wayne Rauh.

8. The idea of a resident commercial theater company operated by individual proprietors or stockholders has largely disappeared except in New York City, where the term "Broadway" has come to represent profit-oriented theatrical ventures. In Pittsburgh, as in other regional cities, a few commercial theater companies continue to operate sporadically (for example, Jude Pohl Productions, Sunn Productions, and Latshaw Productions).

9. In 2006 Pittsburgh ranked fourth among major metropolitan areas in per capita charitable assets. In 2003, 18 percent of that funding went to arts-related activities *(Pittsburgh Post-Gazette,* June 5, 2006, C-3).

10. See, for example, Kreidler, "Leverage Lost"; "The Cultural Dynamics Map."

11. *Daily Post-Gazette,* January 9, 1866, 5; Pittsburgh Cultural Trust, "Mission Statement," http://www.pgharts.org/about/mission.aspx (accessed December 21, 2006).

12. Kaiden, "We Play Harder," 63.

13. Actors who have returned to live in the city include Larry John Meyers, Tom Atkins, the late Caitlin Clarke, Lenora Nemetz, Nancy Bach, Robin Walsh, Holly Thuma, Myrna Paris, Laurie Klatscher, Doug Mertz, Elena Alexandratos, Jeff Monahan, Ken Bolden, and Joe Schultz. Actors who work frequently in Pittsburgh include Ric McMillan, Douglas Rees, Jay O'Berski, Scott Ferrara, Derdriu Ring, David Conrad, Bryn Jameson, Billy Porter, and Simon Bradbury.

14. Stage artists who have taken faculty positions in Pittsburgh since 1990 and work regularly at local theaters include John Shepard, Pei-Chi Su, Rick Kemp, the late Heath Lamberts, Cindy Limauro, Melanie Dreyer, Stephanie Miller, Julie Alderdice Ray, Anne Mundell, Don Mangone, Steffi Mayer, Sheila McKenna, Rich Keitel, Tavia La Follette, Doug Mertz, Mary Rawson, Bruce McConachie, and Doug Levine.

15. Neither theater company has as of this writing chosen to develop a play by a resident Pittsburgh playwright. Geography seems to play a key role in the evaluation of plays and playwrights. I am reminded of a letter I received a few years ago when I was

the resident dramaturg at the Pittsburgh Public Theater. The writer wanted to submit one of his plays to the theater, but he also wanted to assure me that he was a "New York playwright" who just happened to be "living in Vermont."

16. Other resident writers who have also had success both locally and regionally since 1990 include Jeanne Drennan, Lissa Brennan, Mark Clayton Southers, Attilio Favorini, Lynne Conner, Scott Sickles, and James McManus, who received the 2006 Princess Grace Playwriting Award.

17. Supporters of new plays include Pyramid Productions, Genderbridge, the Upstairs Theater New Play Festival, Pittsburgh Playwright's Theatre, Pittsburgh New Voices, Acorn Theater Company, Red-Eye Theater Project, Future Ten, Pittsburgh Playback Theater, Sunday Night Live, the Gemini Theater New Play Festival, City Theatre's Young Playwrights' Festival, the CLO/CMU New Works Project, the Stages in History Program at the Heinz History Center, Pittsburgh Pride Theater Festival, and the Pittsburgh Playwright Theatre's Festival in Black and White.

18. Wilson's comments from a conversation with Javon Johnson, a playwright and actor trained at the University of Pittsburgh in the late 1990s. See Javon Johnson, "A Dialogue Between August Wilson and Javon Johnson," Dramatic Publishing, http://www.dramaticpublishing.com/AuthorsCornerDet.cfm?titlelink=9483&artnumber=1 (accessed December 21, 2006).

BIBLIOGRAPHY

Archival Sources

Carnegie Library of Pittsburgh, Pennsylvania Room

Foster's National Theater Programs, September 1857–September 1858
Nixon Theatre Playbills, 1917–1965
Nixon Theatre Programs, 1936–1952
Pittsburgh Playhouse Programs, 1945–1965
Pittsburgh Theatre Programmes, 1917–1938
PlayGoers Magazine, 1928–1932
Scrapbook of Pittsburgh Theatre Programmes, 1868–1942
Scrapbook of Programmes of the Alvin Theatre, 1899–1902
Theater and Drama Clipping Files

Curtis Theatre Collection, University of Pittsburgh Library

Anna Pearl McMunn Scrapbooks, 1909–1914
Barth Scrapbooks, 1905–1967
Cap and Gown Collection, 1909–1979
City Theatre Records, 1974–1991
Clippings Files, A–Z
Cultural Trust Archives
Don Brockett Papers
Drama League of Pittsburgh Papers
Edith Skinner Papers, 1929–1978
Federal Theater Project Bulletins, 1935–1936
George Baird Clipping Collection, 1915–1960
Ironclad Agreement Records, 1975–1985
John Radovic Collection, Programs and Clippings, 1916–1931
Kenyon Family Papers
Lovelace Marionette Theatre Records, 1952–1984
McHugh Family Collection, 1909–1930

Merriman Scrapbooks, 1865–1942

New Group Theatre Papers

99 Cent Floating Theatre Festival Archives, 1974–1981

Pittsburgh Playhouse Records, 1934–1973

Pittsburgh Savoyards Records, 1939–1974

Pittsburgh Theater Collection: American Ibsen Theater, Benedum Center for the Performing Arts, Carnegie Institute of Technology, Carnegie Mellon University, Civic Light Opera, Heinz Hall, Mountain Playhouse, New Group Theatre, Pittsburgh Laboratory Theatre, Pittsburgh Metropolitan Stage Company, Pittsburgh Public Theater, Upstairs Theater, White Barn Theater, William Penn Playhouse

Ralph Allan Burlesque Skit Collection

Row-Bernhardt Papers, 1910–1922

Steel City Collection, 1974–1977

Three Rivers Shakespeare Festival Records, 1979–1995

W. A. Solomon Papers, Theater Programs, 1869–1871

Fine Arts Archives, Carnegie Mellon University

American Conservatory Theatre (ACT)

Chester Wallace Players Collection

Elizabeth "Bes" Kimberly Collection

Scotch 'n' Soda Collection

William Ball Papers

Library and Archives of the Historical Society of Western Pennsylvania, Senator John Heinz Pittsburgh Regional History Center

A. B. Palmer Papers

Agnes M. Hays Gormly Scrapbook, 1870

Donald Butler Collection, 1920–1998

George Scully Scrapbooks, 1875–1903

Hill House Records

Irene Kaufmann Settlement House Records

Pittsburgh City Directories, 1815–1930

Pittsburgh Theater Programs

Pittsburgh Theaters: Nixon, Alvin, and Pitt, Records, 1906–1972

Pittsburgh Miscellaneous Playbills and Billheads, 1912–1928

Thaw Family Papers

Walter Worthington Papers

University of Pittsburgh

K. Leroy Irvis Papers
Kuntu Repertory Theatre Archive, Department of Africana Studies, University of
    Pittsburgh

Newspapers on Microfilm, University of Pittsburgh Library

Daily Pittsburgh Gazette
National Labor Tribune
New Pittsburgh Courier
Pitt News [University of Pittsburgh]
Pittsburgh Commercial Gazette
Pittsburgh Courier
Pittsburgh Daily Dispatch
Pittsburgh Daily Gazette
Pittsburgh Daily Gazette and Advertiser
Pittsburgh Daily Morning Post
Pittsburgh Evening Telegraph
Pittsburgh Evening Telegraph Weekly
Pittsburgh Gazette
Pittsburgh Gazette and Manufacturing and Mercantile Advertiser
Pittsburgh Gazette-Commercial
Pittsburgh Gazette-Times
Pittsburgh Post
Pittsburgh Post-Gazette
Pittsburgh Post-Gazette and Sun-Telegraph
Pittsburgh Press
Pittsburgh Sun
Pittsburgh Sun-Telegraph

Interviews Conducted by the Author

Attilio Favorini, February 16, 2006
Vernell Lillie, June 23, 2004
Marc Masterson, January 20, 2006

Works Consulted

Addams, Jane. *Twenty Years at Hull House, with Autobiographical Notes*. Urbana: University of Illinois Press, 1990.

Alberts, Robert C. *Pitt: The Story of the University of Pittsburgh, 1787–1987*. Pittsburgh: University of Pittsburgh Press, 1986.

Alger, William Rounseville. *Life of Edwin Forrest, The American Tragedian*. Vol. 1. Philadelphia: J.B. Lippincott, 1877.

Anderson, Barbara, and Cletus Anderson. *Costume Design*. New York: Holt, Rinehart and Winston, 1984.

Anderson, Edward Park. "The Intellectual Life of Pittsburgh, 1786–1936: The Theater." *Western Pennsylvania Historical Society Magazine* 14 (1931): 225–32.

Anderson, George. "PPT's Shaktman Led City's Theatrical Renaissance." *Pittsburgh Post Gazette*, June 28, 1982, 19, 22.

Andrews, J. Cutler. *Pittsburgh's Post-Gazette: The First Newspaper West of the Alleghenies*. Boston: Chape and Grimes, 1936.

Apple, R. W. "Where Steel Was King, a New Spirit Reigns." *New York Times*, July 30, 1999, B-31, 37.

Arian, Edward. *The Unfulfilled Promise: Public Subsidy of the Arts in America*. Philadelphia: Temple University Press, 1989.

Baldwin, Leland D. *Pittsburgh: The Story of a City*. Pittsburgh: University of Pittsburgh Press, 1937.

Bank, Rosemarie K. "Archiving Culture: Performance and American Museums in the Earlier Nineteenth Century." In *Performing America: Cultural Nationalism in American Theater*, edited by Jeffrey D. Mason and Ellen Gainor. Ann Arbor: University of Michigan Press, 1999.

———. *Theatre Culture in America, 1825–1860*. Cambridge: Cambridge University Press, 1997.

Barca, Dana. "Adah Isaacs Menken: Race and Transgendered Performance in the 19th Century." *Melus* 29 (Winter 2004): 293, 306.

Baskind, Sanford. "A 1937 Stroll Down Murray Avenue." *Jewish Chronicle*, May 12, 1994.

Batcheller, J. D. "A Comprehensive History of the Theatre in Pennsylvania with Particular Stress upon the Early Developments in Philadelphia and the Early Companies in the West." PhD diss., Carnegie Institute of Technology, 1936.

Baton, Maisha, as told to Eugene J. Douglas. "August Wilson and Me: The Early Years." *Acting Now.com*, November 2005, 1–5.

Baumol, William J., and William G. Bowen. *The Performing Arts: The Economic Dilemma: A Study of Problems Common to Theater, Opera, Music, and Dance*. New York: Twentieth Century Fund, 1966.

Baynham, Edward Gladstone. "A History of Pittsburgh Music, 1758–1958." Manuscript, University of Pittsburgh Music Library, 1970.

Bean, Annemarie, James V. Hatch, and Brooks McNamara, eds. *Inside the Minstrel Mask: Readings in Nineteenth-Century Blackface Minstrelsy.* Middletown, CT: Wesleyan University Press, 1996.

Beeson, William, ed. *Thresholds: The Story of Nina Vance's Alley Theatre.* Houston: Wall, 1968.

Benedict, Stephen. *Public Money and the Muse: Essays on Government Funding for the Arts.* New York: Norton, 1991.

Birchard, Carl. "The Curtaineers: A Study of an Interracial Dramatics Project of the Irene Kaufmann Settlement of Pittsburgh from Its Inception, November 1943 to February 1948." Master's thesis, University of Pittsburgh, 1948.

Bishop, Janet L. "In the Shadow of the Dream: The Black Pittsburgh Community 1850–1870." Bachelor of Arts thesis, Princeton University, 1982.

Blank, Edward. "What Happened to All the Old Theatres?" *Pittsburgh Press,* July 10, 1983, 225–36.

Bode, Carl. *The American Lyceum: Town Meeting of the Mind.* New York: Oxford University Press, 1956.

Boucher, John Newton, ed. *A Century and a Half of Pittsburgh and Her People.* New York: Lewis, 1908.

Brackenridge, Henry Marie. "Pittsburgh in the Olden Time." *Literary Casket* 3 (July 1842): 12.

———. *Recollections of Persons and Places in the West.* Pittsburgh: John Kay, 1834.

Brantley, Ben. "The World That Created August Wilson." *New York Times,* February 5, 1995, Sec. 2: 1–2, 5.

Brignano, Mary. *Curating the District: How the Pittsburgh Cultural Trust Is Transforming the Quality of Urban Life.* Pittsburgh: Pittsburgh Cultural Trust, 2000.

———. *Pittsburgh Civic Light Opera: How the Dreams Came True.* Sewickley, PA: White Oak Publishing, 1996.

Brockett, Oscar, and Franklin J. Hildy. *History of the Theatre.* 9th ed. Boston: Allyn and Bacon, 2003.

Brown, Jared. *The Theatre in America During the Revolution.* Cambridge: Cambridge University Press, 1995.

Buchanan, Singer Alfred. "A Study of the Attitudes of the Writers of the Negro Press Toward the Depiction of the Negro in Plays and Films: 1930–1965." PhD diss., University of Michigan, 1968.

Buck, Solon J., and Elizabeth H. Buck. *The Planting of Civilization in Western Pennsylvania.* Pittsburgh: University of Pittsburgh Press, 1939.

Buni, Andrew. *Robert L. Vann of the Pittsburgh Courier: Politics and Black Journalism.* Pittsburgh: University of Pittsburgh Press, 1989.

Burleigh, Louise. *The Community Theatre.* Boston: Little, Brown, 1917.

Butsch, Richard. *The Making of American Audiences.* Cambridge: Cambridge University Press, 2000.

Carnegie, Andrew. *The Andrew Carnegie Reader*, edited by Joseph Frazier Wall. Pittsburgh: University of Pittsburgh Press, 1992.

———. "A Great Gift to the People." *Pittsburgh Post*, November 6, 1895, 1–2.

Carson, William Glasgow Bruce. *The Theatre on the Frontier: The Early Years of the St. Louis Stage*. Chicago: University of Chicago Press, 1932.

Chansky, Dorothy. *Composing Ourselves: The Little Theater Movement and the American Audience*. Carbondale: Southern Illinois University Press, 2004.

Chapman, T. J. "Amusements in Early Pittsburgh." *Pittsburgh Post*, January 18, 1903.

Cheney, Sheldon. *The Art Theater: Its Character as Differentiated from the Commercial Theater; Its Ideals and Organization; and a Record of Certain European and American Examples*. New York: Knopf, 1917 (rpt. Kraus Reprint Co., 1969).

Claeren, Wayne Henry. "Bartley Campbell: Playwright of the Gilded Age." PhD diss., University of Pittsburgh, 1975.

Clark, Barrett H. *Favorite American Plays of the Nineteenth Century*. Princeton: Princeton University Press, 1943.

Cockrell, Dale. *Demons of Disorder: Early Blackface Minstrels and Their World*. Cambridge Studies in America Theatre and Drama no. 8, 1997.

Cohen, Harold. "Plays at Fort Pitt Were Forerunner of Pittsburgh Theatre." *Pittsburgh Post-Gazette*, September 26, 1936, 11.

Coleman, Emily. "Theatre USA: The Pittsburgh Playhouse." *Theatre Arts* 42 (February 1958): 59–60.

Collins, John F. *Stringtown on the Pike: Tales and History of East Liberty and the East Liberty Valley of Pennsylvania*. Ann Arbor, MI: Edwards Brothers, 1978.

Connelly, Eugene LeMoyne. "The First Motion Picture Theatre." *Western Pennsylvania Historical Magazine* 23 (March 19, 1940): 1–12.

———. "The Life Story of Harry Davis." *Pittsburgh Sun-Telegraph*. January 3, 1940, 15, 23.

Conner, Lynne. "National Endowments for the Arts." In *Oxford Encyclopedia of Theatre and Performance*, edited by Dennis Kennedy, 916. New York and London: Oxford University Press, 2003.

———. "A Public Theater." *Pittsburgh Public Theater 2000–2001 Season Guide*. Pittsburgh: Pittsburgh Public Theater, 2000.

———. "611 and 621 Penn Avenue: A Tale of Two Buildings." *Pittsburgh Public Theater 1999–2000 Season Guide*. Pittsburgh: Pittsburgh Public Theater, 1999.

———. *Spreading the Gospel of the Modern Dance: Newspaper Dance Criticism in the United States, 1850–1934*. Pittsburgh: University of Pittsburgh Press, 1997.

———. "'What the Modern Dance Should Be': Socialist Agendas in the Modern Dance, 1931–38." In *Crucibles of Crisis: Performing Social Change*, edited by Janelle Reinelt. Ann Arbor: University of Michigan Press, 1996.

Cotkin, George. *Reluctant Modernism: American Thought and Culture, 1880–1900*. New York: Twayne Publishers, 1992.

Couvares, Francis G. "The Plebeian Moment: Theatre and Working-Class Life in Late Nineteenth-Century Pittsburgh." In *Theatre for Working-Class Audiences in the United States, 1830–1980,* edited by Bruce A. McConachie and Daniel Friedman. Westport, CT: Greenwood Press, 1985.

———. *The Remaking of Pittsburgh: Class and Culture in an Industrializing City, 1877–1919.* Albany: State University of New York Press, 1984.

Craig, Neville B. *History of Pittsburgh.* Pittsburgh: J.R. Weldin, 1917 (rpt. of J. H. Mellor, 1851).

Cramer, Zadok. *The Navigator: Containing Directions for Navigating the Ohio, and Mississippi Rivers; With an Ample Account of These Much Admired Waters . . . And a Concise Description of Their Towns, Villages, Harbors, Settlements, etc. With Maps of the Ohio and Mississippi to Which is Added An Appendix, Containing an Account of Louisiana, and of the Missouri and Columbia Rivers, As Discovered By the Voyage Under Captains Lewis and Clark.* 8th ed. Pittsburgh: Cramer and Spear, Franklin Head Bookstore, 1814 (orig. publ. 1801).

"Crash Recalls Great History of Old Alvin." *Pittsburgh Post-Gazette,* November 15, 1940, 5.

Crouch, Stanley. *One Shot Harris: The Photographs of Charles "Teenie" Harris.* New York: Harry N. Abrams, 2002.

Cullen, Jim. *The Art of Democracy: A Concise History of Popular Culture in the United States.* New York: Monthly Review Press, 1996.

Cultural Activities in Pittsburgh and Allegheny County. Pittsburgh: Allegheny Conference on Community Development, 1952.

"The Cultural Dynamics Map: Exploring the Arts Ecosystem of the United States." Report issued by the Cultural Dynamics Working Group, 2005.

Cuming, Fortesque. *Sketches of a tour to the western country: through the states of Ohio and Kentucky, a voyage down the Ohio and Mississippi rivers, and a trip through the Mississippi territory, and part of West Florida, commenced at Philadelphia in the winter of 1807, and concluded in 1809.* Pittsburgh: Cramer, Spear and Eichbaum, 1810.

Dahlinger, Charles William. *Pittsburgh: A Sketch of its Early Social Life.* New York: G.P. Putnam's Sons, 1916.

Davis, Christine. "A Phase I Cultural Resource Survey of the Proposed Theatre Square Project; City of Pittsburgh, Allegheny County, Pennsylvania." Report prepared for the Pittsburgh Cultural Trust, August 1983.

DeGovia, C. J. *The Community Playhouse.* New York: B.W. Huebsch, 1923.

Demarest, David P., ed. *The River Ran Red: Homestead 1892.* Pittsburgh: University of Pittsburgh Press, 1992.

Dickens, Charles. *American Notes for General Circulation.* Middlesex: Penguin Books, 1985.

Downes, Randolph C. *Council Fires on the Upper Ohio.* Pittsburgh: University of Pittsburgh Press, 1969.

Druckenbrod, Andrew. "Green Light for Culture." *Symphony: The Magazine of the American Symphony Orchestra League,* July–August 2004, 70–76.

Dudden, Faye E. *Women in the American Theatre: Actresses and Audiences, 1790–1870.* New Haven and London: Yale University Press, 1994.

Dunlap, William. *The History of the American Theatre.* New York: Burt Franklin, 1963 (orig. publ. 1823).

Durham, Weldon B, ed. *American Theatre Companies, 1749–1887.* Westport, CT: Greenwood Press, 1986.

Elam, Harry, Jr. *The Past as Present in the Drama of August Wilson.* Ann Arbor: University of Michigan Press, 2004.

———, and David Krassner, eds. *African American Performance and Theatre History: A Critical Reader.* New York: Oxford University Press, 2001.

Ellsler, John A. *The Stage Memories of John A. Ellsler.* Cleveland: n.p., 1950.

Elvgren, Gillette, and Attilio Favorini. *Steel/City: A Docudrama in Three Acts.* Pittsburgh: University of Pittsburgh Press, 1976, 1992.

Emerson, Ken. *Doo-Dah!: Stephen Foster and the Rise of American Popular Culture.* New York: Simon and Schuster, 1997.

Epstein, Abraham. *The Negro Migrant in Pittsburgh.* New York: Arno Press, 1969.

Evans, Henry O. *Iron Pioneer: Henry W. Oliver, 1850–1905.* New York: E.P. Dutton, 1942.

Faires, Nora. "Ethnicity in Evolution: The German Community in Pittsburgh and Allegheny City, Pennsylvania, 1845–1885." PhD diss., University of Pittsburgh, 1981.

Favorini, Attilio, and Gillette Elvgren. "I Sing of Cities: The Musical Documentary." In *Performing Democracy: International Perspectives on Urban Community-Based Performance,* edited by Susan C. Haedicke and Tobin Nellhaus. Ann Arbor: University of Michigan Press, 2001.

Fenton, Edwin. *Carnegie Mellon 1900–2000: A Centennial History.* Pittsburgh: Carnegie Mellon University Press, 2000.

Filippelli, Ronald L., and Mark D. McColloch. *Cold War in the Working Class: The Rise and Decline of the United Electrical Workers.* Albany: State University of New York Press, 1995.

Fleming, George T. *History of Pittsburgh and Environs.* Vol. 2. New York and Chicago: American Historical Society, 1922.

———. "Old Theaters and Theatricals," *Gazette Times,* April 30, Sec. 5, 3; May 14, 1922, Sec. 5, 2.

Fletcher, Edward Garland. "Records and History of Theatrical Activities in Pittsburgh, Pa., from Their Beginning to 1861." PhD diss., Harvard University, 1931.

Frick, John W. *Theatre, Culture and Temperance Reform in Nineteenth-Century America.* Cambridge: Cambridge University Press, 2003.

Gaer, Joseph, ed. *The Theatre of the Gold Rush Decade in San Francisco.* N.p., 1935.

Gangeware, Robert. "An Interview with Three Directors." *Carnegie Magazine,* February 1976, 54–87.

Gard, Robert E., and Gertrude S. Burley. *Community Theatre: Idea and Achievement.* New York: Duell, Sloan and Pearce, 1959.

————. *Grassroots Theatre: A Search for Regional Arts in America*. Madison: University of Wisconsin Press, 1955.

Gardner, Dorothea Breitwieser. "History of the Nixon Theatre." PhD diss., University of Pittsburgh, 1959.

Garff, Wilson B. *Three Hundred Years of American Drama and Theatre*. Englewood Cliffs, NJ: Prentice-Hall, 1973.

George-Graves, Nadine. *The Royalty of Negro Vaudeville: The Whitman Sisters and the Negotiation of Race, Gender and Class in African American Theater, 1900–1940*. New York: St. Martin's Press, 2000.

Gillespie, Charles H. "Old Time Actor." *Pittsburgh Press*, August 23, 1908.

Glasco, Laurence. "Double Burden: The Black Experience in Pittsburgh." In *City at the Point: Essays on the Social History of Pittsburgh*, edited by Samuel Hays. Pittsburgh: University of Pittsburgh Press, 1989.

————, ed. *The WPA History of the Negro in Pittsburgh,* compiled by J. Ernest Wright. Pittsburgh: University of Pittsburgh Press, 2004.

Glazier, Willard. *Peculiarities in American Cities*. Philadelphia: Hubbard Brothers, 1884.

Golden, Margaret. "Directory of Theatre Buildings in Use in Pittsburgh, Pa., Since Earliest Times." Master's thesis, Carnegie Institute of Technology, 1953.

Goldstein, Malcolm. *George S. Kaufman: His Life, His Theater*. Oxford and New York: Oxford University Press, 1979.

————. *The Political Stage: American Drama and Theatre of the Great Depression*. New York: Oxford University Press, 1974.

Gottfried, Martin. *A Theater Divided: The Postwar American Stage*. Boston: Little, Brown, 1967.

Gottlieb, Peter. *Making Their Own Way: Southern Blacks' Migration to Pittsburgh, 1916–30*. Urbana and Chicago: University of Illinois Press, 1987.

Grimsted, David. *Melodrama Unveiled: American Theater and Culture, 1800–1850*. Chicago: University of Chicago Press, 1968.

Gutkind, Lee. *The Glory of the Stanley, the Inspiration of the Benedum*. Pittsburgh: Pittsburgh Trust for Cultural Resources, 1987.

————. "Pittsburgh Public Theater: Is It Pittsburgh or Public?" *Pittsburgh Magazine* 9 (November 1978): 41–43, 94–95.

Hale, R. Nelson. "The Pennsylvania Population Company." *Pennsylvania History* 16 (April 1949): 122–30.

Haller, Robert A. "Film Arrives in Pittsburgh in 1896." *Field of Vision* 5 (Winter 1978–79): 2.

Harley, Thomas Roger. "Alvin Theatre: History of a Pittsburgh Institution." Manuscript, December 4, 1979, Curtis Theatre Collection.

Hay, Samuel A. *African American Theatre: A Historical and Critical Analysis*. Cambridge: Cambridge University Press, 1994.

Heimbuecher, Ruth. "Pittsburgh's Black Theater Is Involved." *Pittsburgh Press Roto*, July 11, 1976: 6–11.

Henderson, Archibald. *Pioneering a People's Theatre*. Chapel Hill: University of North Carolina Press, 1945.

Henderson, Mary C. *The City and the Theatre: New York Playhouses from Bowling Green to Times Square*. Clifton, NJ: J.T. White, 1973.

Hewes, Henry. "The Drama Prospers in Pittsburgh." *Theatre Arts* 36 (October 1952): 33–34.

Hewlitt, Barnard. *Theatre U.S.A.: 1665–1957*. New York: McGraw-Hill, 1959.

Hill, West T. *The Theatre in Early Kentucky, 1790–1820*. Lexington: University of Kentucky Press, 1971.

Hine, Al. "Pittsburgh." *Holiday*, October 1949, 34–48, 50–51, 128.

Hinshaw, John. *Steel and Steelworkers: Race and Class Struggle in Twentieth-Century Pittsburgh*. Albany: State University of New York Press, 2002.

Hirschl, Beatrice Paul. "Lillian Russell: Actress Played a Part in Pittsburgh." *Pittsburgh Tribune Review*, August 25, 2002, 8–11.

Historical Society of Western Pennsylvania, "Beyond Adversity." Pittsburgh: Museums Programs Division, Library and Archives of the Historical Society of Western Pennsylvania, 1993.

Hoerr, John. *And the Wolf Finally Came: The Decline of the American Steel Industry*. Pittsburgh: University of Pittsburgh Press, 1988.

Hoover, Bob. "The Place to Be: 100 Years of Pittsburgh's Hottest Spots." *Pittsburgh Post-Gazette*, April 18, 2004, G-1, 10, 11.

Hornblow, Arthur. *A History of the Theatre in America From Its Beginnings to the Present Time*. Vols. 1–2. Philadelphia and London: J.B. Lippincott, 1919.

Hughes, Glenn. *A History of the American Theatre, 1700–1950*. New York: Samuel French, 1951.

Humphrey, Arthur Luther. *Pittsburgh and the Pittsburgh Spirit*. Pittsburgh: Chamber of Commerce of Pittsburgh, 1927.

Iggers, Georg G. "From Macro to Microhistory: The History of Everyday Life." In *Historiography in the Twentieth Century: From Scientific Objectivity to the Postmodern Challenge*, 101–17. Hanover, NH: University Press of New England, for Wesleyan University Press, 1977.

The Iron City : A Compendium of Facts Concerning Pittsburgh and Vicinity, for Strangers and the Public Generally. Pittsburgh: G.W. Pittock and K. McFall, 1867.

James, Reese D. *Old Drury of Philadelphia: A History of the Philadelphia Stage, 1800–1835*. New York: Greenwood Press, 1968.

Johnson, Claudie D. "That Guilty Third Tier: Prostitution in Nineteenth-Century American Theaters." *American Quarterly* 27 (1975): 575–84.

Jones, Chris. "Homeward." *American Theatre*, November 1999, 14–17, 69–70.

Jukes, Donald. "American Ibsen Theater: Rising and Falling in the Master's Shadow." PhD diss., University of Pittsburgh, 1993.

Kaiden, Elizabeth. "We Play Harder: Theater Artists Are Turning Pittsburgh's Conservatism into an Asset." *American Theater* 20 (April 2003): 61–67.

Kann, S. L. *Show Places, Know Places, Go Places in Pittsburgh*. Pittsburgh: Lee-Art Publishing, 1932.

Kelly, George Edward, ed. *Allegheny County: A Sesqui-Centennial Review, 1788–1938*. Pittsburgh: Allegheny County Sesqui-Centennial Committee, 1938.

Kenyon, Elmer. "Old Pittsburgh and Her Young Theatres." *Storegram,* May 1927.

Killikelly, Sarah H. *The History of Pittsburgh: Its Rise and Progress*. Pittsburgh: B.C. and Gordon Montgomery Co., 1906.

Kimberly, Elizabeth Scrader. "A History of the Drama Department of Carnegie Mellon University." Carnegie Mellon University, 1982.

Klehr, Harvey. *The Heyday of American Communism: The Depression Decade*. New York: Basic Books, 1984.

Kleinberg, S. J. *The Shadow of the Mills: Working-Class Families in Pittsburgh, 1870–1907*. Pittsburgh: University of Pittsburgh Press, 1989.

Kloostra, Christine. "Top 25 Arts Cities." *American Style Magazine,* June 2006.

Korol, Paul S. "When Electricity Came to Pittsburgh." *Pittsburgh Senior News,* March 2004.

Kreidler, John. "Leverage Lost: The Nonprofit Arts in the Post-Ford Era." *In Motion Magazine,* February 16, 1996.

Krich, John F. "The Amiable Lady Charms the Iron City: Adah Isaacs Menken in Pittsburgh." *Western Pennsylvania Historical Society Magazine* 51 (1968): 259–78.

Kugemann, Monika. "In Between Cultural Heritage, Identity and the Integration Process: German-American Life, Theater, Music, and Social Events in Pittsburgh 1843–1873: A Historical Case Study." PhD diss., Friedrich-Alexander-Universität Erlangen/Nurnberg, forthcoming.

Kuntz, Leonard Irvin. "The Changing Pattern of the Distribution of the Jewish Population of Pittsburgh from Earliest Settlement to 1963." PhD diss., Louisiana State University, 1970.

Larson, Carl F. W. *American Regional Theatre History to 1900: A Bibliography*. Metuchen, NJ: Scarecrow Press, 1979.

Lears, T. J. Jackson. *No Place of Grace: Antimodernism and the Transformation of American Culture, 1880–1920*. Chicago: University of Chicago Press, 1994.

Lee, Alfred McClung. "Trends in Commercial Entertainment in Pittsburgh." Master's thesis, University of Pittsburgh, 1931.

Lemon, Brendan. "For Pittsburgh, the Latest Stage in a Long Revival." *New York Times,* December 26, 1999, Arts and Leisure, 4, 18.

Leslie, James Edward. "Thirty Years of Pittsburgh Theaters." *Pittsburgh Dispatch,* December 8, 1912, Sec. 6, 5.

Levi, Giovanni. "On Microhistory." *New Perspectives on Historical Writing,* edited by Peter Burke, 93–113. University Park: Pennsylvania State University Press, 1992.

Levine, Lawrence. *High Brow/Low Brow: The Emergence of a Cultural Hierarchy in America*. Cambridge: Harvard University Press, 1988.

Lewis, Beatrice. "Pittsburgh's a Poor Road Town, but Just Needs Encouragement." *New York Herald Tribune*, July 6, 1941.

Lewis, Emory. *Stages: The Fifty Year Childhood of the American Theatre*. Englewood Cliffs, NJ: Prentice-Hall, 1969.

Lewis, William J. "The Passing Show—A Drama Editor Glances Backward." *Pittsburgh Sun-Telegraph*, September 15, 1941.

Londré, Felicia Hardison, and Daniel J. Watermeier. *The History of North American Theater From Pre-Columbian Times to the Present*. New York: Continuum Publishing Company, 1998.

Lorant, Stefan. *Pittsburgh: The Story of an American City*. New York: Doubleday, 1964.

Lott, Eric. *Love and Theft: Blackface Minstrelsy and the American Working Class*. New York: Oxford University Press, 1993.

Lowrie, James Allison. "A History of the Pittsburgh Stage, 1861–1891." PhD diss., University of Pittsburgh, 1943.

Lowry, W. McNeil. *The Arts and Public Policy in the United States*. Englewood Cliffs, NJ: Prentice-Hall, 1984.

Lubove, Roy, ed. *Pittsburgh*. New York and London: New Viewpoints, 1976.

———. *Twentieth-Century Pittsburgh*. Vols. 1–2. Pittsburgh: University of Pittsburgh Press, 1996.

Ludlow, Noah Miller. *Dramatic Life As I Found It*. New York: Benjamin Blom, 1966 [orig. publ. 1880].

Macartney, Clarence E. *Right Here in Pittsburgh*. Pittsburgh: Gibson Press, 1937.

MacGowan, Kenneth. *Footlights Across America*. New York: Harcourt, Brace, 1929.

Mackay, Constance D'Arcy. *The Little Theatre in the United States*. New York: Henry Holt, 1917.

Mahar, William J. *Behind the Burnt Cork Mask: Early Blackface Minstrelsy and Antebellum American Popular Culture*. Urbana and Chicago: University of Illinois Press, 1999.

Mallett, William J. "Redevelopment and Response: The Lower Hill Renewal and Pittsburgh's Original Cultural District." *Pittsburgh History*, Winter 1992–93, 176–90.

Marinelli, Donald. "Final Curtain." *Pittsburgh Press*, April 24, 1983, 1, 2.

Marsh, John L. "Dick Powell: The Pittsburgh Years." *Western Pennsylvania Historical Magazine* 65 (October 1982): 309–21.

Martin, Scott C. *Killing Time: Leisure and Culture in Southwestern Pennsylvania, 1800–1850*. Pittsburgh: University of Pittsburgh Press, 1995.

Mason, Jeffrey D., and Ellen Gainor, eds. *Performing America: Cultural Nationalism in American Theater*. Ann Arbor: University of Michigan Press, 1999.

McClintock, D. M., and George Swetnam. "The Amazing Alvin." *Pittsburgh Press*, April 23, 1961, Family Magazine, 6.

McClure, David. *Diary of David McClure*. New York: Knickerbocker Press, 1899.

McCollester, Charles. "Less Than Miraculous." *Nation*, March 17, 2003, 21–23.

McConachie, Bruce A. *American Theater in the Culture of the Cold War: Producing and Contesting Containment, 1947–1962.* Iowa City: University of Iowa Press, 2003.

———. *Melodramatic Formations: American Theatre and Society, 1820–1870.* Iowa City: University of Iowa Press, 1992.

———. "Narrative Possibilities for U.S. Theater Histories." In *Writing and Rewriting National Theatre Histories*, edited by S. E. Wilmer. Iowa: Iowa University Press, 2004.

———, and Daniel Friedman. *Theatre for Working-Class Audiences in the United States, 1830–1980.* Westport, CT: Greenwood Press, 1985.

McKinney, William Wilson. *Early Pittsburgh Presbyterianism: Tracing the Development of the Presbyterian Church, United States of America in Pittsburgh, Pennsylvania From 1758–1839.* Pittsburgh: Gibson Press, 1938.

McLean, Albert F. *American Vaudeville as Ritual.* Lexington: University of Kentucky Press, 1965.

McNulty, Timothy. "You Saw It Here First: Pittsburgh's Nickelodeon Introduced the Moving Picture Theater to the Masses in 1905." *Pittsburgh Post-Gazette,* June 19, 2005, E-1, 8.

Meister, Charles W. *Dramatic Criticism: A History.* Jefferson, NC: McFarland, 1985.

Mennen, Richard. "Theater." *Pittsburgh New Sun,* November 6, 1975, 5.

Miller, James M. *The Genesis of Western Culture: The Upper Ohio Valley 1800–1825.* Columbus: Ohio State Archaeological and Historical Society, 1938.

Monahan, Kaspar. "Famous American Theatres." *Theatre Arts* 40 (October 1956): 71.

Moody, Richard. *America Takes the Stage.* Bloomington: Indiana University Press, 1955.

Moore, M. Marguerite. "The History of the Pittsburgh Playhouse, 1934–1958." PhD diss., Catholic University of America, 1959.

Mordden, Ethan. *The American Theatre.* New York and London: Oxford University Press, 1981.

Morris, Lloyd. *Curtain Time: The Story of the American Theatre.* New York: Random House, 1953.

Musser, Charles. *The Emergence of Cinema: The American Screen to 1907.* New York: Charles Scribner's Sons, 1990.

Nassif, S. Joseph. "A History of the Pittsburgh Playhouse School of the Theatre, 1934 to 1969." PhD diss., University of Denver, 1973.

Nathans, Heather S. *Early American Theatre from the Revolution to Thomas Jefferson: Into the Hands of the People.* Cambridge: Cambridge University Press, 2003.

Neil, Dan. "Arms of Steel, Heart of Gold." *Attaché,* December 1999, 5–7, 40–43.

Nevin, Robert Peebles. "Stephen Foster and Negro Minstrelsy." *Atlantic Monthly* 20 (November 1867): 608–16.

"New Harris–Alvin Special Section." *Pittsburgh Press,* August 30, 1934, 17.

Noffsinger, John S. *Correspondence Schools, Lyceums, Chautauquas.* New York: Macmillan, 1926.

Novick, Julius. *Beyond Broadway: The Quest for Permanent Theatres*. New York: Hill and Wang, 1968.

O'Dell, Leslie. "Amateurs of the Regiment, 1815–1870." In *Early Stages: Theatre in Ontario 1800–1914*, edited by Ann Saddlemyer, 59–89. Toronto: University of Toronto Press, 1990.

Ohler, Samuel R. "The Penn Theatre." *Carnegie Magazine* 45 (September 1971): 291–95.

O'Mahony, John. "American Centurion." *Manchester Guardian*, December 14, 2002.

Orvell, Miles. *The Real Thing: Imitation and Authenticity in American Culture, 1880–1940*. Chapel Hill: University of North Carolina Press, 1989.

Parke, John E. "Reminiscences of the Old Third Street Theatre." In *Recollections of Seventy Years and Historical Gleanings of Allegheny Pa*. Boston: Rand, Avery, 1886.

Parton, James. "Pittsburgh." *Atlantic Monthly* 21 (January 1868): 17–35.

Payne, Ben Iden. *A Life in a Wooden O: Memoirs of the Theater*. New Haven: Yale University Press, 1977.

Pearson, Talbot. *Encores on Main Street*. Pittsburgh: Carnegie Institute of Technology Press, 1948.

Peebles, Sheila Elaine. "A History of the Pittsburgh Stage, 1871–1896." Master's thesis, Kent State University, 1973.

Peiss, Kathy. *Cheap Amusements: Working Women and Leisure in Turn-of-the-Century New York*. Philadelphia: Temple University Press, 1986.

Phillips, Mary Gaylen. *The Alliance Theatre Company of Atlanta: A Regional Theatre's First Twenty-five Years, 1968–1993*. N.p., 1993.

Pittler, Alexander Zerful. "The Hill District—A Study in Succession." Master's thesis, University of Pittsburgh, 1930.

"Pittsburgh Bicentennial." Pittsburgh Bicentennial Association and Gilberton Co., 1959.

"Pittsburgh in 1816." Compiled by the Carnegie Library of Pittsburgh on the One Hundredth Anniversary of the Granting of the City Charter. Pittsburgh: Carnegie Library of Pittsburgh, 1926.

Pittsburgh Survey. 6 vols. New York: Charity Organization Society of the City of New York, 1909.

"Pittsburgh's Oldest Theatre to Be Closed," *Gazette-Times*, April 11, 1912, 1.

Poggi, Jack. *Theater in America: The Impact of Economic Forces 1870–1967*. Ithaca, NY: Cornell University Press, 1966.

Postlewait, Thomas, and Bruce A. McConachie, eds. *Interpreting the Theatrical Past: Essays in the Historiography of Performance*. Iowa City: University of Iowa Press, 1989.

Powell, Matthew. *God Off-Broadway: The Blackfriars Theatre of New York*. Lanham, MD: Scarecrow Press, 1998.

Power, Tyron. *Impressions of America*. London: Richard Bentley, 1836.

Rankin, Hugh F. *The Theater in Colonial America*. Chapel Hill: University of North Carolina Press, 1960.

Rawson, Christopher. "On Stage: A Look Back at a Century of Theatrical Pittsburghers and Their Feats." *Pittsburgh Post-Gazette*, December 29, 1999, 1–4.

———. "The O'Reilly Theater: Charting 20th Century Black America." *Pittsburgh Post-Gazette*, December 5, 1999, G-14.

———. "The O'Reilly Theater: Curtain Rises on Cultural Trust's $20 Million Crown Jewel." *Pittsburgh Post-Gazette*, December 5, 1999, G-1, 16.

———. "The O'Reilly Theater: Wilson Again Proves Home Is Where the Art Is." *Pittsburgh Post-Gazette*, December 5, 1999, G-13, ·15.

———. "Pittsburgh Playwright Who Chronicled Black Experience." *Pittsburgh Post-Gazette*, October 3, 2005, A-1, 4–5.

———. "Triumphant Triumvirate." *Pittsburgh Post-Gazette*, December 5, 1999, G-8–9.

———, and Caroline Abels. "The Company That Dares to Be Different." *Pittsburgh Post-Gazette*, October 3, 1999, G-3–4.

Reed, Ishmael. "In Search of August Wilson." *Connoisseur*, March 1985, 95.

Rieser, Andrew C. *The Chautauqua Moment: Protestants, Progressives, and the Culture of Modern Liberalism*. New York: Columbia University Press, 2003.

Rishel, Joseph F. *Founding Families of Pittsburgh: The Evolution of a Regional Elite, 1760–1910*. Pittsburgh: University of Pittsburgh Press, 1990.

———. *The Spirit That Gives Life: The History of Duquesne University, 1898–1996*. Pittsburgh: Duquesne University Press, 1997.

"Rob Penny: Curriculum Vita." Kuntu Repertory Theatre records, Department of Africana Studies, University of Pittsburgh.

Robinson, Phyllis C. *Willa: The Life of Willa Cather*. Garden City, NY: Doubleday, 1983.

Rowell, George, ed. *The Repertory Movement: A History of Regional Theatre in Britain*. Cambridge: Cambridge University Press, 1984.

Ruskin, Ryan S. "The Americanization of Eastern European Jewish Immigrants in Pittsburgh: 1893–1920: A Study of Private Sector Initiation and Development of Progressive Social Welfare Ideas and Programs." Bachelor of Arts thesis, Princeton University, 1990.

Samuel, Raphael, Ewan MacColl, and Stuart Cosgrove. *Theatres of the Left 1880–1935: Workers' Theatre Movements in Britain and America*. London and Boston: Routledge and Kegan Paul, 1985.

Sanders, Leslie C. *The Development of Black Theater in America: From Shadows to Selves*. Baton Rouge: Louisiana State University Press, 1988.

Schneider, Martin. "Heinz Hall for the Performing Arts." *QED Renaissance*, September 1971, 23–31.

"Seven Theater Spaces in Pittsburgh." *Carnegie Magazine*, February 1976, 62–69.

Shiloh, Ailon. *By Myself, I'm a Book!* Waltham, MA: American Jewish Historical Society, 1972.

Silver, Reuben. *A History of the Karamu Theatre of Karamu House, 1915–1960*. PhD diss., Ohio State University, 1961.

Smith, Eric Ledell. *African American Theater Buildings: An Illustrated Historical Directory, 1900–1955*. Jefferson, NC: McFarland, 2003.

Smith, Solomon. *Theatrical Management in the West and South for Thirty Years*. New York: B. Blom, 1968.

———. *Theatrical Management in the West and South for 30 Years*. New York: Harper and Brothers, 1868.

Snodgrass, Mary Ellen. *August Wilson: A Literary Companion*. Jefferson, NC: McFarland, 2004.

Sochatoff, A. Fred. "A Theatrical Odyssey in 1918: Recollections of a Day When There Were Eleven Theatres in Pittsburgh." *Carnegie Magazine*, December 1957, 346–50.

Starrett, Agnes Lynch. *Through One Hundred and Fifty Years: The University of Pittsburgh*. Pittsburgh: University of Pittsburgh Press, 1937.

Stein, Charles W. *American Vaudeville as Seen by Its Contemporaries*. New York: Knopf, 1984.

Stepanian, Laurie Anne. "Harry Davis, Theatrical Entrepreneur, Pittsburgh, Pennsylvania, 1893–1927." PhD diss., University of Missouri-Columbia, 1988.

Stryker, Roy, and Mel Seidenber. *A Pittsburgh Album: 1758–1958*. Pittsburgh: *Pittsburgh Post-Gazette*, 1959.

Swoyer, Julia R. "Two Experimental Theaters." *Carnegie Magazine*, February 1976, 83–85.

Szilassy, Zoltan. *American Theater of the 1960s*. Carbondale: Southern Illinois University Press, 1986.

Taubman, Hyman Howard. *The Making of the American Theatre*. New York: Coward McCann, 1965.

Teichmann, Howard. *George S. Kaufman: An Intimate Portrait*. New York: Atheneum, 1972.

Tenney, John. "In the Trenches: The Syndicate-Shubert War." *The Passing Show: Newsletter of the Shubert Archive* 21 (Fall–Winter 1998): 2–18.

"Theaters in Pittsburgh." *Pittsburgh Sun*, December 1, 1973.

Thomas, Clarke M. *Front-Page Pittsburgh: Two Hundred Years of the* Post-Gazette. Pittsburgh: University of Pittsburgh Press, 2004.

Thurston, George H. *Pittsburgh as It Is*. Pittsburgh: W.S. Haven, 1857.

Tompkins, Eugene. *The History of the Boston Theatre, 1854–1901*. New York: Houghton Mifflin, 1908.

Trachtenberg, Alan. *The Incorporation of America: Culture and Society in the Gilded Age*. New York: Hill and Wang, 1982.

Trapani, Beth E., and Charles J. Adams III. *Ghost Stories of Pittsburgh and Allegheny County*. Reading, PA: Exeter House Books, 1994.

Underiner, Tamara L. "The First Twenty Years of Playhouse Junior: A Study of Pittsburgh's Oldest Children's Theatre." Master's thesis, Arizona State University, 1993.

Uricchio, Marilynn. "Setting Stage for Success." *Pittsburgh Post-Gazette,* December 10, 1985, 15, 19.

Van Trump, James D. "And Always the Play: Historic Theater of Pittsburgh." *Carnegie Magazine,* February 1976, 71–79.

Wall, Joseph Frazier. *Andrew Carnegie.* Pittsburgh: University of Pittsburgh Press, 1989.

Walther, Tracey, and Loren Kruger. "A Brief History of the Cultural District With an Emphasis on Theatres." Report commissioned by the Pittsburgh Cultural Trust, 1994.

Ward, Matthew C. *Breaking the Backcountry: The Seven Years' War in Virginia and Pennsylvania, 1754–1765.* Pittsburgh: University of Pittsburgh Press, 2003.

Weaver, William. *Duse: A Biography.* New York: Harcourt, Brace, 1984.

Wemyss, Francis Courtney. *Chronology of the American Stage, from 1752 to 1852.* New York: Benjamin Blom, 1968 (orig. publ. 1852).

———. *Twenty-Six Years of the Life of an Actor and Manager.* New York: Burgess, Stringer, 1847.

Williams, Dana A., and Sandra G. Shannon. *August Wilson and Black Aesthetics.* New York: Palgrave Macmillan, 2004.

Wilmeth, Don B., and Christopher Bigsby, eds. *Cambridge History of American Theatre.* Vols. 1–3. Cambridge: Cambridge University Press, 2000.

Wilson, Arthur Herman. *A History of the Philadelphia Theatre, 1835 to 1855.* Philadelphia: University of Pennsylvania Press, 1935.

Wilson, Erasmus. *History of Pittsburg.* Chicago: J.R. Cornell, 1898.

Witham, Barry B., ed. *Theatre in the Colonies and United States.* Vol. 1: *1750–1915.* Cambridge: Cambridge University Press, 1996.

Zeigler, Joseph Wesley. *Regional Theatre: The Revolutionary Stage.* Minneapolis: University of Minnesota Press, 1973.

INDEX

Index

Theatre Guild, 106–7, 133
Theater in the Courthouse, xviii, 7–9, 11, 18
Theatre in the Garrison, xviii, 6–7, 224n11
Theatre on Third Street, xviii, 1, 11–16, 18,
    21, 23, 30, 40–41, 50, 226n9, 234n37
theater ordinances, 11–12
Theater Owners' Booking Association
    (TOBA), 96, 132, 236n14
Thespian Society, The, 9–10, 224n22
Thomas, Tom, 162, 178
Thompson, Sada, 152, 156
Three Rivers Shakespeare Festival, 197–99,
    201–2, 249n10
Trimble's Variety, xviii, 28, 32, 39, 55
Turner, Sophia or Mrs., 11, 13
Turner, William, 179, 220
Turner, William A., 11, 13–14, 225nn34–35
Tyson, Cicely, 156

Udin, Sala, 169, 174
Uncle Tom's Cabin, 37, 228n40
University of Pittsburgh: 78, 98, 115, 123,
    144, 145–46, 149, 169–70, 188, 197–98,
    201–2, 204–5, 214, 216, 243n19. *See also*
    Pittsburgh Academy; Western Uni-
    versity
Unseam'd Shakespeare Company, 216
Upstairs Theater, 195, 249n10, 252n17
Urban Players, 119–20

Vanguard Theatre Project, 153, 157–58, 168,
    247n47
vaudeville: African American, 96–97,
    236n14; companies and circuits, 57,
    67, 77–78, 89; and moving pictures,

101, 103–4, 108, 131–32; rise of, 71, 81,
    83, 89, 95–96, 234n44, 234n52. *See also*
    continuous vaudeville
Venberg, Lorraine, 198, 205
Veronica's Veil Players, 126, 240n32, 249n10
Victoria Theater, xviii, 89, 101

Wagon Wheel Playhouse, 148, 200
Walker, Marjorie, 183–84, 246n34
Wallace, Chester, 98, 236n18
Western touring theatrical circuit, 11, 13–16,
    22
Western University, 10, 17. *See also* Univer-
    sity of Pittsburgh
Wemyss, Francis Courtney, 22–26, 34,
    226n5, 226n9
Wilkins Hall, 28, 226n2
Williams, Harry, 49, 53–54, 58, 60, 65, 67
Wilson, August: early history, 167–73, 185;
    Fences Pittsburgh debut, 208–9; on
    playwriting, 221; Pittsburgh Cycle,
    196, 204, 209, 219
Wolk, Abraham Lewis, 144–45
Works Progress Administration (WPA),
    117, 141
Worthington, Walter, 119–20, 141–44, 151,
    168, 243n19
Wright, J. Ernest, 115–17
Wymetal, William, 146

Yiddish theater, xii, 122–24
Y Playhouse, 99, 124–25, 129

Ziegfeld Follies, 101, 107–8, 127, 133
Zimmerman, J. Fred, 66, 70–71, 232n4